Confessions of a Record Producer

How to Survive the Scams and Shams of the Music Business

Dan Peterson

Confessions of a Record Producer

How to Survive the Scams and Shams of the Music Business

By Moses Avalon

3rd Edition

Backbeat Books

San Francisco

Published by Backbeat Books
600 Harrison Street, San Francisco, CA 94107
www.backbeatbooks.com
Email: books@musicplayer.com
An imprint of Music Player Network
United Entertainment Media, Inc.

CMP
United Business Media

Distributed to the book trade in the U.S. and Canada by
Publishers Group West, P.O. Box 8843, Emeryville, CA 94662

Distributed to the music trade in the U.S. and Canada by
Hal Leonard Publishing, P.O. Box 13819, Milwaukee, WI 53213

Text Design: Richard Leeds
Composition: Michael Cutter
Cover Design: Richard Leeds—BigWigDesign.com

Library of Congress Cataloging-in-Publication Data

Avalon, Moses
    Confessions of a record producer : how to survive the scams and shams of the music business / by Moses Avalon.-- 3rd ed.
        p. cm.
    Includes index.
    ISBN-13: 978-0-87930-874-2 (alk. paper)
    ISBN-10: 0-87930-874-5 (alk. paper)
 1.   Sound recording industry--Vocational guidance.   I. Title.

ML3790.A93 2006
780.23'73--dc22   2006005013

Printed in the United States of America
 06 07 08 09 10   5 4 3 2 1

● Fast-Forward and Reverse

For over 15 years I made my living sitting behind a large pane of glass. It's the glass you see in a recording studio, the one that separates the performer from people like me: the engineer and the producer. I have worked with hundreds of recording artists in this way, cutting their demos and seeing the hope in their eyes, right through the final mixes of tunes that became huge hits for them. Through it all, I have always found this "separating glass" the perfect analogy for a business that works so hard at separating the artist from their money. Conjure this image: the novice performer sits blissfully in a darkened vocal booth, while on the other side, protected by soundproof walls and expensive machinery, bean counters and executives decide their fate.

Over the years, and in the dim, smoky light of a 2 A.M. recording session, many artists have confessed to me, "If I'd only known better when I signed my first deal." In this moment of crisis, when their manager isn't returning their calls, their girl- or boyfriend is angry with them, their sidemen are getting wasted, the producer is on the phone, and the label won't give them more money, they have turned to me, the unassuming technician, in hopes of a sympathetic ear. They spoke and I listened. This book is the result.

It probably comes as no surprise that these artists feel taken advantage of by the very companies they've made millions for. Are they paranoid, or were their expectations perhaps too high? You will decide for yourself as you learn every trick, scam, and lie they were told—and told back.

What separates this book from the scores of other books on this business is the fact that most other books are written by attorneys and discuss the music business in theory. Certainly there's value in that. But unfortunately attorneys are not always in the best position to speak openly about their clients' business practices. I'm not an attorney. I have no allegiances to protect. I won't bore you with anal interpretations of how things are supposed to work. Here you will only read how things did work when applied to real-life situations. Plus, you will see real dollar numbers showing what everyone makes at the end of the day, from the record company to the recording engineer.

Every account in this book is real. They're designed to illustrate strong examples of how money can slip away from the artist who is not savvy to the way things really work, and give the artist strong ammunition to help them preserve their assets.

The first part of this book looks at the typical recording deal from three distinct points of view: (1) the artist, (2) the producer, and (3) the record label. After reading each section, you will understand why record deals are so complex, and thus, whatever phase of the business you're thinking about entering, you will be well-armed for a negotiation.

The second part of the book can be thought of as an encyclopedia of skullduggery—the first volume ever assembled that catalogues every known way to swindle artists, producers, and even labels out of their hard-earned cash.

It's my guess that most of you reading this book are thinking about a long and successful career in the music industry. Will this book make you paranoid? Well, hopefully it will make you cautious, but will it try to discourage you from getting into the business? Absolutely not. This book is no more than a tool. It's designed to empower you to go forward and deal from a position of strength. Ultimately, it's your talent, passion, and determination that will push you toward a life in music, and that passion will be the beacon for your success.

Within these pages I address the concerns and frustrations of many in this industry—an industry once mired in corruption, but one which in the last decade has traded its "family" ties for ones with multinational conglomerates. The trade-offs are sometimes less noticeable than one might expect.

Tomorrow's music industry has the potential to be the most spiritually powerful business in the world. It is my hope that this book can be part of its growth as the industry moves through the new millennium and on to realize the spiritual image it so realistically feigns.

It is my sincerest wish that this book will someday be obsolete.

❷ Who the Hell Am I?

I entered the business in the early '80s as an engineer in a small 8-track studio. Back then, there were no tell-all books the way there are today. All we had were gossipy stories about people like Morris Levy and the founder of Motown Records, Berry Gordy—paranoid tales of how entrepreneurs swindled naive musicians and songwriters out of their money.

As is common among engineers, after several of the records I worked on charted, I became a producer. I quickly realized that all I had heard as the artist's confessor was true. And, I'm sorry to say, I had become part of that very system, employing many of the same values that I had disagreed with years earlier.

I recalled something a client had told me. He was a successful producer for whom I engineered for years. He said, "No one wants to rip off anybody. Everybody is just doing what they think is right for their client."

Self-serving? Maybe, but I have seen enough over the years to know that in the arena of music, karma often takes a backseat to leverage. What you'll see, after we dissect the pros and cons of major record deals, is that who the good guys and bad guys are is largely a matter of outlook.

❯ Introduction to the Third Edition

Truth rings the town bell, someone once said, and in a business where sleaze runs rampant like a Satyr in a brothel, the truths expressed in *Confessions* seem to be resounding through our community. Since the release of the first edition, readers have sent me in excess of 10,000 e-mails with stories that parallel the ones in *Confessions*. What started out as a subversive alternative to starchy manifestos on the music business has become an established and accepted text in colleges and seminars. *Confessions* is now quoted by reporters in newspapers and in the press releases of hit-makers; its examples have been used by major stars to leverage their labels into better deals, and passages from its pages have been used in legal briefs to demonstrate "industry standards."

This is the good news. However, there is some bad. When the publisher requested updates for a new edition, it was my hope that substantial alterations would be necessary due to the raised awareness and the freedoms offered by the Internet. Unfortunately, after looking over each chapter, the only thing that required serious updating was the math to reflect adjustments for inflation and the addition of new scams *created* by the Internet (see below). This book is, sadly, still far from obsolete.

When scouring through the pages that deal with budgets for albums, one interesting irony that I noticed is that major label recording budgets have not changed very much at all. In fact, the "downsizing" of the business that occurred in 2003–2005 has created more deals where majors buy pre-recorded masters from previously unsigned artists outright, paying mere pennies for finished records. Meanwhile, the price of CDs has increased about 20% since *Confessions'* first printing. This means that labels have succeeded in widening the spread between their development costs and bottom-line profits, while artists' representation has failed to keep pace and capture some of this revenue. To add insult to injury, labels and publishers are now collecting money from new revenue streams created by ringtones, webcasting, downloads, and streaming. Evidence suggests that little of this new money is, as yet, being passed on to the artist in any consistent way.

Let's hope that by the fourth edition of *Confessions*, the content creators of our industry can learn enough to regain some ground. That is the goal of this book.

⧁ The New Guy Out to Get You

This Third Edition of *Confessions* is dedicated to scams born from the emerging power base of the independent music scene.

The first edition of *Confessions* was released in 1998. Back then, unless signed to one of the majors or their publishers, you probably weren't making enough scratch to attract the attention of scammers. Thus the majors became this book's focus and, as a result, readers thought I automatically favored indies.

This edition, written in 2005, sees an entirely new music business landscape: one where artists, producers, writers, and managers are making good livings outside the major label system. A natural reaction to this has been an empire of new ventures that advertise services claiming to help the emerging (or indie) artist in ways that majors used to. They offer things like independent A&R services, digital distribution, low-cost manufacturing, online marketing, instant publicity, e-tailing, and just about every other service that a large label performs for its artists.[1] Some of these companies are legit. Some are not. Since the indie expansion many musicians have opted into bad deals because they put their trust in someone who seemed down-to-earth ahead of reading the fine print, or ahead of common sense. So here is a new rule to think about:

Beware the "nice guy."

Always remember that scammers *must* appear to be charming in order to succeed. This is true whether they emerge from a limo with a linen business card or wear Birkenstocks and have a bitchin' website. When song-sharks worked for the majors they were easier to recognize. But in just the past few years over 1,000 major-label executives were fired, and their jobs downsized. Where did they go? Many started their own companies and are doing what comes naturally to them: targeting artists and seducing their money—but now with a cooler new "indie" vibe.

In my investigations of smaller companies within the music business, I have also discovered that there is such a thing as a "front." That is, a person (often in their

1 In the interest of full disclosure, The Moses Avalon Company is among them. In addition to advocacy efforts and educational seminars, the company offers low-cost independent business affairs solutions to indie artists, basically replacing the "business affairs"/legal component of a major label. Such services include: partnership mediation, dispute resolution, interim management services, contract analysis, career strategies, investigations, business-plan preparation and analysis, deal shopping—and just about anything else to do with the business side of making/marketing music.

20s to early 30s) who is sent to conferences and road shows to promote an "indie" product. But the company who is paying for his ticket and hotel room (and extras) has sent this particular dude more because of his hipness and enthusiasm for music than for his actual industry (or product) knowledge. This person may not actually know that he is pushing something that can hurt artists. (He's probably too stoked at the free ride he's getting on the company dole to even think about it.) He may not even know what his higher-ups or investors are planning in the next year or two or what deals were made without consulting him.

If you think this is far-fetched, I direct your attention to several recent situations where VPs and even CEOs were kept in the dark and made promises that ended up hurting tens of thousands of people: WorldCom, Enron, and the Arthur Andersen firm, the world's largest, oldest, and *most respected* public accounting firm, to name a few known situations; and in the independent music community, MP3.com, Napster (the original one), and several other companies that we'll talk about in this edition, many of which are blindly speeding towards a similar fate.

Let's take a look.

➋ How to Use This Book

Being a musician (and equipment owner) myself, I am very sensitive to the fact that we already have far too many instruction manuals to digest to labor through instructions on how to use a book. So I'll be brief.

Why does this book need a "how to use" section? Couldn't you just read it front to back? The answer is yes, and you would probably get the most out of it that way. But this book has been designed to help you find the answers you need easily, without rummaging through many pages. Simply use the table of contents to find the subject that fits your inquiry best, and turn to the page. Each section of the book is self-contained. (The trade-off for this convenience is that some information is repeated in more than one section.)

To help make this book even more user-friendly, the footnotes can act like a magic tour guide. They contain side comments and supporting facts for the text as well as references to other parts of the book with related information. So, whatever page you open to, you will never be lost.

Part 1, "The Game," is the main component of *Confessions*. It deals with the record deal itself and the people who make it happen. The first section of this part, called "The Players," dissects every person you will have to deal with, their background, what they do, their actual agenda, and how much they get paid for doing it.

Understanding what the other person wants and needs from a deal builds powerful and successful negotiating techniques. The second section of Part 1, "The Deal," breaks down the record deal by looking at both major and independent label deals as well as "baby" production deals. We'll look at the deals from three main points of view: artist, producer, and label/production company. Each faction has its own set of concerns. Here also are the money numbers that you can expect to make from these deals.

Part 2, "Scams and Shams," is a collection of almost 20 years of stories and rumors about how everyone got ripped off by everyone else. The first section of this part deals mostly with the copyright laws and how the strong prey upon the weak to steal material—and what you can do about it. The final section, "Miscellaneous Myths and Untruths," is basically a Q-and-A that will dissolve many of the B.S. rules that you may have heard in your quest for enlightenment about this business.

A Word About the Sidebars

Don't skip them! Not only did it take me a long time to write these things, but they contain some of the most valuable information in the book. Everything has been designed to make what may be the most complicated business in the performing arts simple enough that even your cat will understand it (provided your cat can read). Sometimes a short example can be more useful than pages of detailed explanations. The sidebars tell stories that illustrate the text with a real-life scenario. So take the time to read them.

By the way, if your cat can read, don't waste your time in music—get an agent and call Disney, fast!

Disclaimer No. 1

Every effort has been made to provide the most up-to-date industry information available. It must be noted that the music industry is a constantly changing environment. New laws are changing the way artists will be paid, and companies are sold, resurrected, and merged every day. This book is a guide only, not a road map.

Disclaimer No. 2

Nothing in this book should be misconstrued as legal or professional advice. Enough boring stuff. Let's get to it.

TABLE OF CONTENTS

⊖The Game

Capitalism is convincing somebody that you own something.

—Henry David Thoreau

❧The Players

As in any business, before you get in over your head, it is important to understand what type of players you'll be dealing with. Those who invest in the music business are an unusual breed of gambler. A lawyer friend once explained it to me this way: "The entertainment industry is like a big casino. Motion pictures are the backroom baccarat tables for the millionaires with the $10,000 gold chips. Television is the $100 table for the yuppies, theater the $25 table, and the record biz is the $2 table, essentially for the bargain shopper."

This is not intended to demean musicians, or the other players in the game. On the contrary, to be a player and win at the record game, you will have to place many bets, so they'd better be cheap and shrewd ones. Nor is the above to say that the $2 table is not worth playing; many a large fortune was built on small, carefully thought-out wagers.

In this section we are going to examine the various types of players, both artists and professionals—their roles, agendas, and incomes. But for those of you who've never sat at the $2 table, I can tell you straight out, most of us got our clout from being shrewd, conniving, and, in many cases, lawless.

Welcome, brother and sister.

CHAPTER ONE

⊗The Pros

No matter what aspect of the business you pursue, over time you will find yourself talking to more nonmusicians than actual music makers. Even if you are an artist, as you become more successful, the creative end of music will occupy less and less of your time and you will be dealing mostly with lawyers, accountants, managers, business affairs people, label promotion personnel, distributors, publicists, and more lawyers.

There is a natural feeling of dread many of us experience when dealing with high-priced professionals. We often believe that because they went to a fancy school, or have framed degrees on their wall, they must be more astute than we are. In the music business, this does not always apply. Here's a big secret:

Most music industry pros, at one time or another, dreamt of being some type of performer.

I remember a piece of advice I received from a successful friend. He said that when meeting important or intimidating people he would try to imagine them naked; all their grandeur would instantly wilt. Building on that advice and looking at the line in bold above, try to imagine the pompous pro in front of you playing in a rock band, arguing over chord changes and how he should wear his hair tonight.

Though not all industry professionals were artists, you should be cautious about the ones that were seriously considering it. Even though they've given up the spotlight, their heart may still be there. The best pros are the professionals who love music and may even be musicians but have made peace with the path they have chosen. They are centered and secure with their station in life. These pros are worth their weight in gold. Even these, however, may have a hidden agenda, as we'll see in the upcoming chapters. The key, when dealing with them, is to relax, listen carefully to what they say, and don't panic. No matter how impressive they try to make themselves out to be, remember that they too are sitting at the $2 table.

➲ Lawyers

Let's start with everyone's favorite target, the lawyer. As stated earlier, until recently most books on the music industry have been written by attorneys. As a result, these books tend to overlook the lawyer's contribution to certain problems in this business. Whether this is done out of convenience or naiveté is anyone's guess. So, for the lawyers out there reading this, consider what follows as equal time.

Before any record deal is done, it must go through a lawyer, usually several in fact. The reason: if both sides of the deal are not properly represented, the entire contract may be disputed down the line. That's the actual law! (As practiced by lawyers.)

Because lawyers are centrally placed on all sides of the deal, they have the ear of every important person you will need to know.

Fees for attorneys normally range anywhere from $125 per hour to $600 per hour, although sometimes the lawyer will work for a percentage of the deal instead of an hourly fee (often about 5%). The size of the deal—whether with a major label, a small indie, or a production company—will usually determine the size of the lawyer's fee.

Lawyers typically come from educated upper-middle-class backgrounds and earn anywhere from $60,000 to $500,000 a year. The cream of the crop have been reported to make $1,000,000 per year and up. Clive Davis started out as an attorney and became the president of Arista Records. In 1995, his contract was renewed for $5 million per year (not including a bonus).[1]

However, you shouldn't think that just because the lawyer you've been speaking to has platinum records and framed law degrees on his wall he or she has great knowledge of the law. Many music biz lawyers are more salesmen than litigators. The mainstay of their day revolves around meetings and lunches to rope in business. They are often called "rainmakers."

Behind them, kept well out of sight of the clients, are what I call "the worker bees."

[1] Davis was ousted from Arista by upper management and replaced by hit-maker LA Reid. They then gave Davis his own label: J Records. His first release was Alicia Keys. He now earns about double what he did at Arista. Meanwhile, Reid laid off about half of Arista's executive staff in his first year as CEO, starting a three-year trend that would downsize the major label environment by about 30% and lead to the eventual closing of Arista completely. Financial pressure eventually trickled down and in 2004 led to the crack-up of the largest legal powerhouse that services the music industry (*Grubman Indursky Shlinder*, now just *Grubman Indursky*). They used to represent the bigs like Madonna and Puff Daddy. The future is uncertain.

They stay in the office well past 9 P.M., drafting the contracts and making sure the rainmakers, who promised the world to the client, can actually deliver. The worker bees aren't slick like the rainmakers. They get less glory, but they are the ones who really know what's going on and what you can and can't get away with. One way I can always tell a rainmaker from a worker right off the bat—workers wear less jewelry.[2]

[2] This is not a hard-and-fast rule, just an observation.

One other type of lawyer is one I call "the crusader." Crusaders tend to be young attorneys just starting out in business. They've picked up all the book smarts in law school but have yet to learn how to apply it to real life. As with most people who are new, they tend to be somewhat idealistic about how things actually work. The result can be that they over-negotiate a deal into nonexistence. Afterward they will justify their actions by saying it was a lousy deal anyway.

New attorneys tend not to understand that business is about people, not clauses, especially in the music business. It's about relationships. Keeping an eye on the bottom line can be shortsighted in a business where most people are not initially making a huge living. Unfortunately, lawyers are trained to see things in an arbitrary fashion, so sometimes they can do more harm than good, especially when negotiating small money deals. My friend Larry, who is a music industry attorney, says he would never hire a lawyer who wasn't, at some time, in business for himself. I agree, but this isn't always practical.

Some crusaders mature into excellent lawyers; some don't. Until you can deter-

LAWYER LOGIC

It is all too easy for a lawyer to simply say, "Forget this deal."

Consider the lawyer's logic: If he tells you to sign a contract and something goes wrong, you will likely blame him, but if you never do the deal, he can remain forever wise.

Unlike your best friend or family member, lawyers are accountable for the advice they give. Bad advice can lead to a lawsuit against them. So it is in the lawyer's best interest to lean away from a deal (usually after they've racked up a few billable hours examining it). This is not to say that every deal the attorney tells you to pass up is a good one, but you have to always consider the source when asking for advice.

mine which way they will go, my advice is to steer clear of the crusader. A typical example of how crusaders can muddy the waters is illustrated in the sidebar, "My Friend Don."

Conflicts of Interest

An important point about lawyers is to understand their career goals. For example, if you were negotiating a contract with Atlantic Records, would you hire an attorney who was thinking about working for that company soon after your contract was completed? Would this make you a bit suspicious? Would you wonder how hard your lawyer was going to push for you, knowing that he was trying to suck up to the label?

MY FRIEND DON

Don came from an affluent family and had been working in the music business for several years when he decided to start his own production company. He hired a lawyer to draft a standard production agreement for him to use when negotiating with his clients. The contract, which was very professionally done, was about nine pages long, with lots of fine print. It cost Don a small fortune, too.

I had been operating my own production company for several years, and I tried to warn Don that his contract would never work. He said to me, "But it's a very good deal for the artist."

It *was* a very good deal for the artist. The problem was that the artist usually wouldn't read it because it was too complex and intimidating. I suggested that he do what I did—a simple three-page agreement in plain English. Don's attorney complained that my agreement was unprofessional and left many things out that should be addressed; he insisted that Don keep the agreement that he had drafted. Don did just that.

For about a year he produced no one. No artist he came in contact with had the patience or the money to have a lawyer explain the meaning of the nine-page novel. Out of frustration, his prospective artists chose to look elsewhere rather than deal with Don's business practices, *even though it was a good deal for them*. After 15 months and no new business, Don threw the contract out and Xeroxed mine.

Many attorneys dream of being executives of major labels and see representation of artists, producers, and managers as a mere stepping stone. Other attorneys' main mission is to represent the biggest artists in the business, negotiating against the corporations. Which side of the fence your lawyer is on is important.

But besides this, there is one other oddity that is unique to the music business: it is not uncommon to have attorneys from both sides of a lawsuit working *at the same firm*. By the letter of the law, this is in fact illegal. But in the music business, it happens every day. How can we trust that we are being represented fairly when opposite sides of a dispute sometimes literally share a file cabinet?

We can't. The only answer is to be very cautious about who you get in bed with. Don't go just on instinct that you are being well served. Almost all attorneys who work in large firms ask their clients to sign a document that makes the client aware that conflicts of interest do occur. The client, by signing the contract, agrees to give up their right to have any recourse against the firm if it causes a problem. If a situation arises where the closeness of the two attorneys could bias the outcome of a case, then the ethical attorney would, at that point, tell their client to seek a different lawyer. But not all attorneys are ethical.

A few humbling facts about lawyers:
1. Most lawyers in the U.S. don't earn much more per year than the average sanitation worker.
2. Most lawyers have never taken anyone to court.
3. The most ethical entertainment lawyers make the least money.
4. Most lawyers are not as ethical as they think they are.

❯ A&R

The A&R people work for record companies and are paid by them to find and sign talent that will record hit records for the label. Today, they are not generally supposed to dictate the creative content to the artist; however, this was not always the case. First, some history:

A&R stands for *Artists and Repertoire*. Up until about 1960, A&R men[3] were the "producers" of the records. They spent time with the artists, developed the material, and were responsible for the *sound and quality* of the record. The A&R person would, more often than not, cowrite the songs and assist with the arrangements, yet they would not receive a single royalty because they were employees of the record company—it was part of the job.

[3] There were no A&R women at the executive level until about 1965.

As the business went through its first major consolidation in the 1960s, labels began to cut expenses and farm out various functions, one of which was the producing of the record. With this element no longer part of the A&R responsibilities, those A&R persons who excelled at production became "independent producers." Record companies hired them on a project-by-project basis, giving them a fee for producing and a percentage of the profits (usually 3% after recoupment of expenses). With the creative part of the job now filled by an independent contractor, the role of staff A&R was reduced to that of buyer for the record label.[4]

A typical day for an A&R person consists of arriving at the office around 11 A.M. and taking phone calls and meetings (including lunch) until about 6 P.M. Then they go to a club to see an act they are interested in (often called a showcase). They will spend the better part of the evening talking to band members, managers, and producers, all in an attempt to put a deal together between the band and the label they work for. This can go well past midnight.

A&R people start off, in most cases, as assistants. They make a starting salary of just under $30,000 (at most large labels in major cities), and this can go up to $150,000 at the executive level, once they've survived in the game for a while. On rare occasions, an A&R person may prove so vital to the label that his combined salary and bonus exceeds $750,000 a year.

The position of assistant A&R, which leads to an A&R executive position, seems to be the most nepotistic job in the industry. Most people who get these jobs are in some way related to the higher echelon of the label's management, or they have parents who know someone high up in the label's holding company. This is starting to change as the industry consolidates much of its middle management and smaller indie labels start to seem more efficient to the majors. Smaller labels, who don't have any room in the budget for waste, prefer to hire producers, managers, or people who have worked in the industry as A&R rather than the nephew of a CEO.[5]

It is not uncommon for an A&R person—even a successful one making a six-figure salary—to leave a label after a year because they have fallen out of grace with the higher-ups or get a better offer from another label. The A&R position is a rather tenuous one. They become an easy target for blame in the failure of many projects. It's a worthwhile risk, however, because if the band is a success, the A&R person gets a lot of recognition for his/her forecasting.

Often the most successful A&R people will try to get their own label spun off of the major label they were working for. (This is important information. Remember this when we're talking about the recording deal in the section called "Super-Duper Cross-Collateralization" in chapter 12 and when we discuss one-deep and two-deep labels on page 58.)

[4] Unfortunately, somebody forgot to tell many of today's A&R people that this transfer of duties took place. Today, A&R people who have the clout to muscle in on the creative process sometimes do so under the title of "executive producer" (EP). They can, and sometimes will, attempt to dictate the sound of the record. This is not always a bad thing. Some A&R people have built excellent reputations as having "golden ears."

[5] For an illuminating expansion on this subject see my book *Million Dollar Mistakes* and the chapter called "Friendly Firings."

At smaller labels, the A&R person is usually the owner of the label. Chances are they once worked for a major label and have now grown their own legs. To do so, they've found an investor who is, in essence, investing in the A&R/owner's judgment as to what is going to sell.

Many of these little labels don't last long. But if an A&R/owner can survive the first two years, they have good potential for success. Some examples are Rick Rubin and Russell Simmons, co-founders of Def Jam Records (who released the Beastie Boys and LL Cool J), and Steve Gottlieb of TVT, who discovered Nine Inch Nails.

A few humbling facts about A&R:

1. Despite A&R people's alleged expertise, 75% of all acts signed by them fail to sell enough records to turn a profit and less than 10% earn enough to pay the artist any royalties.[6]
2. The average tenure of an A&R person at a major label is about two years.
3. A&R people are rarely welcome guests at recording sessions.
4. In fact, they're rarely welcome anywhere near the creative process.

[6] For the reason why, see the chapter "Major Label Deal from the Artist's Point of View."

❥ Managers

Yes, yes, managers. What exactly do they do, and how valuable are they in the grand scheme of things? This is complicated, because managers seem to come from every corner of the business.

So, let's say you're a recording artist (or hope to become one) and you're looking for a manager. What will he or she do for the 15% to 20% that they will take off the top of your gross earnings? Well . . .

- Managers shop and negotiate the deal between the artist and the record label. *But wait, doesn't the lawyer do that?* Well, yes.

- Managers make sure that the artist gets their proper royalty payments. *But wait, wait, doesn't an accountant or business manager do that?* Well, yes.

- Managers help the artist select material for the record and help develop the sound. *But wait, doesn't the producer do that?* Well, yes, he does.

- Managers make sure that the venue conditions are the ones agreed upon in the tour contract (i.e., that there's enough beer backstage and the instruments are in tune). *But don't we have tour managers and stage managers for that?* Yup, we do.

- Managers get the act great gigs on the road, like opening up for a national act. *But can't a booking agency do that for 10%?* Uh, yeah.

- Managers supervise the artist's interviews and press releases. They make sure that nothing too negative leaks to the press (unless they want it to). *But don't we have publicists for that?* Most definitely.

- Managers help mold the artist, like with the proper look. *But can't you get a stylist or image consultant to do that for a few bucks?* Sure.

Give up? This description may, on the surface, seem like I'm down on managers, but I'm not. A manager is a classic example of the whole being greater than the sum of the parts. Each function could be delegated to one of the other pros. But the manager has his or her hands in all of these areas and, if he or she's a good one, keeps the machinery oiled with funny stories, rounds of drinks, free tickets, and the three "R's" of the record industry—relationships, relationships, and relationships. But what makes a good one? Are there tests or qualifications that a local government makes one go through before they let someone handle your money? You are about to read a surprising answer.

SUPER MANAGER

Legendary record man "Swervin'" Irving Azoff once managed the mega-group the Eagles. During a tour at the height of their career, one California hotel was unable to provide adjoining suites for the "Hotel California" songwriters. Swervin' Irving drove to a hardware store, purchased a chainsaw, went to the hotel, and turned two separate rooms into one suite by sawing down the wall between them.

Being prudent and realizing that he would not be able to be there whenever the Eagles needed on-site remodeling, he had a carrying case made for the saw so that the group could take it on tour with them.

Now that's hands-on management.

In California, the entertainment capital of the U.S. (if not the world), there are special laws that bar someone from collecting a commission off of a person's earnings unless they are a bonded and licensed "employment agent." This is to protect actors, directors, and writers and insure that the person representing them and collecting their money does not mishandle it. The personal bond insures that they won't run to Mexico and have a wild weekend with your cash. It also weeds out wannabes who have no real professional experience.

However, the record industry succeeded in getting an exception carved into the law, allowing *anyone* to act as an agent if they are procuring a "record deal."

This exception is a double-edged sword. Managers in the music space can literally be anyone an artist chooses. Unlike California agents in other creative fields like acting, writing, and directing, in music managers can make deals *and* collect money, and not even have to have a driver's license or high school diploma. Is this a good thing? The record companies think so. They argued (through their lobby group the RIAA) that this exception is necessary. They claimed that because of the esoteric nature of the music business, *artists* should have the right to choose anyone they want to be their representatives. But who do you think really benefits from this lowered standard of professionalism?

So do you need to get involved with this funky dynamic? Yeah, you do. Just make sure you get a good one. The best way to think about managers is as toll booth attendants. You could bypass them and take a longer road to get to where you want to go. But if you want to get there faster and safer on a nice paved interstate highway, you have to pay the 20% toll. Good managers keep everyone talking to each other. They are master schmoozers, and because there are only two qualifications for the profession—(1) that they are good talkers, and (2) that they have lots of contacts—many people from many backgrounds call themselves managers. (See "Drop-Kicked from the Roster," page 77.)

Here's my definition of a good manager: "Someone who pays attention to how things get done, as opposed to *what* gets done."

Some unfortunate facts about managers:
1. Managers often hide valuables when their clients come to their house.
2. Managers spend less than 6% of their waking time at their primary residence.
3. It can take a manager up to an average of three years to develop a new artist and get them signed.
4. Managers are often dumped by their clients after three years.

⊘ Publicists, Booking Agents, Tour Managers, and Image Consultants

See above.

⊘ Consultants

In the first edition of *Confessions* (1998) there was really little need to highlight the "music business consultant." There were very few and they consisted mostly of old guys who were once label presidents. Their fees were staggering and accessible only by big labels in need of juice. Once in a while you heard about one of them being called to testify in a big case involving a pop star. As an artist you would never need to speak to one. Your lawyer or manager *was* your consultant.

Much has changed. The 2004–2005 label consolidations have produced a surplus of unemployed label execs, and many have hung out shingles as "consultants." Many have also retooled their services to meet the needs of emerging artists. Why? Well, this is where the new business is going.

The growth of this area brings with it new elements both good and bad. On the good side most consultants will offer services that many a lawyer is hired to do for a fraction of the lawyer's price. (With the caveat that most of what a music lawyer is hired to do has little to do with the practice of law.) One needs no law degree to negotiate a contract in most U.S. states or to give you an opinion of whether a contract is "industry standard." A manager who charges 20% over five–seven years to shop a record deal can also be replaced by a consultant hired for a few thousand dollars. Instead of paying a producer 3–5% to produce your record, hire a consultant to executive-produce your record. You make the creative decisions, they do the paperwork, rights clearances, etc., and negotiations with musicians, studios, and even labels.

While the up-front costs can be more than engaging a traditional pro (who would tend to work on a back-end percentage), in the long run most any reasonable up-front fee is going to be far less than a back-end percentage, especially if you think you really have a shot at making it. They are also willing to supply services to folks who normally wouldn't generate enough commission to capture the attention of a seasoned pro. Best of all, you are not bound to a consultant if you decide after the fact that they suck. The no-strings-attached model allows for full ownership of songs and masters. So a consultant could get an artist/writer a record deal and doesn't necessarily get a piece of his publishing in exchange, as most managers would.

On the down side, like any growth field you get a lot of people whose skills at marketing themselves are greater than their actual industry expertise. Whereas managers will help develop an act from the ground up on spec and lawyers as well will take on some "charity cases" in hopes of their hitting it big, conversely, consultants are not known for their vision or their loyalty. They are more like sprinters than long-distance runners. They get in, do a job, and get out. Cash up front and no long-term commitments. Some artists find this attitude disingenuous. But this is mostly their egos talking (and often their pocketbooks). Managers and lawyers can be just as mercenary, signing acts to long-term *and binding* agreements and then becoming too busy to deal with their client's petty needs. With consultants you can usually fire them at will if they get too uppity.

Consultants will typically charge a small fee for a basic consultation of anywhere from $200 to $1,000. Some work on monthly retainers (like lawyers) of $500–$1500 a month with a three-month minimum. Others perform services à la carte for $200–$1000 per service. This emerging profession is working on a trade organization, the Music Business Consultants of America, that will set standards and practices.[7]

[7] **The Moses Avalon Company is one of the founders of the MBCA.**

CHAPTER TWO

⊜The Creators

The other types of players are the creative entities who make the music. I divide them up into five categories: *musicians, songwriters, engineers, artists, and producers.*

Don't let the word "artist" confuse you. In general, the use of the word "artist" in the music business is much the same as the use of the word "talent" in the film industry. It is a description of the person's role and not a reflection of the quality of their work. As used in this book, it refers to a career recording artist.

⊜Musicians

The people in the music business that I have the most profound respect for are the musicians. They work the hardest and, as a group, get paid the least. As I said earlier, almost everyone in this business started off as a musician, but after a few professional (or less than professional) encounters, many opt for something more steady. The ones that stay with it seem to do so for one main reason: they feel a burning passion to create. They did not choose music, music chose them! It's a dedication that is often underappreciated by labels.

Musicians fall into two general categories: *The Survivor* and *The Jobber*. (Note: It's important to understand that this book is about the pop record industry. Therefore, the comments about musicians in this section don't necessarily apply to other genres like classical or jazz. Also not included in this section are singers, whom I have classified under "Artists," below.)

The Survivor

Typically, this musician is a male between the ages of 17 and 29. He has a day job that pays him $17,000 to $38,000 per year before taxes. After his survival expenses, he spends most or all of his surplus income on musical equipment. He reads some trade magazines but mostly the ones that cater to his particular instrument, like *Keyboard*, *Guitar Player*, or *Modern Drummer*—rarely *Billboard*, *Variety*, or any business-oriented trade mag. He plays in at least one band and maybe as many as three, gigs out at least one to three times a month, and makes about $25 per gig.

MY FRIEND STEVE

Steve was a singer and cowriter in a five-piece band and was about to sign a major record deal. It had been agreed that Steve would share the publishing of the songs with the entire band. The label recognized Steve as the driving force in the band's material and wanted him to sign a copublishing arrangement with them—a common request from major labels (for the reason why, refer to "Publishing Deals," page 81). Steve and the rhythm guitarist, who cowrote most of the material, had no problem with this, but the drummer, bassist, and lead guitarist, who started the band and whose connections brought Steve to the label, didn't feel comfortable giving up half of their publishing. The issue became a deal-breaker.

So one week later, Steve and the guitarist quit the band (effectively firing the others) and regrouped. Within a few days, they had a new rhythm section. The new players were excited just to be in a band that was going to be signed. They didn't care about the publishing. The deal went forward and everyone was happy, except for the now-out-of-a-gig drummer, bass player, and lead guitarist, who undoubtedly felt screwed.

It's important to keep in mind that record companies are primarily interested in singers and songs. To them, the rhythm section is replaceable. The side players in Steve's band felt the need to assert their power, not realizing that *their hand was weak*.

Many survivors play with a wedding band on the weekends, which could gross $400 or $500 per gig for them. Occasionally he or she gets session work, usually on the recommendation of a producer/engineer friend who believes in them.

This type of player is easy prey for those looking for a bargain on talent. Because this musician doesn't involve himself in the industry, he's at a disadvantage when it comes to negotiating a good pay rate or copyright share, so he will often be hired to work for little to no money. The trade-off for this exploitation is the hope that the job will lead to something bigger. Long odds for these little gigs, even on a good day.[1]

Ninety percent of the people who call themselves musicians are covered by the above description. A small percentage of them will be attached to an act when it gets signed to a deal with a good label that pays on its contract. About a year and a half after the deal is signed they may, if the record is doing well, start to make enough money to quit their day job.

But the survivor often doesn't grasp the concept that getting a record deal is the beginning of the race, not the end. Most bands break up after three albums, and then the survivor is often back to square one. If they have songwriting credit, then at least they will get publishing royalties (see "Publishing Deals," page 81). But for various reasons the survivor rarely contributes to the actual copyright of the songs on the record and so has little to show for the experience save the box of complimentary CDs in the corner of his basement.

Most survivors that I know move into other areas of the business. Some try to get their own deal as an artist. Some go on to be producers and/or managers. There are several who have found bigger success as A&R people than they did on the road as musicians.

[1] The survivor could try to assert him- or herself and say something to the producer/friend who's hiring him, if he knew exactly what to say. But then again, from the producer's point of view, he probably wouldn't have hired his buddy, the survivor, if he had a budget to pay people. Instead he would have gone with a jobber (described next).

THE ULTIMATE SURVIVOR

After penning and performing the megahit "U Can't Touch This," rapper M.C. Hammer just couldn't seem to bounce back. His next album sank to the bottom of the charts faster than lead in a swimming pool.

Husband and father to three children, Hammer declared bankruptcy in 1996 and went to work as a telephone salesman.

He once was worth $30,000,000.

The Jobber

At one point in their career this musician looked a lot like the survivor. But they hung around a few more parties, or read music better, and eventually got a break on an album as a side player or on a jingle or some high-profile gig that earned them a reputation. This break can come at any time, but usually happens when they are about 27 or 28 and generally occurs after they have been hanging around the scene for some time. When the break does come, they quickly become session players, getting hired often, usually with language like, "We have to get so-and-so, he's hot now."

Jobbers have no day job. They sleep during the day, sometimes do a session in the afternoon, and play with a heavy act that's in town at night. Or they're on the road with a national pop act, or playing in the pit band of a Broadway show or with a big orchestra. They often make as much as doctors, from $60,000 to $300,000 per year. If they're vocalists, they can make even more by doing national radio spots. Obviously, the supply-and-demand factor here is much different than for the survivor, and the competition for these jobs is murderous.

A subcategory of this same group is the writer/producer. This person is a heavy jobber but also writes songs and/or jingles. Because they are meeting and interacting with the top performers in the industry, they are in a choice position to hawk songs to them. As mentioned above, typically these same jobbers also write jingles and soundtracks whenever they can get the work. They rarely commit themselves to a single scenario, like a band, because they make too much money by staying uncommitted and floating from situation to situation. They always have a pet project that they're developing,[2] and I have yet to meet one who wouldn't chuck all the money they make for a good offer from a record label to do an album of their own stuff with themselves as the artist.

But these offers are rare to none. Ironically, the jobber is too overexposed to be of interest to labels, who mostly look for artists that are younger and are discovered under serendipitous circumstances.[3] Jobbers, however, will often network themselves into a producing position because they're good musicians, are personable, and have a lot of studio experience.

Some ironic facts about musicians:

1. Most pop musicians can't read music.
2. Many successful pop musicians never took a formal music lesson.
3. Up-and-coming pop musicians often live with their girlfriends.
4. Successful pop musicians usually don't allow their girlfriends to live with them.

[2] This is usually an artist that they have signed to a production deal (see "The Baby Record Deal," page 143).

[3] See "Gigging a Lot Is Good Exposure to the Industry," page 244.

WHO IS THE SONGWRITER
IN RAP MUSIC?

In rap, the question of who writes the "song" is a bit more complex. Rap usually has no melody to speak of. Since the Copyright Act recognizes the writer of the "melody" as a 50% owner of a song's copyright, how do we attribute ownership? Solution: The rapper-artist agrees to share writing credit between the writer of the rap and the arranger of the music bed, which is called "the beats."

Rap is not the only area where the definition of "songwriter" becomes unclear, but it is the most common. Consider the following scenario: You write a musical arrangement using only instruments and sampled loops. You arrange and, if you're using a computer, program the drums, bass line, and chords. But when it comes to the lyrics, you give it to a partner to write the words and a melody that fits into your musical groove. Who does the law recognize as the writer of the song? The answer is your partner, not you. If push comes to shove, your music bed, unless it is very unique, can be reproduced by another arranger. You get nothing, *nada*, no rights, no money, not even the home version of the game, and there will be little you can do about it[4] (unless you enjoy taking people to federal court—this is a subject we will revisit in several forms throughout the book).

Obviously this is unfair. The reason it works this way is because of left-over loopholes in the copyright law, which has yet to deal with the fact that songwriting often involves the scenario I just described. But people in the know recognize that the arrangement of a song can be, and often is, as important as the lyrics and melody. In fact, many arrangers have argued that since most lyrics in pop songs are unintelligible—the melodies buried under a wave of electric guitars, drums, loops, and synthesizers—what people are really hooking into when they buy a song is the arrangement, the sound and the production.

Hopefully the law will soon be updated to recognize the importance of the arrangement. Until then, lyric and melody writers will have the lion's share of the leverage when cutting their deals with arrangers.

[4] See "Sound-Alikes," page 192; and "Sample Rights," page 84. Oh, and for the lawyers out there reading this and thinking that I'm wrong because of the "collaboration argument," I say this: unless you're willing to take such a case on contingency, save your long-shot legal theories for those who can afford your fees.

⊜ Songwriters

Although it is easy to lump songwriters in with musicians or artists, I prefer not to. Songwriters have a unique place in the creative process in that they make the foundation for all other creative work. Plus, it is a misconception that most recording artists write their own material—most do not, particularly in the R&B area.

Also, many songwriters are not traditional musicians. Some don't even play an instrument; instead, they will collaborate with arrangers by humming the melody to their lyrics. An arranger/cowriter figures out the chords and composes the accompaniment that makes up the musical bed. This is an exception, though. Many writers play one if not several instruments. These days, computers have made it possible for one person to play many instruments without having to go through the trouble of learning music theory or playing technique.

Most writer/arrangers who share ideas with lyricists agree to split the writer's credit 50/50 regardless of who wrote what. It seems to be a simple way to end nasty arguments and keep the marriages friendly.[5]

If figured in dollars per hour, songwriters are the highest-paid professionals in the business. Songwriters who are *not* recording artists can make anywhere from zero to millions of dollars per year. If a writer has just one song on an album that goes platinum in the U.S., he or she stands to make about $65,000 on record sales

[5] The producer is often responsible for arranging the songs, and yet gets no cowritership. For this service he or she is generally compensated with an arranger's fee separate from their producer's fee, but it is a pittance if the song becomes a huge hit. (See "The Major Label Deal from the Producer's Point of View," page 87.)

SO YOU THINK YOU WROTE A SONG?

Think again. Ironically the word "song" is never mentioned in the Copyright Act, so there is no legal definition for it. So if the law can't define a song, how can we, as writers, copyright it? Remember, you can't copyright something unless it's fixed in a medium (like a piece of paper or a CD). So a song is really a "work" *that is the embodiment of a "literary work" accompanied by a musical composition "fixed" in a tangible medium in its "best edition."* Not too sexy. Imagine approaching the spotlight with, "Thanks for the encore. And now for our next fixed sound embodiment in its best rendition. . . ."

To make things simple, the word "song" as used in this book is exactly what you'd think it means.

alone, even if his song is the worst one on the record.[6] If their song is the hit single, then in addition to record sales they can look forward to royalties from the radio airplay. A typical hit song plays for six weeks, many times a day, on hundreds of stations throughout the country. It will earn an average of $150,000 for that year, depending on which Performing Rights Organization the writer is affiliated with.[7]

If you are a working songwriter and you manage to get even one average-sized hit a year, you can look forward to $200,000 to $300,000 for the year. If you're a superstar writer like Andrew Lloyd Webber, Babyface, Billy Joel, or the artist now once again known as Prince, you can multiply those numbers by ten.

These figures can be deceiving, though, because most writers have deals with publishing companies, agents, and managers, all of whom take a cut, but still it's not too bad for a profession that doesn't even require a high school diploma.

In 1997 the artist Sting signed one of the largest publishing deals in history— $32 million. Included in the deal were his rights to his older hits with the Police and several future albums. Also included was the money earned from sampling his hit "Every Breath You Take" for the rap hit "I'll Be Missin' You"—an estimated $600,000.

Some ironic observations about songwriters:
1. Most songwriters don't sing well.
2. A successful songwriter will earn more money in one year than the President of the United States will earn during his entire four-year term in office.
3. Almost no songwriters know the words to "Louie Louie."
4. George W. Bush knows the words to "Louie Louie," and has quoted them in speeches.

[6] See "9-to-1 Publishing," page 201, and "Publishing Deals," page 81.

[7] See "Performing Rights Organizations," page 37.

WRITE ME A KILLER TUNE

Serial killer/songwriter Charles Manson earned an estimated $66,000 on songwriting royalties when the '80s rock group Guns N' Roses used his lyrics for a cut on one of their albums.

Manson never saw the money. Authorities forced him to donate the cash to the families of his victims and the state for the cost of his prosecution. He wouldn't have much use for the money anyway.

➤ Engineers

This is a category close to my heart, because it is the group from which I came. Engineering is both a fantastic and a thankless task. Producers usually get the credit for the engineer's good work, and paying dues is murderous. But the engineers often are the hub of the entire creative process, like the lawyers are the hub of the business process. Engineers sit in on a lot of different projects, and they hear what everybody is working on well before the public does. They will often be asked their opinion by a producer for this reason. By way of this dynamic, the engineer will often become the psychiatrist of every person on the gig, especially the producer (who is usually pulling his or her hair out because of some insurmountable problem that could only be fixed if there was another $50,000 in the budget or by rewriting all the choruses in all the songs).

Usually, if there is no designated producer on hand, the engineer, by default, will end up in control of the session. Two or more band members may get into a dispute over a part, and in order to settle the argument the engineer will be consulted. Once requested, his opinion is rarely challenged.[8] It's easy to see why many engineers go on to be producers, but this was not always so.

[8] An important note: The engineer, unless he is close to the group personally or has clout, will *never* get credit or points for his coproduction advice.

In the '50s and '60s an engineer was someone who had a background in electronics and worked his way up, first spending time as a maintenance assistant for a number of years. Then, gradually, they were booked on sessions by studio managers, and—here's the important part—engineers became employees of the recording studios.

Today, studios don't generally employ engineers. They retain, on an independent contractor basis, studio assistants. Producers bring their own engineer, whom they are comfortable working with.

Most engineers today who work in larger commercial studios, especially remixers, have only basic electronic knowledge. They rely on the studio maintenance technician to know the internal workings of the machinery. An engineer's main responsibility today is to concentrate on keeping the session happening.

[9] Something that you may want to consider before embarking on the career path of engineer: As people invest in home studios, the need for engineers decreases, while the supply of them increases with each graduating class from dozens of audio engineering schools.

While successful engineers can make over $200,000 per year, the average working engineer makes about $40,000 if he works studio gigs regularly in New York or Los Angeles, and $125,000 if he's out on the road three-quarters of the year. Many engineers started out by investing anywhere from $5,000 to $10,000 in audio school to learn the techniques of engineering and then interned in a studio for little or no money. After a year or so, they became assistants and earned about $6 to $10 per hour before taxes.[9]

Almost 85% of the engineer interns/assistants are men, and they take home about $375 per week. Because they usually live in the major cities, it's easy to see that they must have some financial assistance, beyond studio work, to pay their bills. While it's true that there are many young interns and assistants who work hard and live frugally while paying their dues, the reality is that most come from middle- to upper-middle-class families who support their offspring during this hazing. And then there are those who, unfortunately, supplement their income by acting as procurers of controlled substances for their clients. I don't condone this, but I have known it to produce good results for some of my peers.

Another important point about engineers—they lead a very high-stress existence. They are constantly getting fired—usually for political reasons, but it's to be expected when you consider that the engineer usually gets the job because of political reasons. In order to attract clients, up-and-coming engineers often discount their work enormously, or give large commissions to the producers who hire them.[10]

[10] See "Kickbacks," page 95.

Some ironic facts about engineers:

1. In general, recording engineers know more about electronics than airline pilots.
2. The most important part of a half-million-dollar recording project, aligning the tape machine's electronics, is often done by the engineer's apprentice, who makes little more than minimum wage.
3. Many engineers are addicted to *Star Trek*, *Myst*, and *Grand Theft Auto*.
4. An alarming number of engineers are either heavy smokers or using the patch.

❥ Artists

Since this book is by and large very pro-artist, I'm going to take this opportunity to dissect some of the artist's more controversial qualities. Those who have had frustrating experiences with artists may want to pull up a chair.

I have, on more than one occasion, heard an A&R person say, in confidence, "This business would be so much easier if we could just make records without artists."

This statement is echoed by many in the industry. But why? If it weren't for the artist, we would have no music to enjoy and profit from, yet many pros roll their eyes in frustration or hide under their desks at the mere mention of "the artist."

To get an idea, we should consider all the problems that artists face.

Although there are the Britney Spearses who come from supportive families, I believe most artists come from working-class backgrounds. If they did come from money, they have divorced themselves from their families and are now self-reliant. I base this belief on the fact that many of them enter smaller record deals with poor representation and accept amounts of money that wouldn't impress people who are financially savvy. The facts would indicate that most recording artists are living in situations where they can be easily compromised into signing deals that give away a lot of their rights. In a moment of drunken fragility, most record execs will admit that a disenfranchised artist is often a cooperative one.

Most artists start trying to get a record deal when they are about 20. Although in recent years we've seen several superstar artists who are younger than 18, most don't generally sign a deal until roughly age 23 if they're women and 25 if they're men. Since it's often their second or third album that puts them on the map, they don't start to make a decent living until they are in their late twenties.[11]

[11] For the reasons why, skip to "The Major Label Deal from the Artist's Point of View," page 63.

Artists also face other complications that are dissuading. Because the industry has become so visual, artists often have to emphasize their looks to gain the attention of the pros. Many artists find these values distasteful as it instills the axiom that though love may be blind, lust is surely deaf! Compromise, to the artist, seems to translate as "selling out." Sometimes they're right, but often they're shooting themselves in the foot. (See "What Are the Odds?" in the sidebar below.)

WHAT ARE THE ODDS?

Consider the following fact: The average major record company receives between 10,000 and 12,000 demo tapes a year. Depending on the size of the annual A&R budget, each company can only sign between 5 and 40 acts a year.

These are not very good odds—1 in 300 under the best of circumstances. One might think that with so much working against them, artists would be willing to play ball with a record label *at any cost*. Many aren't. Stubborn artists will hold out for better terms, usually overstaying their welcome in the loop of people that they're dealing with. If the artist isn't willing to give up something, they will not get a first deal. Since the people who are shopping them only get paid if a deal is consummated, they will quickly lose interest in a temperamental artist. (See another sidebar in this chapter, "Arrogance and the Record Deal.")

I do, however, have a lot of sympathy for the artist's position. That's one of the reasons I've written this book. Often artists are being asked to compromise, and often it's for a deal that doesn't pay as much as they think (which we'll discuss in more detail in later sections). However, every person in a cutthroat business should understand where they sit in relation to their competition. Many young artists have embraced the business side of music with a fervor and understand the trade-offs that are inherent when art meets finance. These artists, for better or worse, stand the best chances for success.

How Much Do Artists Make?

When it comes to artists' income, it is difficult to speculate, because it fluctuates quite a bit during the course of their career. I'll be discussing different examples throughout the book, but if you need to know now, see "Wrap-Up" on page 167.

A revealing fact about artists: Despite their tendency to express gratitude to God at award ceremonies, most artists can more readily quote the Ludacris than the Bible.

❷ Producers

"Producer" is a confusing term, and often when I lecture I am asked exactly what a producer does. It can be hard to explain to someone who has not sat in on the recording process.

THE YUPPIE ROCK BAND

I have some friends who formed a successful club band called Everyone's Hero. Each person in the band was a professional: there were three lawyers, one real estate broker, and an accountant. They asked me if I could help them get a deal. They had a good following, and their music was as good as anything else out there on the radio.

I ran down the numbers as to what they could expect to get in the best-case scenario. I foresaw an artist development deal with $100,000 to start and an "all-in" recording fund of $350,000. (See "The All-In Deal," page 90.)

The total advance for the entire deal wouldn't have equaled the yearly salary of any two members of the band.

The producer guides the artist through the recording of their record. They help select the material and determine which takes are keepers and which are losers. Sometimes they compose the arrangements and do the engineering, and they usually supervise the final mix of the record.

Although the average record buyer thinks that the artist—the person whose picture is on the record jacket—is the one making all these decisions, they almost never are (unless the artist is a true co-producer).[12] The producer is responsible for the sound and quality of the record. If the mix is terrible, it's the producer's fault. If the performances are weak, it's the producer's fault. (There are exceptions to this, as you will see later.)

A good analogy is to think about the artist as being like a movie actor. The producer is like the film's director and editor. He or she tells the actor how to play the scene and the best way to communicate the message. More often than not, the producer will have veto power over a first-time artist's creative decisions.[13]

[12] Sometimes I encounter artists who insist on "co-producer" credit. Their rationale is that they made just as many creative contributions as the producer and therefore deserve the recognition. Although this thinking is not unreasonable, I tend to disagree. (Unless the artist is actually paying for the master and releasing it himself.) It's expected that the artist is making creative contributions. That's why they are the artist. What separates the producer from all other people who work on the record is that the producer is the one who is contractually accountable for the completion of the master. This puts a unique responsibility on his shoulders, and it is that which earns him the producer's credit.

ARROGANCE AND THE RECORD DEAL

I remember one group I produced back in 1987, a band that we will call Penny Whistle. They had a sound that was raw, heavily distorted, but with contemporary pop overtones. This sound would, in 1990, be labeled "alternative rock," but in 1987 it was noise to most.

I produced the band in my basement studio and took the tape to my lawyer. He liked it and started to pass it along to some of the people he was doing business with. Eventually one of them, Sony Records (which at that time was CBS), became interested.

My lawyer suggested to me that now would be a good time to secure a contract between myself and the band. He gave me a standard management/production contract from the firm's computer. It was nine pages long. The contract had language in it that obligated the band to fulfill a recording contract that I would negotiate for them, it secured me a 15% commission for all services rendered, and it lasted for three years.

The leader of the band decided that he wasn't going to be bound by any agreement that wouldn't let him quit when he wanted to. I explained to him that there was no way a record company, especially one the size of

In rock, the members of the band are the songwriters and the instrumentalists, and the producer has a more passive role, but in R&B and rap, the dynamics of the producer's role are more intricate. They usually write all the music and do all the arranging of the rhythm tracks. Then they find a vocalist, who will be the artist, to sing the lyric track. In this arrangement the artist/singer almost never has any say in the arrangement or the sound of the final product.

In terms of income, producers that are successful make over a million dollars a year during the peak of their careers, but these are rare exceptions. A typical producer gets a fee of anywhere from $25,000 to $75,000 per album that he or she produces and will produce about three to four albums a year. In addition to this, they will get an override on the records (about 3%) if the record sells big.

Many producers come from an engineering background. These producers often do remixing (the final process where all elements of the sound of the record are fine-tuned and balanced). The going rate for this service is between $10,000 and

13 If you read the liner notes on pop records, you will see that artists rarely use the same producer for their second albums. Usually it's because the artist can now assert the creative control they gave up in order to get their first record deal. This is especially true if the artist signed a "production deal" with the producer. See "The Artist/Producer Production Deal," page 144.

Sony, was going to invest in them if they didn't make a commitment for at least a couple of albums.

The band leader, Jimmy, who wrote all of the songs and was the lead singer, decided no. And so the deal was officially dead. Jimmy then quit, broke up the band, and moved out of town, stiffing me on his thousand-dollar production bill.

Last I heard, Jimmy was delivering pizza in Pennsylvania. One year later, a band with the same sound and look as Penny Whistle hit MTV as a buzz clip on *120 Minutes*. Their name—Nirvana.

I tell this story because it is typical, and it's my hope that you, the reader, can extract some lesson from Jimmy's example. Hold out for a good deal, but don't forget that the record business is just that—a business. Everybody involved needs to see some prospect of being satisfied financially in order to make the deal work. Some artists have difficulty understanding that. They often promise points to people helping them get signed. But if they haven't been through an actual record deal, they probably don't know what they're talking about. And when they see how much the percentage they promised really costs them, they will generally try to renege. We'll discuss why this happens in much more detail throughout the book.

$25,000 per song. If a producer is a remixer, he can do many such jobs a year. It has to be remembered, however, that producers have phenomenal overhead—mostly their special equipment that they use to create their sound. This equipment will get carted around from studio to studio, wherever the job takes them. In cartage alone a producer can spend over $50,000 a year. The equipment and insurance are many thousands more.

Two observations on producers:

1. Many producers have somehow mastered the knack of supervising several projects at once without attending a single recording session.
2. Producers rarely have anything positive to say about recordings they didn't make.

❷ Last but Not Least: Control Freaks

Have you ever had the displeasure of working for someone who distracted you while you were doing the very task they employed you to perform? If you don't acknowledge what they're babbling about, they become offended; if you screw up the job, they become indignant. You may not know it, but you were working for a control freak: someone who must, usually because of neurotic need, control every aspect of every situation all the time.

All right, in truth there is no specific person called "a control freak." I wish they did have labels; that way you would know who they are before you get involved with them. Rather, control freaks go by many more common names: egomaniacs, arrogant pricks, unproduceable, uncompromising sleazebags, and my favorite, "someone with a bad vibe." But no matter what you call them, their presence in the music industry is so pervasive that this particular player warrants his own section in this book.

It's important to point out that not everyone who wants their own way is a control freak. Some individuals are true perfectionists, and their persistence is for legitimate artistic reasons.

I'm not a psychologist, so I wouldn't presume to comment on why these people seem attracted to the music business. Perhaps the music industry's lack of official structure is an invitation to the control freak to "be their own boss." If you've ever found yourself threatening to sue someone because they owe you money for a job, and they say, "Go ahead!," you probably have a control freak on your hands and will in all likelihood never see that money. Control freaks are much happier paying their attorneys twice what they owe you.

In the following sidebar are some of the telltale signs of a control freak. If you find that the person you're working with fits more than four of the examples, start looking for new work.

CONTROL FREAKS...

- Ask many questions at inappropriate times.
- Won't let you off the phone when you are talking to them.
- Interrupt you when you're speaking.
- Want to do everybody's job (write, produce, manage, engineer, etc.).
- Tend to be argumentative and unwilling to compromise.
- Tend to have little professional training at anything.
- Will fire (or ignore) anyone who can outperform them.
- Will fire (or ignore) anyone who disagrees with them and is proven to be right.
- Order an extra dessert when someone else is paying the dinner bill.
- Relentlessly complain about how much things cost.
- Often employ simple-minded and incompetent help.
- Often complain that they have been ripped off.
- Owe money to many people, especially their lawyers, and construct brilliant rationalizations for not paying them.
- Consult expert after expert until one tells them what they want to hear.
- Make deals they have no real way to honor.
- Think they know everything.
- Will overcomplicate situations with misleading and esoteric information.
- Harbor paranoid suspicions towards other people and often generalize with terms like "they," "them," and "those people" without ever clarifying who "they" are.
- Believe that everyone is entitled to hear their opinion.
- Will usually take credit for anything that they can get away with.
- Often sport mustaches.

Counteracting the Effects of the Control Freak

If you are trying to work with this type of person, you must be careful. What they really think of you could depend on how useful you are to them at that moment. Some typical examples are the following: a person who thinks the whole industry is full of shit, but you are the one person they will trust; the producer or manager who insists on contracts with long terms attached to them; people who are interested in establishing their irreplaceability in a project before it is even off the ground; lawyers who want to manage as well as produce an artist but have little experience with anything other than law. I think you get the point.

So how do you deal with someone like this? It's not easy. The first thing I would suggest is to accept that there will be times when you will have to button your lip and play the cards the way that they are dealt. Aside from that, there are a couple of techniques that come to mind for coping with this person.

First, always let them think that you agree with them. You can't change their mind anyway, so just play along. Time and circumstances will usually prevail over their stubbornness. Second, never allow yourself to be caught up in their dogma. Always have a plan when you enter the employ of a control freak. Focus on why you are there and what you are getting out of it. As soon as you've achieved your goal, don't hang around one minute more than necessary. And, as a reformed control freak myself, I can tell you the cardinal rule for this type of person: Make them right. Even if it kills you. Acknowledge them and agree, no matter how absurd what they're saying seems. Remember an old Yiddish saying: "Never try to teach a pig how to sing. It wastes your time and annoys the pig."

CHAPTER THREE

Companies, Companies, Companies

So one afternoon you sat down and wrote a simple four-chord song and made a rough recording on your home hard-disk multi-track. You sent it to a friend who liked it, and the next thing you know a top artist heard it and fell in love. They want it for their next album. A few years later, the song is on the radio and it's a hit. You've won the jackpot. Suddenly, as if from nowhere, your mailbox is being stuffed with large, thick envelopes from various companies. Who are they? What do they want? My god! There seem to be hundreds of them and they all have thick forms and legal documents for you to fill out. You're hearing from record companies, performance rights organizations, publishing companies, promotion companies, the Musicians' Union, publicity companies, rights clearinghouses, and some guy named Harry Fox. At what party did you meet this Fox person, and how did he get your address?

It is staggering how many companies are associated with a marketable song—often referred to as "product."

All right, so the above example is a bit oversimplified, although I have seen songwriters with successes almost that dramatic. The point I'm making is that most artists are at first unaware of the staggering amount of paperwork and legal documentation that goes into the simple four-chord song they wrote and produced in their living room. Here is a basic list of the main types of companies and what they do. They are the entities we speak of when we speak of "the music industry."

⊜ Record Companies

Record companies are in the business of making bets. Every band they sign requires an outlay of cash. If it's a major label or a major-owned indie, it could be anywhere from $200,000 to $2,000,000 per act. If it's an independent, the tab is usually no more than $50,000. In essence, record companies are really banks that specialize in lending money to musicians. Continuing with this analogy, one could compare the A&R person and the business affairs person to loan officers. The idea that a record company *gives* an artist money is the most common misconception among new artists. In reality, record companies loan the artist money.

When you read about an artist getting a one-million-dollar recording contract, it means that the record company loaned that artist a million dollars. The artist is expected to pay it back out of the royalties that their record earns.

Aside from loaning money, record companies offer promotional and distribution services to a recording artist. These services can range from merely supporting distribution for an already finished record, usually for about 25% of the artist's profit, all the way to the other end of the spectrum of financing the recording of the record and then promoting and supporting its distribution. For this, the take is generally up around 90% of the proceeds from record sales.

Tour support and music videos, contrary to popular belief, are not a prerequisite in a record contract, although many new bands may get them. Whether tour support and video money must be paid back out of royalties, or whether they're an outright investment by the record company, is open to negotiation, and depends on the clout of the artist.

⊜ Production Companies

These operate in one way as record companies do—they develop talent—and one vital way that they do not, in that they do not have a specific distribution contract with a distributor to get their recordings into a retail environment. This is no small exception—if you can't get the records in front of customers, you usually can't sell very many of them.

Production companies, which I sometimes call "vanity labels" or "three-deep labels,"[1] are usually owned by producers or recording studios. They sign artists and produce demos and shop them in hopes of getting the artist a record deal.

[1] See the chapter "Vanity Labels" to get a complete understanding; I define this term a bit differently than others.

Many production companies dream of being record companies and often seek an affiliation with a major label or distributor to handle their product. But don't be fooled. Unless the production company has secured a distribution contract with a legitimate distributor or has found a way to independently release their recordings, they are no more capable of selling records en masse than you or I. For more on this see "Distribution Companies," page 46.

❯ Publishing Companies

The role of the publishing company is easy to comprehend, even if publishing deals themselves are not. Simply put, publishing companies safeguard the copyright by dealing with the complex renewal regulations, and they collect the money that is due to the songwriters they represent. They also litigate on behalf of their authors in case of infringement, and they shop your songs to various other companies to use in movies, commercials, TV shows, and so on. In exchange for these services writers agree to hand over the copyright of their songs in exchange for a

---

DISTRIBUTION DIATRIBE

I have known of several situations where XYZ Records (a fictitious example) had a distribution deal with a major label. Thinking that the major would get the record to the store for them, XYZ signed artists and went into production. Then the major's president was fired. The new president decided to trim the fat and let go of the "little labels" (sometimes called boutique or vanity labels) that they had been distributing, including XYZ Records. Now, overnight, XYZ is reduced in status to just a production company. If you are an artist and you are signed to such a company, watch your back. Your "record company" may lose their distribution. If it does, you might want to consider trying to get out of your agreement with them. Better still, when signing a contract with such a company, try to get language included in the contract that will give you an out should this situation arise.

percentage of whatever the songs earn—usually anywhere from 25% to 50% of the monies they collect for a songwriter's catalog.

If you've written a song that is going to be released on a major record label, you are going to make money. Because the Copyright Act of 1976 requires record companies to pay for the use of a song on a record, the major labels have agreed to pay an amount of money called a "compulsory rate" (sometimes called the "statutory rate") to each person who writes a song that's on any record they distribute. As of January 2006 the rate is 9.1 cents per song for each record distributed.[2]

[2] **See "Publishing Deals," page 81.**

So, to continue our mock example, you wrote a song that will now be on a big record. The record company must pay the owner of the copyright a compulsory licensing fee of about 9 cents for each song on a record, for each record sold. (See the sidebar, "What Do Doctors and Songwriters Have in Common?") A million-seller has huge potential.

The publishing company sees an opportunity to collect some easy coin, so they will try to make a deal to collect writers' royalties, since writers seldom want to go to the trouble of pounding the phones and hiring accountants to do this nasty work themselves. The publishing company will also collect the synchronization license fees for a song. A synchronization license is the fee that a movie or television company pays for the right to use the song as part of the soundtrack in a film or TV show. These fees can be quite high. For the use of Sonny and Cher's "I Got You Babe" in the movie *Groundhog Day*, the film's producers paid the song's publishers $80,000. Not bad. In recent years publishing companies have found new sources of revenue in "clearing samples." Samples are the small sound bits used mostly in rap and R&B to make up pieces of the groove of a song. The publishing company owns the rights to the songs embodied in the samples, so they can negotiate a fee for use of the sample in a new song.

As an artist or writer, you may be asking yourself, "Why do I need this? Can't my lawyer or manager (or consultant) do that?" Well, you may not. Starting in the '60s, many artists who wrote their own material realized that they were giving up 50% of their money to a service that they didn't require, because they were the artist recording the material. Why hire a company to sell the material to others? They began to make publishing arrangements directly with the record companies. In order to compete with this new trend, publishing companies started handing out big advances to new artists, as high as $1,000,000 for a new act. In fact, this still is not an uncommon practice. But still, why would an artist accept any amount of money to give away 50% of their music when they don't have to? For the answer to that and other perplexing questions, you will have to wait for chapter 6, "Publishing Deals." In the near future the need for publishing companies may be completely undermined by a new entity in the music business: the copyright administration company.

❯ Copyright Administration Companies

Over the past few years, in an attempt to compete directly with publishing companies, several entities have sprung up that will gladly collect a songwriter's (or publisher's) money and enforce his rights for a mere 10%. They call themselves copyright administration companies. They don't generally shop songs (but most publishing companies don't do that either these days), nor do they give you large advances. But if you haven't tied up your rights with a publishing company when luck strikes and one of your songs is placed in a major project, signing with one of these has huge advantages. You retain most of your rights, and these companies perform most of the same services that you would expect from a publisher. Some of these companies also administrate the copyrights of *sound recordings,* something traditional publishing companies do not do as yet.

Because these companies are new and innovative, many have embraced the advantages of the Internet with greater aplomb than the old-regime publishers. For example, some have online forms you can fill out to license a song. Its ease of use eclipses the old method of having your lawyer call the publisher to negotiate permission to put a cover song on your record or use it in a movie or TV show.

In the future you'll probably be seeing more of these entities and, in response, you will also see publishing companies doing all sorts of creative things to win back songwriters.

❯ Performing Rights Organizations

The one type of revenue that publishing companies and copyright administration companies let others collect for them are *performance royalties*—that is, the royalty that the writer/publisher of a song gets for each time that song is performed publicly on media like radio or network TV.

In the music business, "perform" has a unique definition that goes beyond the normal use. When you see a musician play a song on TV live, you're obviously watching a performance. But did you know that when a DJ spins a record in a club, what you're hearing is a "performance" as well, even though it's originating from a machine?[3] This also goes for cover bands playing at weddings, as well as jukeboxes in bars, VHS tapes, DVDs, CD-ROMs, turntables in nightclubs, and any other type of music that is experienced in a "for profit" public place. So, yes, the common interpretation of law says that each time a radio station plays a song for its hundreds of thousands of listeners or a DJ spins a mix in your favorite dance club, the writer should get paid a few pennies for the "performance." If the song is a hit, this can add up to quite a few pennies. But how can you ever know how many times each station or club plays a song, or how many wedding bands are turning your cool hit into "the bride cuts the cake"?

Enter the PROs, that is, the Performing Rights Organizations: ASCAP, BMI, and SESAC. (Also called "Societies.") In the United States, they represent the writers, the little guy out there trying to make a buck in the super-duper Big Brother environment of the broadcast industry. They stand for:

ASCAP: American Society of Composers and Performers

BMI: Broadcast Music Inc.

SESAC: Doesn't stand for anything. (They bought the name from a European company. The acronym doesn't translate into English, but they kept the letters anyway. Recently the Society of European Stage Authors & Composers has been added.)

These three companies monitor clubs, venues, theater, and the airwaves and keep track of who plays what and how many times. They collect performance fees (which vary according to the approximate listenership of each station or size of each venue) and distribute this money to the writers who are registered with them. Because the costs of negotiating millions of transactions would be prohibitive, a system has evolved using these societies in similar ways that unions represent laborers with collective bargaining. Each society negotiates a "blanket license" (kind of like a set annual payment) that permits broadcasters and venues to play music by its members.

Since you cannot belong to more than one PRO at a time, and since hit songs earn a ton of cash, these organizations compete fiercely for membership. The rivalry between ASCAP and BMI has filled the pages of several other books, all worth reading before you venture into joining either. To attract members, each sometimes offers cash advances to a new artist/writer who just signed a big deal (although they "officially" deny this practice), and each also boasts about its unique monitoring system. BMI's pitch is that they have the largest membership in the world. But is this a good thing? Here's some statistics to chew on that may put the whole game in perspective.

3 This should not be confused with a "mechanical royalty, also known as a "compulsory license." See "Publishing Companies," page 35, "The Harry Fox Agency," page 49, and "Publishing Deals," page 81, for what that is.

Society	Total membership (2004)	Total annual revenue 2004	Average annual (mean) earnings per member 2004
ASCAP	220,000	$700,000,000	$3181.81
BMI	300,000	$730,000,000	$2433.33
SESAC	6,000	$65,000,000	$9208.33

WHAT DO DOCTORS AND SONGWRITERS HAVE IN COMMON?

The law protects writers in a way that no one else in the music industry is protected. It guarantees that you are entitled to be paid. The only other professional in the United States who has a law guaranteeing a specific payment is a medical doctor. Behold . . .

> [Excerpt of the 1976 Copyright Act, Section 115:] ¶c-3 . . . the royalty under a compulsory license shall be payable for every phonorecord made and distributed in accordance with the license. For this purpose, a phonorecord is considered "distributed" if the person exercising the compulsory license has voluntarily and permanently parted with its possession. With respect to each work embodied in the phonorecord, the royalty shall be either two and three-fourths cents, or one half of one cent ($.005) per minute of playing time or fraction thereof, whichever amount is larger.

In English, this means that if you make a CD and give it to someone and have no intention of getting it back (even if you gave it away for free), then you, as the "record company," must pay this fee for each song on that record. Since most pop tunes are about 3.5 minutes, the compulsory license fee is more than the fee calculated by playing time (.005 x 3.5 = .0175). Because of increases in the fee after the 1976 Copyright Act, the compulsory fee is now a minimum of 9.1 cents, up from 2.75 cents. Oh, yeah—"phonorecord" is an antiquated bit of legal mumbo jumbo for CDs and tapes.

This fee is often called a "mechanical license," and it must be paid to the writer within a few months of the record's distribution.

4 There is no dispute
that at present
BMI's overhead is
slightly more than
ASCAP's. BMI is fa-
mous for sponsor-
ing large showcase
events to "shop"
their members,
whereas ASCAP
prefers more inti-
mate workshops
and salons where
pros come to
speak.

The above chart uses crude math and averages each society's annual cost for do-ing business at 15%.[4] So don't worship its results. It's just designed to show that more members does not necessarily mean more payment to those members. It also does not take into account that some writers earn millions a year through the societies, while others (the majority) get little to nothing. ASCAP and BMI claim complex se-cret formulas to figure out how much money each member makes. They hire peo-ple to listen to the radio all day and make logs of what songs are being played, al-though they both claim to be developing more modern methods in the coming years. SESAC has a more high-tech approach: they use an on-air monitoring service that recognizes the recording's digital wave when it's played over devices (like a radio). Regardless of claims by each, writers in all three societies at similar levels seem to make about the same amount of money.

There is currently much debate over how fair the systems for ASCAP and BMI are because to some it seems as though the payouts favor certain writers or types of music. SESAC has managed to dodge this bullet for the moment, since they use an "objective" computerized monitoring system—but it is likely that they, too, will be under scrutiny soon as their membership grows. See the chapter "ASCAP vs. BMI: PRO Pontification" (page 253) for more details on this.).[5]

There are other PROs in other countries. In fact, each European, Asian, and South American country has its own versions of ASCAP, BMI, and SESAC, but you need not concern yourself with them. For those with international hits originating in the U.S., the three main PROs mentioned above will attempt to collect from each of the smaller ones in the individual countries.[6]

Internet PROs

Due to the Internet, a new type of PRO designed strictly for collecting the per-formance royalties for digitally streamed sound recordings has been created. These days "digital streaming" means through the Internet and over satellite radio. Why is this new? Well, in the U.S., sound recordings were never paid a royalty when publicly "performed." That means, in simple terms, when a song played on the ra-dio, the songwriter made a royalty but the people who own the sound recording of that song made zilch. This includes the record company and the artist who per-forms the song. Hard to believe, but true. (In Europe and Australia both the song and the sound recording of the song are subject to performance royalties.)

However, a new statute that allows for the collection of royalties from "digital sources" has opened up a fresh revenue stream for artists and their labels. This roy-

5 Originally, SESAC
was interested
only in classical
music and royal-
ties from European
broadcasting, but
recently they have
been aggressively
pursuing more
members in the
U.S. pop arena. To
date they are still
the underdog and
remain in a distant
third place to
ASCAP and BMI.

alty is supposed to be split between the artist, the label, and the collective other musicians who played on the record in a 50%/45%/5% split respectively. (The musician's share actually gets paid to the AFM, which supposedly distributes it to members using its own formulas. See page 42.)[7]

While it's true that so far the only sources for earning "digital sound recording performance royalties" are things like Internet steaming/downloads and Internet and satellite radio, it's a given that in the not-too-distant future many forms of transmissions (and distribution) will be digital, and thus we will see artists now making additional money from these "performances" of their records. Examples might be the digital "beaming in" of music to restaurants and stadiums, as well as cell-phone ringtones and many other places.

As of now there are only two PROs vying to collect this money: Sound Exchange and Royalty Logic.[8] Sound Exchange has the largest amount of members and the largest amount of dollars distributed to date. But there is a down side to this company: It has strong ties to the major labels. This represents a conflict of interest (especially if you are an artist on a major label) since you will be relying on this company to "fairly" split the money between you and your label. Considering how "fair" labels have been to artists in the past, this connection must be watched carefully.

By way of a comparison, this is the same argument that ASCAP uses when competing with BMI. They say, BMI is owned by a coalition of broadcasters—the very entities that are supposed to be paying these fees to BMI writers. So joining BMI, if you're a writer, is like joining a union that is owned by the company you're working for. Or so ASCAP's pitch goes. Likewise, Sound Exchange was once owned by RIAA and still has strong ties to its former owner. Sound Exchange says that after they deduct a "reasonable" administrative fee, they will divide this money up fairly, giving 50% to record companies (that is, the companies they recognize as real record companies—read: RIAA members and their affiliates), 45% to featured vocalists (artists, in other words), and 5% chopped up between side players, background singers, and band members. We'll see.

❂ The Unions

Before I talk about the unions that hover around the U.S. music world, I feel that in all fairness I should disclose some of my political beliefs in this area. So if you're interested please see the sidebar "The Union Jack."

[6] (From previous page) Unfortunately, it seems that PROs in other countries are not as heavily regulated as the ones in the U.S. and sometimes don't pass on the money they collect to the writers. In some countries, like Spain, the only PRO is a company called SGAE: Society of General Autores (Authors) and Editoriales (Publishers). This company also distributes records and functions as a publishing company. This triple hat has many wondering if there are conflicts of interest within the organization.

[7] In Europe and Australia the split is only two ways: 50% to the label and 50% to all collective performers on the record.

[8] Royalty Logic is owned by a company called MRI, which does independent accounting (some would say oversight) of ASCAP and BMI on behalf of broadcasters.

The AFM

Unless you are the producer of the record, you will probably not have to deal much with the musicians' union (the American Federation of Musicians), which represents, according to them, about 15% of the known musicians in the U.S., or about 120,000 members. The AFM wants to know if the players on a recording were union musicians, and if they were paid standard union wages.

If the musicians were not union, then the AFM will try to get them to join and pay dues. Joining is a good idea for any musician who plans to play on a lot of big

THE UNION JACK

Truth be told, when it comes to artistic endeavors, I'm not very pro union.

I know, unions stand up for the little guy. In theory this is true, but the reality doesn't seem to work out that way anymore these days. Unions make individual trade agreements harder. Plus, graft accompanies some of the unions' activities in the entertainment industry to the point where one starts to wonder who they are really serving in the long run.

Now, I don't hate *all* unions. Clearly factory workers who are paid 1/1000th of what their CEOs are making need a collective group to stand up for their rights. But actors making millions a movie? Artists making millions in royalties? Don't they have expensive agents and lawyers protecting their rights? In addition, people who support the union agenda will avoid admitting that since the creation of the Taft-Hartley Act (the law that gives unions their power) we have had a radical evolution in labor law—the common law has caught up with the gaps that Taft-Hartley was supposed to close and we in the U.S. really don't need unions the same way we did in 1945.

"What would be a viable alternative, Moses," say you? I'll tell you. Instead of unions we should have "trade organizations." What's the difference? A union has the power of law behind it to *force* a company to hire its people, even if they are mediocre. Unions have no real incentives to train their members because the law *demands* that a corporation negotiate

record projects or jingles, the reason being twofold. One, as a result of a collective bargaining agreement between the union and record companies, the musician is entitled to collect a performance royalty for each new use of his or her work—for example, if you play on a record and it ends up in a movie. Or vice versa: if you play on a soundtrack and it ends up a CD. (Yes, even if you are responsible for playing the two-bar pennywhistle solo.)[9]

The second reason, and I believe that this is the more important of the two, is that no major label will give you credit on a record unless you are a member of the

[9] That's why producers normally require their non-union musicians to "sign off" their rights before the player enters the session. This does not mean the players don't get paid; they still get their union-scale session fees, which at the time of this writing start at about $120 an hour.

with them, or the corporation could face criminal penalties! This is why it's very, very hard to fire an inferior worker when he belongs to a union.

Doing business with a trade organization is voluntary. If your organization's tradesmen are good at their jobs, people will want to do business with them. To me that's the spirit of good capitalism. The best rising to the top. Not the one with the most powerful union.

Trade organizations can have pensions, just like unions, and they could have health benefits and all the trimmings that a union offers. We could have several trade groups within a field, giving tradespersons a choice as to which one they would join. Does an actor have a choice of unions if he appears in a Hollywood movie? Or a musician if he performs on a major label recording? No. There is only one union for each area. Where is the competition to keep these unions doing their best for the little guy? At present, there is none. That is capitalism at its worst.

Hard-core liberals will see this as a setback. And they might have a point. But I feel the bigger setback is losing billions of dollars a year to a runaway industry because the law in this country forces entrepreneurs to retain lazy or ill-trained workers. Yes, I'm stating my case in an extreme way to make my point, but I would take back everything I just said if the unions did half of what they advertise in the area of advocacy for members' rights. Both of the two unions discussed in this chapter have advocacy branches, but I'm just not feeling them. Maybe things will change when they realize that copies of this book are in the hands of their members.

Musicians' Union, even if you are a featured performer. (See "Getting Credit Where Credit Is Due," page 281.) Major labels also pay a small royalty (several cents per record sold) to the union for a "special payments fund," which goes to all musicians who worked on the record. Why are the labels so generous? The law requires labels to negotiate with unions, and because musicians are not only laborers when they play on records but also "authors," the AFM—according to the Copyright Act—is entitled to extract (although some would use the word extort) far more money from labels than they already do. The current label/union agreement is a compromise born out of a conflict between copyright law and labor law. But how much of the money for the "special payments fund" actually gets passed on to musicians is debatable.

Recently, in Latin music, the majors have been taking advantage of a loophole and not paying the minimum union scale to musicians who record for their Latin division. Labels claim that the Latin components of their family of labels are separate companies and therefore not bound by the agreement reached between the AFM and the parent label. So for example a label pays union wage, but its Latin label does not. The AFM has championed this cause and fought to get musicians (even non-AFM members) more money for their work when recording for the Latin subsidiaries of these majors. Meanwhile, labels often wonder what the union does for them in exchange for the money they are required to pay. The AFM claims that their members are the highest quality of performer available. But the AFM currently does not maintain a program for quality control of its members' skill or professionalism level, as other unions that service the arts do. Also, many musicians feel burdened by the AFM, as they are required to pay several hundred dollars a year in dues. The organization also does not secure employment for them, nor does it create a standard contract for recording artists like other unions, such as SAG or AFTRA do for actors.

AFTRA

AFTRA is the American Federation of Television and Radio Artists. How will this apply to you if you are an artist? Well, if and when you appear in a music video and that video is aired on MTV, technically you are a "television actor." The good news is that this means by law you're eligible for all kinds of royalties for the airing of your TV performance. And AFTRA is the union that is supposed to enforce and collect them, like the AFM does for "reuse fees" on master recordings.

The bad news is that AFTRA hasn't gotten around to negotiating a standard payment for these royalties with record labels and MTV, even though MTV has been on the air for over 20 years. They're getting to it, they claim. But AFTRA has been busy with other things. In 2003 they secured a health-and-benefits package that record companies will have to pay into. Major labels are now required to pay into a program for *every* artist they sign, including the ones that don't sell many records. But for reasons that are too complex to go into here (and too boring), most artists on majors won't get to see these benefits. But AFTRA's Health and Pension Fund will still collect on them.[10] The AFTRA website encourages all of its members to join SoundExchange, a company that is aligned with major labels (see page 41). I suppose SoundExchange has a reciprocal understanding

However, on a good note, AFTRA does enforce the recognition of a singer as an artist separate from the other musicians that play on a record. It ensures that an up-and-coming singer in need cannot be exploited by an unscrupulous producer or major label who makes them sign away rights for mere pennies. For this, AFTRA should be acknowledged.

[10] For an analysis of the reasons why, you can go to www.MosesAvalon.com and read the November 2003 Moses Supposes article called "*AFTRA Gets Labels to Cough Up Cash for Acts They Can't Sell: New Deal Might Hamper Artist Development.*"

❷ Publicity Companies

If your song is getting airplay and being nominated for a Grammy, you will at some point be approached by a publicity company. What do they want from you? Information. Your background, your influences, your next work, your former lovers, whatever they can get from you. This information is valuable to them because they sell it. You might be thinking, who would want to pay for this kind of crap? The only safe answer I can give is, you'd be surprised who wants to know. Magazines, news companies, competitors, and so on. If you become famous and your information starts to become very valuable, you will then hire a publicist to handle incoming requests and outgoing responses to any and all inquiries. A publicist is sort of like a press agent, except that they are not actually making statements of "fact" directly to the papers. Therefore they can get away with being "creative." Publicists work mostly for PR (public relations) firms, although many are independent.

❷ Independent Promotion Companies

Usually, record companies have their own promotion departments that handle their records, but the trend, for the artists that can afford it, is to hire an outside promotion company to support promotion of a new record.

The promotion company contacts radio stations and begs them to play a single off the artist's new record. Since airtime is limited, they have to beg hard. It is not unheard of for these companies to offer the program director of the station a "gift" if he puts the song in what's called "heavy rotation" (frequent play on the air). Many a hit has been "bought" in this way. (See "Airplay & Webcasting," page 121.)

❯ Distribution Companies

The distributor's job is to ship the records to record stores, keep track of how many are selling, collect the money from the record stores, and pay the label. Sounds easy enough, right? Most people think that a record company actually ships the records to the record store, but they don't. The record company sends the master recordings to a duplication factory with instructions on how many units to manufacture and which distributors to send the thousands of CDs, cassettes, 12-inch platters, and so on, to. The factory ships it all to the distributor's warehouse and the distributor sends the records to the record store on the record store's request. If the record store doesn't request the record, then it will stay in the warehouse.

Now here's the catch. All records are classified as a consignment item. This means that if you own a record store and you ordered a record that didn't sell, you can ship it back to the distributor for a full refund. Good news for the store, bad news for the artist.

As you can imagine, the potential for corruption and the tendency toward kooky accounting is great in such an environment.

Because the records can be returned, distribution companies keep what's called a "reserve" against artist's royalties. Even though they shipped 50,000 units to the record store, the distributor is not going to pay the label its share until they are sure that those records are not going to be returned. (To understand how this affects the artist and producer, see "Returns, Reserves, and Cutouts," page 73.) The label then in turn keeps a "reserve" against the artist's royalties and does not pay the artist their full amount due until the distributor pays them. An example of this is WEA/Maverick. WEA is a distributor that ships records and collects money from the retail stores for the sales of the records produced by artists signed to Maverick Records. WEA holds a portion of the money before passing it on to Maverick. Maverick then, in turn, withholds a portion of that money before passing it on to their artists.

Now you may be asking, what about things like iTunes and Yahoo? How does a distributor play a role there? At the moment distributors still are the key interface with online retailers, but this is certainly going to change soon. Once every man, woman, child, and dog has access to the Internet and wants to buy music that way, it's unclear why a label would want to give up a healthy percentage to a distributor when it can make direct deals without them. The future will be interesting.

E-tailers

The Internet has given birth to a new type of "distributor," the e-tailer. The biggest example is Amazon.com. These entities allow a customer to order a record off their websites, and then the e-tailer sends them the record via snail-mail.

These companies have been very useful to emerging artists who cannot yet justify a distribution deal with a major due to small sales numbers. E-tailers handle very small lots (as little as several units) and will usually charge about 30% for both warehousing and mailing. Aside from being a bit expensive, there is nothing wrong with this, but some e-tailers like to twist the meaning of the word "e-tail" to suit their particular business model and then call themselves a "distributor"when they are not. A distributor sells to retailers. E-tailers sell to the end user—Joe Public. Now, this might seem like a moot point, but it's really not. E-tailers generally have no contractual obligations to their clients in regard to the logistics of bulk inventory or insurance for payment. Nor do they compete with other distributors by marketing and promoting their artists, like real distributors do. In fact, e-tailers are not distributors even if they might like to think that they are. Making a deal with them is *not* the same as making a deal with distributors like ADA, BMG, or Virgin, whose job it is to market and promote your record to retail stores and keep track of thousands of units. Yet the fees some e-tailers charge is usually higher than what a major label will charge to do actual distribution.

❷ Digital Rights "Aggregators" (or Digital Distributors)

With the digital age comes a new middle-man to deal with. Aggregators sign up small labels (or independent artists with their own "vanity labels"—See "The Vanity Label," page 151, for more on this) with the nebulous promise of getting their music onto some of the more prestigious digital retailers, iTunes & Yahoo being the biggest at the moment, with a Microsoft strategy in the works as of this writing.

Why do small labels need aggregators? Why can't you just sign up to these services yourself? Well, because in many cases, despite their advertising, they won't

[11] Note: e-tailers do not engage in such practices. Another important difference between distributors and e-tailers: e-tailers do not "push" records. See "Distribution Companies," page 46.

take you. Services like iTunes have a lot of liability—or so they claim—and they don't want to do business with a fly-by-night that might be posting music it doesn't have rights to. This would make the digital retailer guilty of facilitating copyright infringement. So the retailer wants to be able to make a singular party responsible for "aggregating" the rights and clearing them, and then making sure the content is properly formatted (glitch free) before it gets to their pretty online store.

So the aggregators were born. They call themselves all kinds of other names that sound far sexier; "digital distributors" is the most common one (although technically they do not "distribute" as the term is used in the music business). Other names are "digital labels" or just plain old "indie labels"—ones that specialize in the on-line sales space. They charge anywhere from 15% to 25% of the total amount of money they collect for the artists/labels they handle.

Now, these are not companies to be suspicious of on their face, but, conversely, you should not allow their we're-too-hip-to-have-a-real-office-where-you-can-come-see-us philosophy put you at ease about signing over your rights. These deals can be tricky, and many aggregators don't really "clear" the rights they aggregate, leaving themselves and their clients open to litigation. (See "Digital Deceptions & i-Tunes Scams," page 208.)

⊙ Rights Clearinghouses

This is a relatively new branch of the industry. If your song is going to be used in a movie or TV program, the producer of that show will have to get the rights to do so. In order to facilitate this process, he or she will probably hire a "music supervisor" to handle the negotiating for all the popular music used in the film.

These supervisors act as clearinghouses for the rights and compensations to use the music. Almost without exception, they deal directly with the publisher of the song that has been requested. If you publish your own songs and you want them in the movies, be prepared to talk to the rights clearinghouses.

⊘ The Harry Fox Agency (the HFA)

Remember the 9.1 cents mentioned above in "Publishing Companies"? Well, how do we know that record companies are paying the songwriters their total required royalties and mechanical license fees? The Harry Fox Agency is a for-hire policeman that periodically checks up on record companies to make sure that they are living up to the provisions of the Copyright Act, which requires record companies to pay the 9.1 cents, called a "compulsory license" (or mechanical royalty) to songwriters and their publishers. The HFA charges publishers and writers affiliated with them a commission of 4.5% on any royalty money they collect. They also issue the license to labels that want to put a cover song on their record, and they are supposed to make sure the label pays the original writer/publisher his 9.1 cents per record sold.

The concept of the Harry Fox Agency is a noble one, but since its inception the record industry has evolved from several major record companies to over ten thousand smaller ones. Since the HFA earns money on a commission basis, their priority is not in the small profits to be gained by auditing little indie labels and their small runs of 10,000 units. And so, unless you are an artist signed with a large record

HOW MANY RECORDS CAN SLIP THROUGH THE CRACKS?

In 1983 ABC Records was sold to MCA.[12] When the accountants went through ABC's old warehouse, they found over nine million backlogged records collecting dust. These were sold to a "shady" distribution company for 35 cents apiece. No writer or artist was ever paid a royalty on this sale. MCA made close to $3 million in cash and barter.

[12] MCA is now owned by Vivendi Universal.

company, Harry Fox is a white elephant. I know for a fact that many smaller indie labels don't even bother to get a license from the HFA if they are going to put a cover song on their release. They just do it and let the chips fall where they may. And some big artists don't use Harry Fox anymore either because they don't want to pay the administrative fees. As the Internet makes "direct licensing" of music easier and easier for writers and small publishers, it's foreseeable that the Harry Fox catalog will diminish and, in time, and so too will its significance.

The HFA has been jockeying for position recently in some important negotiations regarding online music. (See Internet PROs, page 37.) Regardless, I feel the future of this company becomes more tenuous as the digital landscape develops and new forms of untraceable distribution (like downloadable music) become more common.[13] There are also several Harry Fox competitors that, for some reason, you never hear about. The main one is the AMRA (American Mechanical Rights Agency), located in Los Angeles. They work the same way and charge the same amount.

➲ The RIAA

In 1998, when the first edition of *Confessions* was released, there was little reason to mention the RIAA when discussing the companies an artist would have to interact with. RIAA stands for Recording Industry Association of America. It is a trade organization, or "club," so to speak, that represents the major labels (and their affiliate labels) in various legal matters. For many years it was most known for positive things like issuing the Gold and Platinum record awards when sales of a particular album reach certain levels (only to their members, though). These days they are most famous for suing a 12-year-old girl (as well as over 10,000 others) for illegaly downloading music from the Internet. The RIAA feels highly justified in this action by claiming that the companies it represents lost an average of $1,000,000 a day to piracy in the years 2000–2003. It also claims that because of file sharing the industry has seen a global decline of album sales to the tune of about 7%.[14]

But don't shed a tear for the majors or the RIAA too quickly. In 2001, the RIAA successfully positioned itself as the middle man collection agent for massive amounts of new revenue intended for record companies, artists, and musicians. This is due to a new law that creates a royalty for the "performance" of music when it is digitally transmitted, such as streamed through the Internet. Those eligible to receive this new royalty are the authors of the "sound recording" (the record, in other words). That would be the label, the lead singer, the songwriter, and the musicians. (See SoundExchange, page 41.)

[13] A legal controversy rages over whether a download on a service like iTunes is a strict mechanical sale or a "performance" (see "Performing Rights Organizations," page 37). ASCAP, BMI, and SESAC say it's a "performance," and Harry Fox says it's a "sale." Who wins will determine who gets the rights to collect millions in royalties each year. Place your bets.

[14] An article I did in April of 2004 that based its conclusions on SoundScan sales results impeached the RIAA's claims of lost sales during this time. Much of that article is encompassed on page 249, "Illegal File-Sharing Is Killing the Music Business."

Some strongly objected to such a close connection, asking why the RIAA should be trusted to collect all of this money, which some experts say will amount to tens of millions per year, instead of just the portion intended for its members. The RIAA boasted that it was the most qualified candidate because its members distribute 85% of the music in America. However, this number is a self-postulated reality. According to industry trade magazines, major labels release about an average of 83,000 records per year in recent years, while independent labels in that time were responsible for a little over 200,000 releases per year. Unfortunately, the RIAA's statistics are not measured by releases, but by units shipped. And since the four major distributors—the key participants in the RIAA—control all the major sales channels in the western world, the 200,000 releases on independents are not likely to be tracked with any degree of accuracy. So a small indie that distributes 5,000 to 10,000 CDs per year through local mom-and-pop record stores and nets about $150,000 per annum would not show up on the RIAA radar nor qualify as a "real" record company. When you account for all of this "under the radar" music, a more likely estimate of the RIAA's U.S. representation, according to some, is about 34%.

≥The Deal

I have on occasion compared the record industry to a football game. Imagine that you're trying to explain the rules of football to someone who never even heard of the game. Sure, the basic concept is fairly obvious, but sometimes it's the finer rules like offsides and holding that hold the key to the game's strategy. Without an understanding of the subtleties, a football game would just appear to be a bunch of people running back and forth willy-nilly as they chase a pointy brown ball.

This section breaks down the scrimmage of the record deal. As you'll see, the comparisons to football are more than incidental.

CHAPTER FOUR

⮞Understanding Distribution,
or Why Are There So Many Logos on the Record?

⮞ The Big Four

Before we can talk about a deal with a major record company, we must first define exactly what a record company really is. If we think of a record company as a company engaged in the production, manufacture, and distribution of records, by this definition there are only four record companies in the entire free world (ignoring China and the former Soviet bloc countries). They are BMG/Sony, UMVD, EMI and WEA.[1] (And it's likely that by the end of 2006 WEA and UMVD will merge as well.)

In fact, one could define a "major label deal" strictly as a deal to create a record that will be distributed by one of these four companies or their wholly owned subsidiaries.

To help create a picture that makes this clear, think about it as four trees with one distributor as the trunk of each tree. At the first branching off of the tree trunk, you would have each of the distributor's major affiliates. For example, WEA's main companies are Warner Bros. Records, Elektra Records, and Atlantic Records. These three companies make up the first three and largest branches of the tree. From these branches come the smaller twigs—the other labels. (For

[1] Starting in the mid-1980s, independent avenues for sales tightened and labels merged. By 1987 most significant independent labels had joined one of the six main distributors. Arista joined RCA. RCA joined BMG. Chrysalis went to EMI. A&M merged into PolyGram, making 90% of the national major label product controlled by six companies. At the end of 1998 PolyGram became part of Seagram's, who owned Universal Music as well. They then sold it only two years later, in 2001, to the Vivendi Universal, making it an almost neck and neck tie with Warner Bros. Records (WEA) as the largest music distributor in the world. WEA was bought by Internet giant America Online in 2001, which then sold it off in 2004. BMG and Sony merged in 2004, narrowing the distribution pipeline down to only four majors.

2 Recently the trend is for major-distributed "indies" that have shown an ability to create a unique voice to assert their autonomy. In the future you'll be seeing fewer multiple label names on videos and records. So, for example, Motown and Mercury, although both are distributed by Universal, don't feature the Universal name on some of their product. Also, if you are fond of watching the MTV shows that feature videos from the 1980s, you'll notice a longer chain of of names on the videos than you do on videos released these days.

3 This might be because PolyGram's actual corporate parent name used to be Groeilampenfabrieken N.V.—known in America as Philips Electronics—and they make most of their money selling computer circuits. How many recording artists would care to boast that they're employed by a Dutch components conglomerate? They were bought in 2001 by the Vivendi Corporation. Vivendi does healthcare and waste management. Most of their money comes from construction and selling bottled water.

a more complete picture of how the industry is structured as of this writing, you can refer to the "Major Label Family Trees," page 306.)

Here are a few examples:

1. From the Island/Def Jam branch of UMVD comes Mercury Records.
2. From the Atlantic Records branch of WEA comes Elektra.

Sometimes it can get confusing, because a Big Four distributor can have the same name as one of their record divisions:

3. From the RCA Music Group branch of Sony/BMG Sales Group comes RCA Records—not to be confused with the RCA Nashvile, a record company that is also distributed through Sony/BMG Records Group.
4. From the Island/Def Jam distribution branch of UMVD comes Def Jam, from which, in turn comes the famous classic label, Island Records.

A family tree of the distribution channels expands every day, with more and more offshoots of labels splitting the branches thinner and thinner until you get to what I call "vanity labels"—small labels that have only one act on them. (See "The Vanity Label," page 151.)

When you look at a CD you'll notice that there are several logos on the mirrored surface. These logos make up the pipeline of the act's distribution. These same names appear at the base of the TV screen when you watch the group's video. Some examples are "BMG/Arista" and "Sony/Epic/Crescent Moon."[2]

❷ What Is a Real Independent Label?

The independent label enjoys a certain freedom that majors do not. They are not managed by a multinational conglomerate so they don't have the pressure of annual financial reports to live up to (see "The Big Picture," page XXX). They are owned and operated usually by one or two people with a love of music and a brash entrepreneurial spirit. But these days there seems to be an underlying desire for many record companies to market themselves as "independent" when in fact they are controlled wholly or in part by one of the majors. PolyGram, for example, when it existed, had almost 100 smaller labels under them at one time, some of whom would refer to themselves as independent.[3]

The term "production company" is often misrepresented as an indie label. For example, consider Shady, a "record company" owned by the artist Eminem. It's displayed like this: UMVD/Interscope/Shady. The last label in the distribution chain, Shady, is, in reality, only a production company. They sign the artist and develop the act. The next label in the chain, Interscope, usually markets and promotes the act, and the last label, UMVD, one of the Big Four, distributes the record.[4] (Use of Shady as an example is not meant to imply that they are trying to misrepresent anything. It's only an example.)

It starts to get confusing as to whether a label is a true independent. Logic would simply define independents as labels that are not distributed by one of the Big Four. But consider this example: Favored Nations (considered by many to be independent) is distributed by independent distributor RED. But RED, one of the largest independent distributors in the world, is 60% owned by Sony. Does that mean that Favored Nations is no longer an indie label? Sony claims it's a silent partner with RED, allowing them to maintain their own clientele of mom-and-pop record stores. Of course, this might change in time.[5]

To add to the difficulty in defining "independent" is the fact that a single indie label could have several distributors. For example, at one time the indie distributor Vernon Yard was partially distributed by another indie distributor, Caroline, and partially by its parent major label, Virgin. Yet parts of Caroline are also distributed by Virgin, and all of Virgin is distributed by EMI, slated to be owned by Warner in 2006. Confused?

In the early part of the 1990s the industry saw a serious readjustment: the sale of MCA to beverage behemoth Seagram (makers of the famous vodka). Following this was the forming of DreamWorks with record industry guru David Geffen. Both had ripple effects throughout the industry that resulted in a great deal of consolidation.[6] Because of this consolidation, nowadays it's common to find labels that are not controlled by one of the Big Four, yet have some of their product distributed by them. These labels have crossbred the family tree of majors with independents to become what some have called "the major/indie."

God help us.

And then there is yet another criterion that must be considered: the actual contract that the artist will sign. The theory behind signing with an indie is that the business will be more relaxed. More creative control and less suit-and-tie crap. But most of the so-called indies that we're talking about here use the same contract that majors employ. Why? Well, because many an indie has dreams of being bought out someday by a major. Having a contract that is too radically different from the majors' could nix a deal. Also, many so-called indies don't have the money to develop their

<aside>
[4] Part of the confusion of major vs. indie has roots going back to 1975, when major labels were appalled by a new brand of music called punk. Punk's violent anti-social lyrics offended the sensibilities of major label A&R, but small labels recorded these bands and were able to sell millions of records through little mom-and-pop stores. Many of these labels, called indies because of their non-mainstream taste and because they had no direct distribution ties to major distributors, were literally run out of people's bedrooms. Majors eventually caught on and bought out many of these "bedroom labels," but by then the trend had faded. The bedroom labels, now clearly extensions of the corporate machinery that bought them, still called themselves "independent," perhaps as wishful thinking and in keeping with the political climate of the time.

[5] In fact, it already has. Massive consolidation in 1998 and again in 2004 has dissolved many of the indie distributors, and mom and pop record stores.
</aside>

6 (From previous page) The MCA sale sparked a huge restructuring at Warner Bros. Records and EMI Records. Both of these giants consolidated, letting go hundreds of people. The Time Warner Corporation eliminated many of their sub-labels, allowing smaller companies direct contracts with the parent label/distributor, Warner Bros. Records. EMI followed by dissolving several of its middle management divisions and became EMD (which stands for EMI Music Distributors).

7 A trend in the last few years—since the most recent consolidation of labels in 2004–2005—is to take labels that have had excellent success and create a hybrid of the major label and the parent label called a "group." A "group" is not usually an individual label (with some exceptions). A group takes several catalogs of older labels where only a few artists are still active and bundles the catalogs under the management of one parent label; in essence these

own legal templates (which costs thousands of dollars to do from scratch). They use existing contracts, figuring that these are the best since they were produced by major labels. So, considering these circumstances, it can be argued that any label that uses the same contractual structure as a major is seriously thinking about selling out to one, and should be disqualified from being able to hold its head up as a true "indie." (See "Indie in Disguise," page 137)

So who's left? If every label is somehow tied to the Big Four in some way, what alternatives do we have? Well, there are many small labels that are not distributed by the Big (Brother) Four but rather by smaller distributors such as Dutch East India. These distributors function just like Big Four labels in that they shift the burden of warehousing and shipping the records to stores off of the label and charge them a fee of about 25%. Indie volume demands are also much lower. An indie distributor would be happy to ship from 5,000 to 50,000 or more records a year from one label. These numbers would be a joke to a Big Four company.

By strict interpretation there is only one company that is presently independent and has annual sales equivalent to a major label—the Walt Disney Company. They produce, manufacture, and distribute everything themselves. But we don't think of them as an independent, for obvious reasons.

❯ One-Deep & Two-Deep Labels

Rather than get all hung up about who is and is not a true indie, I'm going to invent my own jargon. For the purposes of this book, I'm going to call all record deals for which the records end up being distributed directly by one of the Big Four "major label deals," and all the parent labels that are wholly owned by them "major labels." So, for example, some major labels would include Interscope and Atlantic, and so on. These days many of these have the word "Group" attached to them.[7] The labels that are branched out from major labels (or groups) will be called "one-deep labels." Take Bad Boy Entertainment, which is distributed by Universal, but marketed under the Universal Motown Group. The chain would read "UMVD/Motown/Bad Boy" on the CD; on the video these names are sometimes reversed, such as "Bad Boy/Motown/UMUD." Regardless, since Bad Boy is one step away from the actual parent distributor, I'm therefore going to call the deal on Bad Boy a "one-deep label deal."

As you've probably guessed by the way the proverbial distribution tree branches, there will be two-, three-, and four-deep label deals as well. For example the alternative "indie" label called Flip is actually marketed through Interscope, and distributed by UNI. The chain would look like this: UNI/Interscope/Flip. A deal on a label like Flip I will call a "two-deep label deal."[8]

Anything that falls outside of Big Four distribution will then be called "indie distribution," or "indie deal." Bear in mind that there are many indies who actually do take their records to the store themselves in a van or a car. We have to admire this kind of determination, because it is these individuals who discover and cultivate most of the best music. These people look at talent first and the bottom line second. Therefore, we shouldn't begrudge them the few dimes more that these records cost, because a world without indies would be a gray world indeed.

However, the odds of making any serious money with this self-delivery method are long odds indeed. Since most artists want to make a lot of money, they invariably look to the major labels, thinking that should be their first way to go. In many cases this can be exactly the wrong approach. To understand why, let's look at how a major label record contract works.

"groups" are the new parent labels. Examples include "Universal Motown Group" "Island/Def Jam Music Group," "Verve Music Group," "Columbia Records Group," and, in the most notable growth from small production company to major player, "Zomba Label Group." See the last chapter of this book, "The Big Picture," for a complete outline of who owns what (Page 293).

[8] Since the contract with Flip will read very much like one with its parent label, MCA, I therefore classify Flip as a major label, though the A&R staff there might take issue with me.

Flow of Ownership

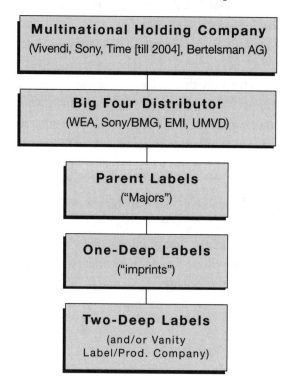

Multinational Holding Company
(Vivendi, Sony, Time [till 2004], Bertelsman AG)

Big Four Distributor
(WEA, Sony/BMG, EMI, UMVD)

Parent Labels
("Majors")

One-Deep Labels
("imprints")

Two-Deep Labels
(and/or Vanity
Label/Prod. Company)

Sample Family Tree

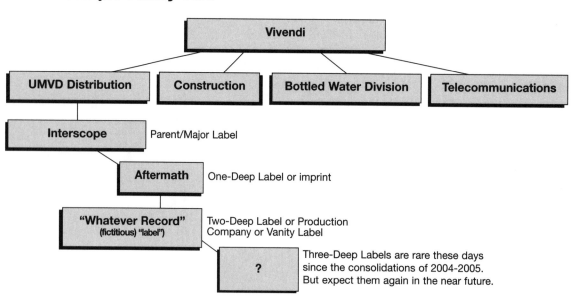

Vivendi

UMVD Distribution   **Construction**   **Bottled Water Division**   **Telecommunications**

Interscope   Parent/Major Label

Aftermath   One-Deep Label or imprint

"Whatever Record"
(fictitious) "label")   Two-Deep Label or Production
Company or Vanity Label

?   Three-Deep Labels are rare these days
since the consolidations of 2004-2005.
But expect them again in the near future.

UMVD Distribution

UNI

Geffen Records
413
Chess
Drive Thru
Fiddler
Flawless
Flicker
I Am
Geffen
DGC
Experience Hendrix
Radioactive
Rawkus
Never So Deep

Universal Motown Group
Bad Boy
Blackground
Brushfire
Casablanca
Cash Money
Cherry
D Block
Enjoy
Fo' Reel
Moonshine Conspiracy
Motown
Next Plateau
Polydor
Republic
Rocket
Street
Strummer
SRC
Strummer Recordings
The Ultimate Group
Universal

Fontana Distribution

Universal Music Latino
CJ Latin
Flow Music
Fonosound
Gold Star
Guitian
Infinity
Karen
Latin World
Mas Flow
Music Haus
Musimex
New Records
Perfect Image
Pi
Pina
Pimient
Pina Records
Planet Rhythm
Platano
Big World
Music Up
Protel
Revolú
RMM
Universal Music Latino
Vale Music
Vivamusic

Universal Classics & Jazz
Classics
Decca
Decca U.S.
Decca Broadway
Deutsche Grammophon
Archiv
ECM
Philips
Mercury Living Presence

Universal Music Enterprises
Chronicles
Hip-O Records
New Door Records
Universal Special Products
UTV

Universal South

Univision Music Group
Univision Records
Fonovisa Records
Ramex

Varese Sarabande Records
Fuel 2000
Sunswept Music
Water Music

Verve Music Group
Blue Thumb
GRP
Impulse
Verve
Verve Forecast

E2 Music
Empire

Walt Disney Records
Buena Vista
Walt Disney Records
Disney Sound

Island/Def Jam Music Group
American Recordings
Def Jam
Def Jam South
Def Soul
The Inc.
Roc-A-Fella
Island
Kemado
Mercury
MonarC
Murder Inc.
Roadrunner

Concord Records
Concord Records
Concord Picante
Peak Records
Playboy Jazz
Stretch Records
Concord Jazz
Fantasy
Contemporary
Good Time Jazz
Kicking Mule
Milestone
OBC
OJC
Pablo
Prestige
Riverside
Specialty
Stax
Takoma

Interscope/A&M
A&M
Interscope
Almo
Aftermath
Amaru
Beat Club
Cherry Tree
Flip
G-Unit
Kickball
Nothing
Ruff Ryders Ent.
Shady
Vagrant
Weapons of Mass Ent.

19 Records
ABKCO Records
ARK 21
Mondo Melodia
Bungalo
Disa
Procan
DreamWorks Nashville
DreamWorks Records
Fonovisa
DMY
Garmex
Oro Musical
Platino

Hollywood Records
Lyric Street
Mammoth
Skaggs Family
Ceili Music

Lideres Records
Ole Music

Machete Music
Los Cangri, Inc.
VI Music

Palm Pictures
Pyramid
Sybersound
Thump Records
B-Dub
Discos Fama
Thump Street

UMG Nashville
DreamWorks Nashville
Lost Highway
Mercury Nashville
MCA Nashville
Rounder
Bullseye
Heartbeat
Marsalis Music
Philo / Zoe

CONFESSIONS OF A RECORD PRODUCER

CHAPTER FIVE

The Major Label Deal

from the Artist's Point of View

L et's say you're in a rock band and your manager calls and says that he has wonderful news: he's negotiated hard with Pacific Records, a huge label distributed directly through one of the Big Four, and he's got you a great deal—the kind you dream about, the kind that will make you famous (Pacific is a fictitious label for the purposes of the example; don't go looking for them).

First off, he's got you a full-color album cover and full-color printing on all promotional materials (Pacific only wanted to give you black and white at first). He's also persuaded them to give you a five-album contract instead of only three, plus the company has agreed to manufacture 100,000 units in your first printing. And, you're gonna make at least one video. You're gonna get $200,000 for the first record and $300,000 for the second, with a sliding royalty scale that goes up with each album you record.

Sounds amazing. Where do I sign?

Well, before you get too excited, remember the football analogy. You need to understand some things about offsides and holding. In reality, a good manager would never let you sign a deal like the one above unless the advance money was so big that no one cared how many records you were going to sell. Are you surprised? Then you're reading the right book.

There is an allure surrounding the major label record deal that seems to have many new artists mesmerized. So much so that they rarely ask the important questions about how the deal really pays off.

On the surface, the concept seems simple enough. A group is "lent"[1] money by a record company to record songs. When the recording is finished, the company markets it to the public and waits to see if the record sells. If it does, they pay the group or artist a percentage of the profit, known as a royalty. If it doesn't sell, then the record company and the group go their separate ways.

Obviously, it's not that simple, or we wouldn't need the pros. What most lawyers, producers, and managers won't tell you (unless you ask) is that a deal with

[1] Many lawyers object to my use of the word "lent," because "advance" has a more precise legal definition. They're being anal.

MATCHING TIE AND AX

When you sign a major recording contract, you are in effect signing an employment contract. The band, or artist, will become an employee of the label. You will perform where they ask you to perform, record when they ask you to record, and re-record if and when they ask you to re-record. They own your work, and they own whatever they can get that your contract lets them have. Most pros won't tell the artist this for the obvious reason—most artists are looking to avoid employment. The idea that if they sign a major record contract they are becoming a "company person" will be an instant turnoff, so it's not generally mentioned. Even though there is language that specifically states that the recording agreement is not an employment contract and that the artist is an independent contractor, this is semantics. The recording contract functions as an employment contract no matter what they call it, except you don't get the health and pension benefits that you would if they called you an employee.

Most large companies compensate their employees with retirement plans, like 401(k) plans. No record company that I've heard of in the United States initially offers their artists any means of squirreling away their earnings (except by recommending "financial planners"), yet they treat their artists like employees by controlling the quality and frequency of their work.

a major label is, in effect, an employment contract (see the sidebar "Matching Tie and Ax").

Even if you express concern over this, a pro will still steer you in the major label direction because, they will say, that's where the most money is, and the best opportunity for success. What they leave out is that that's where the money is for them, not necessarily for you, the artist. Pros usually work on commissions and fees, not royalties. An attorney negotiating a major record deal will bill between $5,000 and $50,000 dollars for that negotiation. The manager gets 15% to 20% of the advance (which might typically come out to about $100,000 for him). The accountant or business manager gets 5%. Since their payoff is directly tied to the size of the advance, their main incentive is to get as much money as possible up front. Producers are of the same mind: the bigger their budget, the bigger their fee.

So what's wrong with commanding high fees and getting a lot of money from a major label? Well, nothing if the artist is popular enough to justify a big advance. But if you are starting out and no one has heard of you yet, it can be disastrous. You're about to see why.

◉ Recoupable Financing—
The Moving Goal Post

As mentioned earlier, record companies do not give away money, they loan it in the form of an advance against future royalties. The only difference between a record company and a bank is that with a bank you have to pay the money back regardless of the success of your venture. With a record company, the artist doesn't usually have to pay back anything if the label drops them. In the finance world, this is called "forgiven debt," and for this privilege record companies feel that they have the right to ask for a disproportionate split of the proceeds. For a new artist, typically the split is 12% artist, 88% record company.[2]

The really sucky part is that the artist pays back the big advance (i.e., loan) out of their 12%. Meanwhile, the record company is recouping their expenses from their 88% end of the stick.

You don't have to be a math genius to figure out that long after the record company has recouped its initial investment, the artist is still trying to recoup out of the 12%. Eventually, if the record sells, the artist will make additional money, but where is that threshold? You'll see soon. (If you're impatient, fast-forward to the Egghead Boxes, pages 67 and 71.)

2 Critics of this chapter (lawyers, usually) argue that no self-respecting lawyer or manager would let their client sign a deal for only 12%. They claim to get at least 15% for their clients. They are forgetting that in just about every scenario there are deductions that bring the 15% (called a base royalty) down to about 12% and sometimes less than that. For more on this see *Secrets of Negotiating a Record Contract* and "The 3/4 Royalty" (page 69).

Unfortunately for the artist, the above example is only the start. Out of the artist's 12%, a quarter of that (3%) goes to the producer. Producers, if they are in demand, traditionally get paid their royalty up front, from record one, meaning that they get paid from the first record sold and not after the recoupment of the artist's advance.[3] In other words, if you owe your label $500,000 and the producer gets paid 50 cents from the sale of each record, and you are paid one dollar from each sale, then if you sell one record, a dollar is subtracted from your debt and 50 cents tacked on. You now owe the label $499,999.50. If you sell two records you owe the label $499,999.00. And so on and so on. If this doesn't make sense now, it's okay. Continue reading. The important thing to grasp is that the record company tends to pay the producer's royalty first with each record sold and tacks what they pay the producer onto the artist's bill. Think of it as each unit sale allowing you to take three steps forward and one step back.

In addition, in most contracts 50% of the money spent on videos, tour support, promotions, and the cost of full-color record jackets also gets added to the artist's recoupable account.

[3] In some situations, an up-and-coming producer may have to wait for the recoupment of the recording fund before he gets his money. It's the same amount of money; he'll just get it later.

❷ The Big Four Deal with Real-Deal Numbers

Let's apply some real-life numbers to this example. Now, it's possible that you will be in high demand, that a huge bidding war will ensue for your masters, and you'll get the type of deal you occasionally read about in the trades: $1,000,000 signing bonus, $500,000 production budget, five-album guarantee with star producer attached and the label throwing in a condo to live in while you're recording, a $1,000,000 video budget with P Diddy as producer, director, and personal shopper. But let's start out a bit more realistically.

A typical major label deal would include giving about $200,000 to the artist for the production of the album and setting aside another $300,000 for promotion, making a total bill of $500,000 to the artist. This bill is called by accountants "the aggregate sum" or "the Schedule of Standard Costs" (SSC). Another, more common name for it is the "recoupment fund." They are all more or less the same thing. Try to remember these terms, as they'll be used over and over again.

Out of the $200,000 production budget, the manager takes 15% of this, or $30,000. The lawyer takes about $5,000 for services rendered in negotiating the deal. Let's say that the producer takes only a $10,000 fee (this is very conservative, believe me).

This leaves the artist $155,000 to make a record and live on while they are in production. Production could be anywhere from three to five months.

I know many artists who spend the entire $155,000 in the studio and have nothing left over for themselves. The producer will try to persuade the artist to do this, because he makes more money.[4] But let's say that the artist holds him down to a $100,000 budget and decides to save $25,000 for unanticipated expenses. This leaves $30,000 left over for the artist. If there are four players in the band, then that will be split four ways, leaving $7,500 for each member of the act—before taxes.

This is all the money that the artist will see from the label on that record until the label has recouped the entire $500,000 advance![5]

So How Long Till I See Some Money?

In our example, the artist's deficit to the label is $500,000 for recording and promotion expenses. They will pay the company back through their royalties. Let's say that the CD's suggested retail list price (SRLP) is $17.00. For each record that sells, the artist gets 12% of that (or $2.04) deducted from their recoupment fund. But remember, for each CD sale the producer gets paid their 3%, or 51 cents, first. This 51 cents gets deducted from the $2.04 above, so only $1.53 actually gets deducted from the artist's debt to the label. Rather than teach an accounting lesson here, I'll give you the break-even number. Using these figures, the artist will have to sell 326,797 records before the record company is required to give them any more royalty money on album sales.

4 See "The Major Label Deal from the Producer's Point of View," page 87.

5 In some cases the label will spend additional money on tour support. But even if they do, this money is invariably recoupable from the artist's royalties. There is also additional income from publishing advances if the artist is also a writer, but we'll deal with that later.

EGGHEAD BOX #1

Let x = the number of records to break even.

Artist's & Producer's share		Aggregate sum (SSC)		Producer's share
$2.04x	=	$500,000	+	$0.51x

$1.53x = $500,000

x = 326,797

➲ Packaging Deductions and Giveaways

But don't get too excited. In most record contracts, major or indie, there are two things to look out for. The first is the now-famous packaging deduction, also called a container charge. This is the cost of the actual case that the record is wrapped in.[6] The amount usually charged to the artist is 25% of the retail sales price of the unit, or about $4.25 in this case, which is deducted off the retail sales price *before* the artist's and producer's royalties are computed. This means that even though the artist is supposed to get 9% of $17, they will really only get 9% of $12.75. Snag. The way this is usually phrased in the contract is a "25% container charge on CDs and a 15% container charge on cassettes and 12-inch phonorecords."[7]

The second pitfall is the "giveaway" clause, also known as "free goods." The record company will argue that in order to promote a new artist they will have to give away many CDs. The distributor of the record will want latitude with "giveaways" as well, in order to induce a record store to pick up a new artist—like, buy two boxes and get one free. For this reason the artist will agree that a royalty will only be paid on actual records sold and not on records that are shipped or are given free as promotion. The programs for giveaways are often called "special goods programs."[8] This deduction is usually another 25%.

➲ Breakage—The 90% Rule

Even within the actual sales (called "bona fide sales" in most contracts) the record company will only pay you on 90% of them because of "breakage." This is an old tactic left over from the time when records were made of brittle vinyl and occasionally broke during shipping. The record company's rap is that the artist shouldn't be paid for broken records.

This was bogus even back then. Now that most records are CDs made of polycarbonate, one of the strongest synthetics in the world, this clause is beyond ludicrous. Add to this the contorted logic of the whole thing: Records are a consignment item—a healthy record can be returned if it's not sold. Certainly then it could be returned if it arrives at the store *broken*. But the clause is still in many major label contracts.

So now we have a royalty base of $12.75, which is only payable on 90% of the sales. (I have seen contracts where the breakage clause is as stiff as 80% of sales.)

[6] With CDs this is called a "jewel box."

[7] We all know that it doesn't really cost the record company $4.25 to package the album. It probably costs about $1, but it is an accepted "give" that artists deal with.

[8] When you reach star status, you can usually negotiate this out of your contract. There is not as large a need to seduce a record store to carry, or a radio program director to play, someone like Garth Brooks.

❯ The 3/4 Royalty

We're not quite done yet. Record companies rarely pay the full royalty promised. On the sale of tapes and 12-inch records they sometimes pay the full royalty, but generally only pay to a 3/4 royalty (that is, three quarters of the 9%, or 6.75%) on CD sales, because CDs are still considered "new technology" (even after more than a decade).[9] Uh-huh. So the alleged research and development cost is passed on to the artist. Artists' representatives have become savvy to this scam, so the "new technology" deduction is slowly falling by the wayside. But record companies have found clever ways of reinserting it. Of late they call it a "new configuration" deduction and are applying it to records sold as MP3s, DVDs, and any kind of Internet download, which will likely account for many U.S. sales in the future.

The 3/4 royalty has several other manifestations —"budget records," for example. If a record doesn't sell for the full $17.00 (which it rarely does), the artist is not entitled to their full royalty but rather only 3/4 (or sometimes 1/2) of it.

Still yet another manifestation of the 3/4 royalty is the "special TV and advertising deduction." In this one, the record company decides that since they are spending "extra" money on your promotion around the time of your release, they will pay the artist only between 3/4 and 1/2 of the normal royalty during these times.

All the above together basically means the only way to earn the full royalty promised is to sell tapes or 12-inch LPs at full price starting at six weeks after the record's release. Best of luck. Hopefully lawyers and managers will soon be able to get the 3/4 royalty clause out of the contract forever.[10]

❯ Download Sales

Now one might ask, "What about downloads? Why should the record company charge me for packaging or 'breakage' when the record is bought from Yahoo or iTunes and there is no packaging and certainly no breakage?" Well, first, here's the lousy but often-given answer—because they can.

The better answer: Record companies know that you know that they know that it doesn't cost 25% of a unit for packaging. They also know that you know that downloads have no ability to break.[11] These are just mathematical devices they use to arrive at a certain "penny rate." A penny rate is the exact amount in pennies that they are paying the artist for each sale. In our example above the penny rate is: $1.14.[12] This is not an untypical penny rate for a new artist. Anything over $1.50 and the profits start to cut into the company's expectation for the artist's costs. Believe it

---

[9] This also includes Minidiscs, and anything else new.

[10] Had car designers made the decision to switch to CD players as standard features in economy cars instead of sticking with cassette players, recording artists might have seen a drastic reduction in their income. Three cheers for the global economy.

[11] Although they can have "damaged data" resulting in a bad tracer and a "return" of sorts.

[12] The math:
($17 − $4.25 = $12.75);
(.75 X 12%= 9%) =
$1.14

or not, these costs don't go down just because it so happens that *that* particular sale didn't happen to have any packaging. There is still the packaging for the thousands of other units they manufactured (and didn't sell). Considering that less than 18% of the world owns a telephone (let alone a computer with high-speed Internet access), it's more than likely that hard-media records will still continue to be the norm for a little while.[13]

However, there is some good news. At least one of the Big Four has dialed back a bit on breakage and packaging deductions. They do not make these deductions for download sales. But don't get too comfortable; instead, get ready for "conversion charges" and other things related to creating and storing "metadata"—the files that hold the sound file and its tracking information.

In addition to this, there is a controversy as to how an iTunes sale should be treated under the normal artist/label contract. Is it a "sale" or a "license"? Why a controversy? Because labels don't actually *sell* records through online download services the way they do through "brick and mortar" retail stores. In regular retail they work through distributors who ship units to the store. But on services like iTunes, the record company *licenses* a catalog of music to the digital retailer (iTunes, Napster, Yahoo, Rhapsody, etc.). It's true that this license is based on per-sale amount (like iTunes paying the labels about 62 cents for each single sale), and under this logic the artist should only make about 9 cents (or 90 cents for an album—before the producer's cut and assuming that the normal deductions *don't* apply). But, the deal itself is structured as a *license*, similar to the way that a movie company might license a song for the opening titles of a film (called a *sync license*). Such licenses are usually split between the artist and the label on a 50/50 basis. In that case the artist would make about 33 cents a single and $3.30 an album. Quite a difference.

Labels just laugh at this argument. They say, "But it's a standard sale," and they will only pay it out that way. But lawyers will continue to fight for this differential, and so should you.[14]

Then there are other types of digital sales, called "tethered sales." These are what you have when someone subscribes to a service and pays a monthly fee for an "all-you-can-eat" approach to their music. The songs you download have a virtual "tether" that communicates back to the mother website each time you put your PLD (Personal Listening Device) online to get more music. The PLD tells the mainframe what tracks you listened to and how many times it was played, and then calculates the appropriate royalty for the artist. It works on a similar theory as a jukebox. You get a penny a play. Or thereabouts. For more on this see "Digital Rights Aggregators," page 47.

[13] And can you believe it, this number has started shrinking as of 2004 instead of growing. Why? As of 2005 close to 20% of the western world no longer have traditional "land lines" in their homes, and that's up from 10% in 2004. Also, this example does not include "ringtones" which are not considered a "record sale." More on this later.

[14] For more on digital distribution deals on indies, see page "Digital Rights Aggregators," page 47.

⊜ Deep in the Hole

When we add all this together, we see that the artist must sell over one million records before he breaks even. Let's do the math:

To make it simple, I just focused on CD sales, ignoring the other types of recordings like LPs and cassettes, because recent history has shown that an artist will usually sell a majority of CDs over other types of records under normal circumstances. The box below shows the equations for calculating the artist's and producer's royalty for CDs.

ARTIST:

SRLP $17 – $4.25 (packaging) = $12.75 @ 6.75% (3/4 rate) = $0.86

PRODUCER:

SRLP $17 – $4.25 (packaging) = $12.75 @ 2.25% (3/4 rate) = $0.28

And now let's plug the numbers into the final equation.

EGGHEAD BOX #2

Again, let x = the number of records to break even.

Artist's & Producer's share		*Aggregate sum (SSC)*		*Producer's share*
$1.14 x	=	*$500,000*	+	*0.28x*

$0.86x = $500,000

x = 581,395

Then this number divided by .75 (75% of sales for "giveaways") = 775,193

Then divided by .9 [90% of sales] = 861,325

GETTING "CUTOUT" OF ROYALTIES

Almost all new artist recording agreements with major labels insist that the artist will not be paid a royalty on "cutouts." Cutouts are the backlogged records that didn't sell and remain in a warehouse where eventually they will be shipped back to the label for a refund. They are called cutouts because the label and/or distributor cuts out the album from the company's catalogue of inventory. Basically, a dead record. You've seen them in the discount bin at places like K Mart.

Record companies traditionally sell cutouts at fire-sale prices (sometimes they sell for as low as 60 cents apiece) to companies who broker them to the "offbeat" retail chains, record clubs, and little mom-and-pop stores or sell them to recycling plants for scrap plastic.

Obviously a record company can't pay the standard royalty to an artist when they're selling the merchandise at below cost. However, when cutout sales top mainstream sales, it starts to smell fishy. In the 1980s, the major labels sold an estimated 200 million records a year as cutouts! It makes you wonder how hard they pushed to sell the record in the initial release.

Artists get angry when they read royalty statements claiming they still owe the label money when their record is selling in the hundreds of thousands. This leads to audits. But these audits usually conclude that the uncredited sales are cutouts and therefore royalty-free.

It's a tough bind. As an artist, it's nice to know that your record is in hundreds of thousands of homes, but it sure would be nice to get paid for it. There is no easy way to solve this problem. Good managers know the game and should always be aware of exactly how much real revenue their client is worth to the label and press heavily in negotiating their next advance.

Now that we've entered the world of downloaded sales you'd think we've seen the last of cutouts, but not so. I've seen several contracts that have substituted the word cutout (or returns) for "transmission errors," meaning that the files were corrupted during transfer and were rejected by the "store" (iTunes, Yahoo, etc.). This requires the label to repost the master on the service. This somewhat digital equivalent of a cutout costs the label very little, but some will still try to deduct it from artists' royalties.

And if the artist is lucky enough to actually sell close to a million records, look how the numbers work out. Remember, break-even is 861,325. Only sales above this number become actual dollars back in the artist's pocket.

Here's the score after 1,000,000 records have sold:

Producer: $241,171
Record company gross: $6,000,000 (approximate)
Artist: $80,500[15]

The record company's average profit per unit is $4.50, meaning they broke even on their "mean cost" after only 111,000 records.[16] But the artist is barely recouping even after 1,000,000 records sold.

What if the record sells 2,000,000 units? After 2,000,000 records sold:

Producer: $560,000
Record company gross: $12,000,000 (approximate)
Artist: $661,000

Finally the artist gets some significant coin. But before you go putting a down payment on a house, there are a few deductions: 15% for the manager and 5% for the accountant leaves the artist with $528,000. Split that four ways for each member of the band, and you've got $132,200 *before taxes.* Which is enough to buy a nice car and live well for about a year.

It's about time you made some money. But wait, there's more. I've saved the best part for last.

❷ Returns, Reserves, and Cutouts

Without a doubt the most Byzantine point of all in the record agreement is the reserve clause.

Records are a consignment item, which means that a store can get a full refund on records that they don't sell. So, just in case the unsold records ship back to the distributor, the label holds the artist's royalties for up to four pay periods (two full years), so that if records ship back, they can make return and shipping deductions from the artist's account. This is no small matter. The reserve clauses tend to be for 20% to 40% of gross sales!

Remember at the beginning of this chapter when the manager told the artist that

[15] Here's the math for those who care: .86 (1,000,000) (.75) (.90) − 500,000 = $80,500.

[16] This equation is based on the assumption that labels average about $6 profit per record. This number is then divided into the artist's advance of $500,000. For the complete breakdown of record company profits, refer to page 303, or review "The Major Label Deal from the Record Company's Point of View," page 101.

the record company was guaranteeing a 100,000 minimum run on the first pressing of the album? Well, that's fine if the artist's market warrants it. But most new artists rarely sell more than 60,000 units on their initial release. If the record doesn't sell all 100,000, the remainder will be shipped back at a charge to the artist. The returned stock will then be sold as "cutouts," and no royalty will be paid on these units (see the sidebar "Getting 'Cutout' of Royalties").

Based on a 20% reserve, if the artist sold two million records and is owed $661,000 for the first year, the company will apply only $528,000 (80%) to the artist's account. The balance of $133,000 will remain in the label's bank for another two years, gathering not dust but interest. At average prime rate (5%), that works out to about $6,650 worth of interest per year—none of which gets passed on to the artist. So, even though the artist should get about $660,000, they get only 80% of that. The rest they will have to wait a year or two for. And during that time they are loaning it to the record company, which gets to make money on it and not pass a dime of that extra profit back to the artist.

It would be easy to understand the record company holding back the royalties and keeping the interest if they were still owed money, but after two million records sold, they have long since recouped and are well into the black. Why hold the artist's money? The cold hard truth is, once again, because they can.

Now in the realm of digitally downloaded sales where a download is not returnable, you'd think that record companies would dispense with the pretense of this withholding of income. But no. As of this writing, three of the Big Four still hold reserves *even* on digital sales. Crazy.

Was I right? Isn't the football game more interesting to watch when you know about offsides and holding? While the record company nets millions, the musicians are surviving on the few thousand dollars they saved from their recording budget. And remember the full-color CD jacket the manager promised? The artist pays for that as well. The more the cover art and liner notes cost, the more money gets charged to the artist's recoupment account for packaging and container fees.

Back in the '60s, rock and roll managers would neglect to tell their clients that all the goodies that the label was promising the band, like color cover art and big psychedelic black light posters and limousines, were being paid for out of the band's advance and would be applied to their royalties.

Oops!

Keep in mind as well that all the above is what's in the standard "boilerplate" recording contract. Your best hope is that many of these ridiculous clauses can be negotiated out of your deal.

I know what you might be thinking: There's always the second album. Remember how your manager said that the budget for the second album would be more than the first? Maybe you can keep some of that money this time around. Except for one thing—the record company insisted that all the records on the contract be cross-collateralized.

Cross-what?

❯ Cross-Collateralization, or Robbing Peter to Pay Paul

"Cross-collateralized" (or, as it's sometimes relabeled in contracts, "offsets") is one of the most important phrases to be on the lookout for in a record contract. Put simply, it means that the debts you run over the course of your deal will be repaid out of *any* profits from future records or publishing. So even though one of your albums may have gone double-platinum, if the others lost money and those losses are more than the profits from your hit album, guess what—you still owe the label money. Debts from one album can be recouped from the profits of the others. (For an astounding and sobering explanation of cross-collateralization, read Donald Passman's book *Everything You Need to Know about the Music Business* [Simon & Schuster]. Or my book *Secrets of Negotiating a Record Contract: The Musician's Guide to Understanding and Avoiding Sneaky Lawyer Tricks* [Backbeat Books].)

But there are other versions of this. If you went over budget $100,000 from the first record and they promised you a $300,000 advance for the second—guess what? You're getting advanced only $200,000 to make the second record, and now you owe them $300,000. The record company takes its $100,000 first. This can get really ugly if the contract states that you're supposed to get an advance of, say, $500,000 to produce your fifth album. Here you are, looking forward to getting a huge check after working your butt off for four albums, and then the record company says, "Sorry, but you went over budget on your last three records by $400,000, so we're only advancing you $100,000 for your fifth record." With this pittance, they will now expect a pop group with a good enough track record to warrant a fifth album to produce a quality recording under low-budget conditions.[17]

So much for scraping some money off your next record's budget. Well, there's still the sliding-scale royalty they promised you. Maybe, maybe not. It depends on your deal.

Atlantic Records in the '70s and '80s had a clause in their standard contract that promised the artist the standard 12% royalty on the first record, a 13% royalty on

17 These numbers are oversimplified. $100,000 an album is considered low-budget by major label standards. See the sidebar "Typical 'Official' Album Production Budget on a Major Label," page 92.

the second, and then a whopping 15% from the third on. The catch was that the artist had to deliver the finished masters of each record no later than eight months after the last one. Anyone who's been in the industry could tell you that between touring and recording and writing, there is little chance of this happening. In the Atlantic contract, if the artists didn't deliver in time, they were kept at the old royalty rate. Nice. (See "Decoding of an Actual Warner Bros. Record Contract," page 232.) And there are still more severe versions of the deal "offset" that would allow the record company to take money the artist owes them out of any source whatsoever—including publishing, touring, merchandising, or anything they can think of. We'll get to that stuff later. But if the artist is smart and has learned from experience, they'll manage their second record advance much smarter than their first one.

❯ A Major Label Deal Is Like Having a Credit Card at 66% Interest

So, what have we learned thus far? We see that the artist is borrowing $200,000 with the understanding that they are going to have to pay back $500,000 ($300,000 going for promotion) and that the $500,000 is a moving goal post, meaning that the record company can spend more at their discretion and charge it back to the artist. Since the initial contract period of these deals lasts about two years and it is within that time that the advance money must be paid, the artist, in effect, is entering into a "loan" agreement at an interest rate of 66.3% per year. And even after they pay back all this money, they don't own the rights to their master recordings—the record company does.

When a lawyer, manager, or producer is talking about shopping you to a major record label, this is the type of deal they are talking about—a short-term loan at 66.3% interest with a forgiven debt feature. They won't mention that this will be the situation, and they usually won't explain about the moving goal post unless you ask them (although since the first edition of *Confessions* more lawyers are breaking the news to their clients up front). This is because long after the artist's record is in the discount bin, the pros will have taken their commissions off the top of the deal, and the producer will have started to collect his or her 21 cents from the first record sold.

But all this funny accounting is only an issue if your record actually gets released. No one says the label has to release your masterpiece debut record, as you'll learn in a moment.

❯ Drop-Kicked from the Roster

The frigid reality of the major record deal is that, in spite of the fact that a label will sign about 20 to 30 new pop acts a year, it may only have the budget to market about six of them effectively. This means that there are going to be several unhappy campers at the end of the fourth quarter when the vice presidents make cuts to their roster.

In my opinion and experience, these decisions are rather arbitrary and often based on politics rather than the quality of the record. Yes, it is important that the artist produce good material, but what if all 30 acts signed that year produce good material? Several will still be cut for economic reasons.

One factor in this decision is the "A&R revolving door." If the A&R person who signed the act is no longer with the company, all the acts that he or she signed that year stand a good chance of being dropped. Since A&R persons tend to label-hop with great frequency these days, the odds of getting dropped are better than not.[18]

For many acts this is disastrous because it means starting all over again. Most artists focus on the getting of the deal as their main form of competition. They don't recognize that once they are on a label's roster they are still competing with other acts for position on the release calendar and promotion money. For this reason it is important that the band have a manager who is well connected to the inner sanctum of the label.

Since the most recent consolidation of the Big Five into the Big Four (and coming soon, the Big Three), labels have decided to sign even fewer artists. Industry blowhards (sometimes called "consultants"—see page 77) say that this signals the "end of the music business as we know it." But I think not. While it's true that fewer signings means labels are taking fewer chances on new acts, it also means that the few they do sign will receive more attention. And believe me, given a choice of (1) getting signed and never released and (2) never getting signed by a major, I'd take choice No. 2 any day of the week and twice on Sundays, even if it hurts the ego a bit.

But for those who are "lucky" enough to get signed, aside from politics, marketing departments also look at the changing needs and whims of the public when considering the release of a record. Herein lies what is probably the single most frustrating part of major record deals: the timing of the release, or what I call "time warp."

[18] See "A&R," page 9, for the reason.

❯ Time Warp: How Long Till the Record Comes Out?

Typically, a manager shops an act to several labels. When one takes an interest, the manager and the A&R person sit down and smoke fat cigars and discuss the deal. When they reach an agreement (and that could take several months), then they "do lawyers" for $30,000. The lawyers argue and debate the finer points of the agreement, ultimately producing a document 50 to 75 pages long. This is the record agreement, also referred to as "The Thick" or "The Long Form." This process can easily take up to six months, and has been known to take as long as 15 months before the thick was finished.

When this is done, the act will go into the studio and record a single or an album. If they are well prepared, this will take an average of about two weeks to six months. After the album is done, it sits on the shelves of the A&R person and the marketing department for another few months while the political wheels turn and decide whether the act will be drop-kicked or move on to be marketed.

By this point, about a year has passed since the label agreed to sign the artist they thought was so special. There's just one problem—that was a year ago, and by now the industry trends may have changed, or the A&R person may have been fired and his or her replacement doesn't want the old A&R's dirty laundry.[19]

[19] Think about it. Would you want to pick up on a former employee's decision? If it fails, you get the blame. If it succeeds, you don't get the credit.

There are at least 500 ways for a label to say "no" to a potential contract signing or a release. The artist or their representation must try to cut down that number. What this really means is that artists competing for a deal or market attention must become like televangelists—they are in the believer business. They must make believers out of all who come in contact with them. This is what is often called a "good vibe"—one that instills confidence in the record company. It starts not with the vice president who makes the ultimate decision, but with the lowly secretary, who often has the ability to get you past security.

Some artists manage to do this with pure arrogance, and some with humility. Whatever works, use it. Because when the record is done, the battle isn't over. There is still the marketing department to contend with, and the publicity department, and the promotion department. You will have to make friends with all of them if you want your record to be a success. (See "Image Molding," page 105.) Remember:

Artists are in the believer business.

Need and Greed: Be Careful What You Wish For

Do you still want a major record deal? Are you sure? Your lawyer told you it was a good deal, and your manager agreed. Even the producer thinks it's the best thing for you. Can they all be wrong?

Yes.

As we've seen, pros and the producer get paid by different schedules than artists. But to be fair to these folks—whom we do not want to alienate—let me state in their defense that there is another reason why nobody mentions all the pitfalls of major label deals to the artist. That is because the artist rarely wants to hear about it.[20]

Most people agree that the standard major label recording contract is unfair, but pros will tell you, the artist, that it's the only real money game in town. They will also bolster their opinion with rationalizations like, "Long before you are supposed to start collecting royalties on your first record, you will be receiving your larger advance for the second record." They'll also tell you that once you become a big star you can negotiate almost all of these pocket-picking clauses out of your contract. You can get bigger royalties payable on 100% of sales with no special goods programs. You can get the record company to pay for the video and other promotion costs instead of passing their cost of doing business on to you.

All that is true. (Somewhat—see the footnote.)[21] But until you prove yourself with a successful record, you'll be facing the standard deal that most new artists live with. Maybe now it's easier to understand why so many artists "sell out" when they sign to major labels.

But if at the outset you are only getting a few thousand dollars to close the deal and then, two years later, $95,000 if you sell two million records, how can you survive? What advice do the pros have for you? What do you have left to sell that is of any worth? (Besides instruments and vital organs.)

Well, how about the right to collect your songwriting royalties? Sounds promising, so let's take a closer look at "the publishing deal."

[20] I've tried on occasion to persuade an act that I was producing to go with an indie label over a major. They look at me cross-eyed. The advance money is drastically smaller on an indie. I try to show them that despite the large advance they will probably never see royalties. It's futile.

[21] Renegotiating was the name of the game until recently when Universal Music decided that it wasn't going to oblige artists anymore. And so this gravy train dried up for all but the really top stars. For more on this see my book *Million Dollar Mistakes*.

CHAPTER SIX

⊛Publishing Deals:
The 200% Pie, or 100% of Something Is Better than 200% of Nothing

I f you are signing with a major label, then in all likelihood a publishing company will want to be involved with you as well. Here's why.

While the record is still in recoupment hell, the authors of the songs on the record are vacationing in Boca Raton. Unlike recoupment negotiating, which inhabits the realm of twisted legalese and creative accounting, writers get paid because there are laws that dictate how and when a writer gets paid.[1]

The Copyright Act establishes a special payment to the songwriter whenever his song is distributed on a CD in the United States. The payment is a "compulsory license" (because writers are "compelled" to license their songs), and the amount that is paid is often called the "statutory rate."

To keep things simple, the current industry-accepted statutory rate (as of 2005) is 9.1 cents for each song on an album for all records distributed. Let me repeat that: for all records distributed. The Copyright Act defines "distributed" as "if the person exercising the compulsory license has voluntarily and permanently parted with its possession." In layman's terms, "sold or given away." Since it would be hard for a record company to argue that they manufactured records without the intent to sell them or give them away, it would

[1] See "What Do Doctors and Songwriters Have in Common?," page 39.

follow that all records manufactured would require that a royalty be paid. But you will only be paid on the ones that actually sell through normal retail and wholesale distribution.[2] So if you're the writer of *all* the songs on your record, let's see what the record company owes you just for the turnkey expense of mass-producing your CDs.

You'll get 9.1 cents per song x 10 songs on a record x 100,000 units (the first run in the hypothetical contract we've been discussing). That's $91,000. But in case you haven't caught on, nothing is as simple as it seems in this business of music.

◗ Three-Quarter Rate

First, record companies will make you agree to only put songs on the record that you wrote and to only charge the label three-quarters of the statutory rate of 9.1 cents (or about 6.8 cents per song) if you want the deal. This is called the *three-quarter rate*. If you are going to use cover tunes, the record company makes you agree to pay any difference between the three-quarter rate and the full rate that the other writers will charge them. Second, they will limit how many songs they will pay for—typically a total of ten songs on the album for an "all-in" rate of 68 cents for each record *"sold."*[1] But with a million-selling record, the three-quarter rate can still spell real money for the writers: 75% of 9.1 cents = 6.8 cents x 10 songs x 1 million records = $680,000.[3]

No wonder there are publishing companies that want to collect this money for you. If the deal looks big enough, they will even offer you a recoupable advance against future earnings of your mechanical license. For a new act on a major label, the advance can be anywhere from $25,000 to $500,000. That's a lot of cash for the artist who desperately needs something to live on while the record company holds royalties in reserve.

But nothing is for free in this world. That advance money is in exchange for the right of the publishing company to control the song's copyright and give the writer 50% of the revenue earned from the song.

Now here is where it can get confusing. First of all, let's turn the pie we are about to split up into a 200% pie. It's just like 100% inflation. Everything that would normally be 10% is now 20%. You can think of the song's pie as a 200% pie that is divided up 100% for the writer and 100% for the publisher. So when you hear people talking about 100% of the "publisher's share" they are talking about 50% of the total money the song earns. Before you go on, reread this paragraph over and over again until it is clear.

[2] It's a foregone conclusion that you never see a dime of publishing royalties from records given away. See "Getting 'Cutout' of Royalties," page 72. Also, "Sold" has a special meaning within the universe of a recording contract. (For more on this see *Secrets of Negotiating a Record Contract*.) In short, it does not mean every record that the record company actually sold.

[3] Instead of $910,000, which would be the compulsory license at full rate. You're already saving your record company $230,000 on a big hit by agreeing to this. You're quite a sport. For reasons why they do this, see "Deductions," page 102.

But why should you want to give 50% to a company to collect the money that should be paid to you by law? The publishing company's argument is a good one: They sell the idea that you, the artist, don't want to go to all the trouble of going around collecting money from all the sources that owe you for the use of your song, like radio stations, movie companies, movie soundtracks, other artists who do cover versions of your song, and most recently, sample rights.[4] (In case you were wondering, this statutory rate of 9.1 cents is chargeable whenever anybody else records the song or uses a sample of the song.) The main reason you sign away 50% of your proceeds to a publishing company is to have them market the song to commercials, movies, TV shows, and so on. You just have to sit back and be creative. They handle all the business, for a cut of every dollar the song makes. Seems reasonable.

There are, as always, a couple of catches. Let's deal with the recoupment clause first.

> # Publishing Advances and Their Deductions

This tends to be a bit confusing, so let's go slow. Example: The publisher "loans" the songwriter(s) of the record (who is usually the artist, on a first record) $100,000 against the money he will earn from record sales. The recoupment formula should be about the same as for record sales, right? Each album sold equals 63 cents of revenue, which means the advance will be recouped when you've sold 158,730 records. (Refer to Egghead Box #3.)

EGGHEAD BOX #3

.68x = $100,000
x = 147,058 records

But it doesn't work out that way, for two reasons.

Administrative Expenses
The first is that many deals have a clause built in for administrative costs; these can be as high as 20%. This comes off the top.

[4] A sample is a piece of a recording usually taken off a record and incorporated into the arrangement of a new song. The act of getting the right to use the sample is called "clearing." See "Sample Rights," page 84.

If the publisher takes only half of the publishing share, then in effect they are taking 25% of all the writer's mechanical royalties. (Remember, it's a 200% pie. So a 75%-25% split becomes a 150%–50% split.) Let's say that the copyright of the song earns $1,000 from sources like record sales, radio play, or a movie soundtrack. In this case, 25%, or $250, goes to the publisher and the remaining $750 gets applied to the recoupment of the writer's advance.

But publishers usually charge administrative costs of only about 10%. These are deducted first, before the split. So, $1,000 minus 10% equals $900. Once the publisher subtracts its cut (25%), the artist is left with $675. By this account, the artist must earn $148,148 to pay back an advance of $100,000. This is roughly the same as borrowing money at 48% interest.

But this isn't so bad, really, especially when you compare it to the record deal in the last chapter. My only real complaint is that a publisher's overhead is nowhere near as massive as a record company's, and their risk is much lower because they usually don't give advances unless there is a distribution deal in place, thus minimizing their risk. They can be wrong about how successful a new artist will be, but it won't cost them anywhere near what it costs a label to take that gamble. Yet they still take a large chunk of the writer's money.

The only dangerous thing to look out for here is the cross-collateralization clause. If you have signed a record deal with one of the Big Four, then they will want you to give them your publishing contract as well. Many managers and pros recommend against this, but I say it can be a good thing for the first album because it will give the record company an extra incentive to work the record for you. But if the contract cross-collateralizes your record deal with the publishing deal, then any money that you earn as a writer will go toward recouping your record deal. This sucks— always, all the time. Don't let them try this one on you, or you will be forever in a bottomless pit of recoupment hell.

Sample Rights

The second way the writer/artist gets gypped out of their money is with sample rights. This is a new form of publishing revenue born in the past 15 years or so.

Most early rap and R&B records "borrowed" bits and pieces from other recordings to make up the arrangement of their new recording. For a while they got away without paying for these, but eventually publishing companies caught on and started asking for a portion of the copyright on the new song. A famous case that comes to mind is the song "Ice Ice Baby," by the artist Vanilla Ice. To make the main groove of his hit recording he used a portion off of a David Bowie record. Bowie's publisher asked for 50% of all the publishing on the recording and the full statutory rate of 5.5 cents in exchange for the right to sample his recording.[5]

Today samples have found their way into almost every form of modern music. Clearing the rights to use the samples is a matter of course and courtesy. If you steal a sample, the consequences can be costly litigation that you are likely to lose.[6] But remember, in the "three-quarter rate," the label made the artist agree to an "all-in royalty" for all mechanical license fees not to exceed 68 cents per album. So who pays for the right to use it?

Nowadays the record company charges the sample rights back to the artist in a clever way. They deduct it from the statutory rate that they pay on album sales.

So, for example, if you are supposed to receive 68 cents for the ten songs on your record, but you use a sample and the publisher of that sample wants you to pay the full 9.1 cents, this will put you about 2.3 cents over the limit of your 68-cent allowance. And guess what? The record company will deduct this 2.3 cents overage from the 68 cents they were going to pay you. If you know anything about music production, you know that songs that tend to use samples rarely use just one to compose the arrangement of a song. Over the course of a typical rap or R&B record, it is not uncommon to find 15 to 50 samples being used. So if this is the case, you can kiss your statutory, guaranteed-by-law licensing fee good-bye. It will be chiseled away penny by penny with each sample you need to license.

What makes this really evil is that even when an artist is signed to a major label and they are using samples that come from their own label's publishing catalogue, the above conditions will still exist. (See "Sample-Alikes," page 195, for a way around this.)

❯ The Workaround for Recoupment Hell

How does one beat this system? Answer: forget royalties. The name of the game is advances! Get as much money up front as you can, then administer it wisely. Assume that you may not get any more money from the label or the publisher. If the first record does well, renegotiate firmly for a larger advance on the second record. It's better to have the label owe you money than vice versa.

[5] 5.5 cents was the rate at the time. The rate has since been increased to 8 cents.

[6] Publishing companies hire listeners called "sample police." These people do nothing all day but listen to new records in search of unlicensed samples.

Collecting Money in the "New Economy"

The buzz word at the start of this millennium was "new economy," spawned largely by the growth of the Internet. Dot-coms, as they have come to be known, sprouted up like weeds, offering the promises of new and cheaper distribution methods and the ability for anyone with a home computer and a phone line to own entire catalogues of music for free. "They" called it "a revolution that would change the music industry forever." It lasted exactly 13 months.

Almost as quickly as you could say "ISP," record companies and publishing companies were just as quick to say the word "lawsuit." Within months, the big payers in the dot-com game were all but dot-gone. The ones that remained were absorbed into Big Four oblivion. However, the dot-com wars left in their wake a new distribution channel: music sales via downloading records directly into a home computer. Record companies initially turned their noses up at this idea, but they gradually began to see it as viable.

Many technical and legal glitches still need to be worked out before it will be possible to get entire catalogs of old favorites and new releases with just a mouse click,[7] but publishing companies are now fighting for their share of the download pie. As this goes to print, lawyers from labels, publishing companies, and the Copyright Office are negotiating a fee, much like the 9.1-cents-a-song fee discussed above, for downloading music. Whatever this fee is, the income to songwriters should increase substantially in the next five to ten years—provided they ever get around to figuring out what the fee will be. (Remember that it took Congress 67 years after the invention of the record player to create the first statutory rate and to agree that a recording should be protected by copyright.)

An important point to keep in mind is that there is nothing really "new" about the new economy. There have been and always will be new ideas for making money, as older, perfectly good systems fade away. And the art of collecting money hasn't changed much despite all the new bells and gadgets, either. The economy is the economy is the economy. However, we tend to be less cynical about things that are new, because despite our skepticism, deep down we would like to believe that "new" means "improved." If the dot-com wars taught us anything, they taught us this is not necessarily the case.

[7] This was true in 2001 when the Second Edition of this book was created, and believe it or not, despite the somewhat successful services like iTunes, it's still true now in 2005 in this Third Edition.

The Major Label Deal
from the Producer's Point of View

The word "producer" is often associated with someone who raises money and puts a deal together. This is most true in the theater, film, and TV world. But in the record industry, the producer is more like the director of a feature film than a financier. The producer will often play a very creative role in the production, directing the musicians the way a film director would direct actors. But there is one significant difference between a film director and record producer—record producers are usually made contractually responsible for the "delivery" of the final master recording. They don't just get to play with the studio toys and order around the musicians. They are responsible for all the paperwork of sample clearances, union issues, and booking studio time. (They usually have assistants do much of this stuff for them, but they are still responsible for it.) This is no small difference. Many artists like to try to leverage themselves a "co-producer" credit without having to take on all these other responsibilities. This is because many artists are not aware that all this menial paperwork needs to be done in a professional, major label situation. And because when they think of a "producer," all they generally relate to are the creative aspects of the job.

The producer on a major label record sits in a very different position than the new artist. Usually they already have a track record of delivering quality product to the label and are commanding high fees for their participation in important records.

Before one can grasp the agenda of the producer, one has to understand exactly who hires him or her. And the conflict that comes with the job.

⊗ The Artist/Producer Conflict

[1] Most artists are young and inexperienced with business, so it is not surprising that they perceive all forms of authority—producers, record companies, and so on—as "the establishment," hungry for the millions that can be made off their music. The recreational drugs that many artists indulge in do not help to eliminate their paranoia, either.

Starting out as a producer is not cheap. Producers are very much like artists. Many, in fact, started out that way. Maybe not as full-fledged recording acts but as a main member of a band or the chief writer for a band. Other producers come from engineering backgrounds. Often, to get his or her business off the ground, a new producer will buy thousands of dollars' worth of equipment for making demos (demonstration recordings) of the artists they will contract and shop to record labels. As you can imagine, the investment in equipment and time can be enormous. This is why new producers often think more like businesspeople than like artists.

But this bottom-line attitude often makes artists leery and fosters an attitude that producers are out to rip off their songs and hijack their publishing rights.[1] Because of this, artists can be less than respectful of the fact that a producer will invest thousands of dollars in time and resources developing the artist's sound. Instead they tend to see only that what they bring to the table is irreplaceable, that they are "the talent" and therefore deserve immediate respect and recognition.

Producers can be equally suspicious of artists, fearing that after they do all the work (usually on spec) the artist will break ties, leaving them out of the windfall loop.

Things would be easier if artists were in touch with the reality that most new acts lose money. But, given the headstrong position of both parties, it's easy to see why the process of record deal-making can be a small miracle in itself.

When a major label does eventually sign an artist and plops down a million dollars to launch their careers, the posture of the producer/artist relationship changes radically. Experience has taught the label that most new artists can't be trusted with a large budget, and since in all likelihood they do not have the studio experience to produce the record themselves, the label will stipulate in the contract that the artist will, "at the artist's expense," hire a producer.

The phrase "at the artist's expense" is somewhat misleading. Since the producer will be paid out of the artist's advance and the producer's royalty will be carved out of the artist's share of 12% (see "Recoupable Financing—The Moving Goal Post," page 65), the artist is the one who hires the producer in the legal sense. But it's the

CHAPTER SEVEN

record company that puts the food on the producer's plate, since without the label the artist wouldn't be able to afford the recording.

The artist may or may not do well, but the record company is here to stay.

Add to this the fact that once a major label is involved, the producer has a lot of emotional leverage. As an old expression goes, "If you pay a doctor for his advice and you ignore him, who are you hurting?" This is the position that most producers will take with a reluctant artist who wants to do something avant-garde or non-commercial on major label money.

Artist: "Nah, man, we don't like that thing you had us do in the chorus, it's too commercial."

Producer: "Well, okay, it's your record. I don't want to ruin your vision."

Following this dialogue, in all likelihood the producer, who often has a close relationship with the A&R person, will tell him that the group isn't being cooperative and he has doubts as to whether they will be able to deliver a hit record. The A&R person will, in turn, talk to the group's manager (with whom he also has a good relationship), and the manager will tell the group that they had better shape up and listen to the doctor.

This is an extreme case, but it does happen often enough to be a realistic example of how the producer's allegiance and leverage works. The band hires a producer more often than not at the insistence of the label and then pays him to protect the record company's interests. Nobody likes to talk about this small conflict of interest, but everyone knows it exists.[2]

On the point of who should have final say over a creative choice on a record, I side with the producer. If you think this is self-serving, remember why a producer is hired in the first place. If artists want to make "art," they don't need a producer or a record company. Anyone can produce a record if they don't care how commercial it is. But when artists sign with a major label, they are signing a contract that says, "Yes, we want to make records that sell in large quantities." The producer is hired as the expert consultant toward that goal. If an artist is not in touch with that reality, they are wasting their time and the record company's money.[3]

The producer also has knowledge that the artist probably does not. They've been around the industry and see how long things take. They know that the time between an artist's signing and an album release could easily be over a year. In that time the fickle market can change direction. To combat this, the expert producer must be somewhat of a fortune teller. He might try to influence the band to incorporate new

[2] *Unless* it's a production deal where the producer and the artist were signed as a package. For more info on this subject see "The Baby Record Deal," page 143.

[3] Given enough time and money, the artist will probably come to the same or similar solutions that the producer comes to. The only difference is that the artist rarely has unlimited time and money. That's why the producer was called in in the first place. So if you pay someone for their expertise and you don't listen to them. . . . You get the point.

4 The label of course
has a great deal of
foresight since
they know all the
other artists that
they have on their
roster, as well as
a good idea of
what's on other
labels' rosters.

5 See "One-Deep &
Two-Deep Labels,"
page 58, if you
don't know what
this means.

6 "All-in" funds can
be distributed for
entire albums as
well, and, while
they are most
common in the
R&B, hip-hop, and
rap fields, they can
be found in the
rock and pop fields
as well.

7 I know producers
who record every-
thing in their home
studios and then
charge the label
the same rates as
professional large
studios (about $150
per hour). They
even go to the
trouble of printing
bogus invoices. So
out of $50,000 they
net almost all of it.
With the popularity
of cheap hard-disk-
based recording,
this has become
more the norm.

elements into their music so that when the record comes out it will sound fresh. The new band almost never understands this concept. They create in the vacuum of their self-contained environment and often don't concern themselves with how they will be perceived after one or two years against the vast tapestry of new releases.[4]

Herein lies the fundamental dilemma of the producer: how to make a commercial record and still be original and faithful to the artist's sound. It's a delicate tightrope to walk. But remember, if the record sells a million copies and the band hates it, that producer will work again. Period. Even if the artist is upset at the way the record turned out. With that established, let's look at the different types of producer deals and their ins and outs.

Note: In this chapter we discuss the elements of the major label deal that the producer will be most concerned with. However, for the up-and-coming producers reading this book, still looking for that breakout deal, you might also want to cover the chapter called "The Baby Record Deal" (page 143), as that chapter addresses more specific issues that arise between the artist, the producer, and the smaller label/production company.

❯ The All-In Deal

A new producer being contracted by a group signed to a one-deep label[5] will ask for and usually receive a $50,000 fee (or about a quarter of the entire recording budget) for producing a rock, pop, country, or jazz album. This fee is for overseeing the record and working with the artist on the arrangements. However, sometimes they will be paid by the song in what's called an "all-in budget," meaning that the record company gives the producer a chunk of money to produce one song.[6]

The producer with an "all-in budget" pays all the vendors involved, the recording studio, the engineer, everything. The budget also includes a sum that the producer "pays" to himself or herself. But if the producer can complete the project for less than the budget allows, then whatever is left over is his or hers to keep. The producer's total advance from the record company, including the amounts to be paid to the various vendors, is usually about $35,000 per song. If the producer is clever and thrifty, he can usually keep about $22,000 of this. While all the money for the recording fund is recoupable from the artist's side of the equation, only the portion that is considered to be the producer's fee is recoupable from the producer's side of the royalties equation (see Egghead Box #1, page 67). This is the factor that gives the producer the incentive to bring in the project for as little as possible. Whatever he doesn't spend, he gets to keep—free of recoupment.[7]

The all-in deal can be very tricky. Most producers prefer it because they can juggle money around and the record company won't know exactly how much things cost or how much the producer actually keeps.

There is one major drawback for the producer in an all-in deal—that's when the record company decides that it wants a remix or re-edit of the final version of the song and expects the producer to pay for it out of his recording fund. Unless the producer has good management or clout, these changes can continue ad infinitum until the producer has gone into his own pocket to complete the record. Generally, the record company will reach a compromise with the producer and offer to pay some or most of the expenses involved in remixes.

● Non-All-In Deals

Most all-in deals described above are found in R&B and rap projects, where you have what I call "producer-driven acts," meaning that the producer often writes the songs and does the arrangements and basically *is* the artist. The producer's own fee in the recording budget is usually the only money that will have to be recouped before the producer will see royalties. For this reason, the producer will want to keep that fee as low as possible, especially if he can get kickbacks from vendors.[8]

8 See "Kickbacks," page 82.

In rock and other types of music where the band is more the focus of the record, not the producer, you tend to have non-all-in deals. In this setup, the producer still prepares the budget, but his or her production fee is paid directly from the label on behalf of the artist. The producer is relieved of administering the budget and will have less opportunity to scam. But it's not impossible. Example: if you have a budget of $100,000 and you charge $30,000 as a producer's fee (normal), then the producer needs to recoup $30,000 off his end before he starts to receive royalties. But if he can siphon $20,000 off the budget and then only charge a $10,000 producer's fee (low), then he still gets to put $30,000 in his pocket and only has to recoup $10,000 off his end.

A veteran producer will get about $150,000 as a fee to produce the album. Depending on his or her clout, this either will or will not be recoupable out of future royalties. If it's not recoupable, that means the producer starts to earn royalties from the sale of the first record, while the artist has to wait until the entire recording fund is paid back to the label before he or she sees any more money from record sales. It's easy to see why artists have love/hate relationships with producers.

As artists get more successful, they usually try to exercise their muscle by taking more control over the production of their record. Most of the time, self-producing is a formula for disaster. It tends to have the same effect as a person giving themselves a haircut without a mirror. Sometimes it works well; there are some artists who have excelled at producing themselves, like the artist now once again known as Prince. But most artists, even many who've been making hit records for years, hire people to at least coproduce their albums.

In the typical rock production, the producer acts as a sounding board for the varied and sometimes conflicting ideas that the artist has for the songs. Often, the producer will help arrange the material, and sometimes he or she writes bridges for songs that are missing that "certain something." The problem with rewrites is that the artist can get a bit touchy about sharing the copyright of the songs with the

TYPICAL "OFFICIAL" ALBUM PRODUCTION BUDGET ON A MAJOR LABEL

Even in an all-in deal, the producer must submit a plan for the recording, but there are still all kinds of ways to hide money in a budget. If the producer is clever, neither the artist nor the label will ever find it. Below is what two normal budgets look like to the untrained eye.

	New artist	Mid-level artist (or one that is in demand)
Basic trax		
Three weeks at large studio ($1,500 per day "card rate") discounted[9]	$9,000	$22,500
Engineer ($400–$750 per day)	Included in studio fees	$13,500
Media:		
Tape (2-inch 24-track) 20 reels @ $150 per reel (old school) or Pro Tools rig rental by the day	- - -	$3,000
3 100-gigabyte hard-disk sidecars ($250 each)	$750	- - -
Union scale—musicians' fees for the backup band— $350 per player per day (four players)[10]	$29,400	$58,800 (dbl. scale)
Overdubs		
Smaller studio ($1,000 per day) for four weeks discounted	- - -	$30,800
Smaller studio ($500 per day) for four weeks discounted	$10,000	- - -
Union scale—musicians' fees for the band— $350 per player per day (two players)	$14,000	$28,000
Side players/guest soloists	$3,000	$10,000
Engineer ($400–$1,100 per day)	$8,000	$30,800

producer (even though a good producer is improving the song; see "When the Producer Wants Publishing," page 96).

❷ The Spec Deal

Speaking of the producer being taken advantage of, the "spec deal" seems like a good place to talk about his or her vulnerabilities.

Unknown acts often seek producers—either by themselves or through their managers—to produce the magic demo that will get them the big deal. If it's a manager coming to the producer, it's usually because he has a very

---

cont'd

Mixing

Mix studio—$2,500 per day (15–36 days)	$37,500	$90,000
Media: Tape—1/2-inch mixdown tape,		
10 reels @ $60 per reel	$600	$600
Digital backup/storage	$200	$500
Mix engineer ($1,000–$1,500 per day)	$15,000	$54,000
Single mix (for radio)	$5000	$50,000
	(1 single)	(2 singles@ $25,000 each)

Producer's fee . . . . $20,000 . . . . $110,000

Miscellaneous

Cartage	artist pays for own . . .	$10,000
Lodging	stay with a friend	$30,000
Strings/sticks/skins, etc.	$500	$1,000
Mastering	$1,500	$10,000

Total . . . . **$154,450 . . . . $553,500**

Note: These figures are the average as of press time.

As you can see, the cost of doing business more than doubles once a plateau of success is established, mainly for two reasons: (1) Vendors are less likely to discount their rates, and (2) the artists pay themselves more and treat themselves to better accommodations.

If you compare the budgets from the Second Edition of *Confessions*, you'll notice that the album budget (and producer's fees) for new (emerging) artists has gone down while the budgets for old (or in-demand) artists has risen.

---

talented group on his hands that seems unable to record anything. Maybe they're too disorganized or don't know their way around the studio. The group tends to have an expectation that the producer, if he likes them, will finance a recording and shop it to a label.

Producers are generally reluctant to take on these type of spec (short for speculative) deals unless the band is both very good and very willing to make the back end of the deal attractive for the producer. Attractive, in this case, usually means:

1. A 15% finder's fee taken off the top of the advance to the artist.
2. The right to produce the record for a fee of no less than $25,000 plus a 3% or 4% royalty.
3. A large participation in publishing—50% if it's rap, hip-hop, or R&B, 25% if it's rock.
4. A demo fee of upwards of $5,000 per track (song).

All the above in exchange for producing a recording and getting the band a deal.

Let's see how those numbers play out in a typical scenario. If the producer gets the artist the deal and they get a $200,000 advance to make the record, they must first pay off the producer. Fifteen percent off the top leaves $170,000. Then there's the demo fee. If the producer did four songs (typical), he will take $20,000 for that work, leaving $150,000 for the artist. Now comes the producer's album fee of $25,000, leaving $125,000 to make the record and for the artist to live on until the royalties start coming in.

This will seem, to the artist, as if the producer is raping and pillaging, but consider three things:

1. The producer has an enormous risk in doing the project at all. He is not financed by a multinational corporation like a major record company, and although he has had some success (or you wouldn't be talking to him), that doesn't mean that he has the 20 or 30 grand lying around to develop the act.
2. The producer has reputation. The artist, at this point in his or her career, has nothing to lose. The producer, on the other hand, can damage his reputation and waste his time by getting involved with a loser act.
3. No one says the artist must hire the producer. If the artist thinks the producer wants too much, then the artist is free to produce the record and get the deal himself.

The artist will quickly see that large labels, as a policy, will not deal directly with them but rather prefer to go through a party they are familiar with.

◉ Kickbacks

Here we get to a dark subject and one that is the source of the most industry quibbles—kickbacks. In the secret code of the industry it's called many things: good business, greasing the wheels, doing the right thing. Others just call it thievery. Consider the following examples:

Kickbacks to the Artist and Manager

Often when the producer gets complete control of the recording fund, as in an all-in deal, the artist's manager may want a little piece of it. He will say the money is for his client, but we know better. If the money ever actually reaches the artist, the manager will likely commission it. But not to worry: it rarely does. The manager will try to convince the artist to let him keep it to recover the costs that he has incurred managing the artist for the past year or two before the record company signed the artist. The artist will often agree, out of guilt or loyalty.

Should the producer elect to pay the manager, it will be somehow camouflaged as some other expense in the recording budget, which means it will be recouped out of the artist's royalties. In other words, the artist pays for this kickback twice— once when they give up the money to the manager and again when it's recouped from their royalties.

The record companies know this goes on; no one is being fooled. There is, however, an accepted level of theft the industry has sustained over the years, a nebulous threshold known only to those who are in on the deal. This is why it can be hard to understand all the ins and outs of the record deal from the outside. Relationships are the foundation of the deals, and therefore everybody is scratching everybody else's back.

Kickbacks from Vendors

The producer also has relationships with studios and engineers. He will in turn sometimes ask for a kickback from each of them to help put more money in his pocket. (See the sidebar "Kickback or Commission?," page 97.) His agenda is that only the producer's fee as listed in the recording budget is recoupable. Therefore, whatever other sources of income the producer can create will be his to keep, free of recoupment.

Kickbacks to A&R

Corruption can go on at higher levels as well. I've heard of an A&R person who had an under-the-table deal in which the producer agreed to give them a kickback if the A&R person convinced his VP to get the recording budget up past $300,000. Once again, the artist pays for this greasing of the wheels.

There is no question in anybody's mind that this is stealing. But record companies have been known to look the other way on one condition—if the record is a hit. If it is, all will be forgotten. If not, the producer may find himself at the wrong end of a lawsuit.

Kickbacks from Musicians

There are more subtle ways that a producer can scam money off the budget and stay in that gray area between right and wrong. For instance, he may ask the side-person (a musician who is not part of the band but is used as a soloist or fill-in player—formerly known as a "sideman" before the days of political correctness) to give him a commission or "finder's fee" for the gig. These fees can run from 10% to 25%. Usually they will be paid from the sideperson to the producer directly and will therefore bypass the album's accounting.

Whatever the producer's angle, this must be done carefully, because at the major label level, everything in the budget goes through the business affairs office—the office that writes the checks that pay the producer's bills. If the producer is not careful and the budget is audited, he might have some explaining to do. On the indie level, the accounting is often less precise, so the producer has more latitude for his creative budgeting.[11]

11 For complete budgets and how to steal money, see "The Virtual Budget," page 153.

❂ When the Producer Wants Publishing

Paranoid ideas have been instilled in artists and writers that their publishing is something that they should never give up—that if a producer or manager asks for part of their publishing, they should run the other way. These concerns are good ones, but they don't tell the whole story. Here's why:

When a song plays on the radio, the law provides that the writer of the song earns a royalty. But what about the record company that put up the money, the producer who contributed scores of arrangement ideas (or who may even have rewritten portions of the song), the musicians who played on the record, and even the engineer

KICKBACK OR COMMISSION?

I was once hired to engineer a big-budget R&B record on a major label. The producer and I had a good relationship that went back two or three years. He had used me on several recordings, which helped build both of our reputations. This deal was his big shot. The budget for the album was over $300,000 "all-in" just for the recording. This was going to mean a lot of money for the producer, if he could be clever about it.

During the production he would frequently show up hours late for the session, leaving me, the artist, and the studio assistant sitting there twiddling our thumbs at a collective billing rate of about $300 per hour. I couldn't figure out why. I knew he had a lot of cash to make this record with, but why waste it? Then it hit me.

When he asked me to work on the recording he said he would pay me $60 per hour. I was delighted, not only to work on what seemed to be an important record but also at twice my usual rate of $30. But there was a catch: I would have to give him back $15 per hour in the form of a commission check. I did it. But what I began to figure out during the course of the production was that every vendor involved, including the studios, was giving him commissions. So while the record company was paying hundreds of dollars per hour in fees and charging them to the artist's account, the producer was making about $100 per hour under the table in addition to his fee. If I were him, I would take my time as well. Yes, this really was an all-in deal. It was "all in" the producer's pocket.

The artist sued the producer when he found out about the kickbacks, even though the record was a hit. The record company held the artist's royalties in escrow until the two parties worked it out. (How nice of them to keep an eye on the several million dollars collecting interest in their bank while the lawyers quarreled.)

I said nothing. Eventually the record company paid off the producer, and he and the artist went their separate ways. When the artist made his second record, he decided to produce it himself. It was a bomb. He has since been dropped from the label's roster. The producer, on the other hand, is still making records for that label. In fact, he called me recently to work on his next one. Get the picture?

Think the artist was wrong for pursuing this? For the reason why I do, see the sidebar "When Artists Steal from Other Artists," (page 99).

who "played" the mixing console, determining the sound of the record? These are all "authors" of the sound recording, yet they receive nothing.

More recently the use of samples has created an even stronger argument for producers to receive a share of publishing. For example, snippets of James Brown records have appeared on literally thousands of records in the form of samples, yet the original producers whose records were sampled haven't seen a nickel for the sample rights on the new recordings.[12]

[12] See "Sample Rights," page 84.

One could argue that the label and producer are not as important as the songwriter, without whom there would be no song to record, but a producer's contributions to the "sound of the record" should be worth some form of authorship royalty, don't you think? Well, the truth is more complex than a simple yes or no.

The Copyright Act of 1976 provided for a clause that could, at some future date, be amended to include a special royalty for the "authors of the sound recording," but to date (with one exception below for "digital transmissions") it has not been ini-

THE RADIO HIT ARGUMENT

It is difficult for some people to justify that if a record is a hit on the radio, only the writer of the song should get a piece of the royalty pie. If it were not for the record company, there would be no money for the recording, and if it were not for the engineer, there would be no quality recording, and if it were not for the producer, there would probably be *a big mess*. That's why producers feel justified in asking for publishing on songs that they contribute to.

Think about it this way: Long after record sales stop, a hit song is still played on the radio—whether it's for a review of the Top 100 of that year, or a "Where Are They Now?" show, or just because it has become part of our culture (like the song "Wild Thing," which is still played hundreds of times a year and is used in film after film). This airplay rarely leads to any substantial new record sales, so does it seem fair that while the record companies, producers, and musicians get zilch, the writer collects on airplay? Denying a producer publishing is the same thing as saying, "You don't have a right to make a royalty if the song is a radio hit," meaning that it gets lots of airplay but the airplay doesn't translate into record sales. Yet despite this inescapable logic, a producer asking for a piece of publishing is still met with criticism.

tiated due to tremendous opposition. The resistance comes largely from TV networks and rights organizations like BMI and ASCAP, all of whom have used their influence to prevent the establishing of a statutory rate for performance of a sound recording. TV companies are fed up with the license fees they already pay (discussed previously). The rights organizations also feel that a new royalty would take money out of their client's, the songwriter's, pocket by splitting the royalty pie even thinner.[13]

Advocates of the sound recording performance rate point out that if record companies and producers had their own publishing money to collect, then they wouldn't have such a strong argument for going after the songwriter's publishing. (Record companies would try to go after it anyway, but that's another matter.) Regardless, both sides will have a chance to prove their cases soon.

A new law called the Digital Millennium Copyright Act (DMCA) has created a new royalty stream for the performance of a sound recording when digitally transmitted. These transmissions will include things like satellite radio and Internet radio, but will not include common radio (called terrestrial radio) because of a "grandfather clause." (Meaning the new royalty will not be chargeable on the old format because it would upset the old format's business standards.) While presently the money generated from sound recordings in the U.S. is not 1/100th of the money

[13] In my opinion, PROs (performing rights organizations) like ASCAP and BMI and SESAC are motivated not by principle but by fear. They're only as powerful as the share of dollars they can control. If their income goes down, they lose power. Don't misunderstand me: This would ultimately be a horrible thing. These companies have made outstanding strides toward reform in the record industry, and I'd hate to see a world where PROs don't have the clout to collect for their writers. This controversy is just another example of having to take the good with the bad.

WHEN ARTISTS STEAL FROM OTHER ARTISTS

Artists who complain that their producer skimmed their budget are forgetting that in many cases they helped do the same thing to another artist. How?

Every working producer has one project he's working with that's paying his bills—the major label deal. But then there's another type of act: the one he's developing and keeping in his back pocket; doing demos and waiting for the just the right combination of song, singer, and timing to shop to a label. But when does the producer have time to work with his back-pocket artist if he's **blocked out a studio** with his major label artist for weeks at a time.

Well, if you haven't guessed, he's skimming late-night time off the big artist to develop the little artist. Technically this could be considered stealing. But I have never heard an artist in development complain or object.

that songwriters earn for terrestrial radio, in the next ten years it's bound to add up. In Europe, Canada, and Australia, sound recordings are paid performance fees on terrestrial radio, and they total hundreds of millions a year. This might be a good indicator for the future.

The company that collects the royalty generated from U.S. transmissions is SoundExchange. (see Performing Rights Organizations, page 37), but the usual suspects, ASCAP and BMI, are also vying for a piece of this pie.

There is an equitable solution to the "producer wants publishing" argument that I've known some artists to agree to. In many cases it may be agreed that the producer will get a 10% to 15% interest in the writer's share of the publishing but will not share in any publishing advances or have the right to administer (control) the copyright.

This means that if the artist has a 50/50 publishing deal as described earlier, then the writer is retaining 75% of the pie, and the producer will get 15% of the 75%, or 11.25%.

14 If you are confused by the formulas and don't know what a 50/50 publishing deal is, then please go to "Publishing Deals," page 81.

In real dollars this is hard to translate, but figure if the record sells a million copies, the publishing rate payable to the artist, assuming the artist wrote all ten songs on the record, is around $600,000 (at the three-quarters rate), of which the producer would get $67,500. However, this does not include the radio and TV royalties, which are based on the number of times the song is played and about how many people are watching the broadcast.[14]

CHAPTER EIGHT

⊛The Major Label Deal

from the Record Company's Point of View

At last, we get to hear from Father Christmas. I needed to save him for last because, as you can see, these deals can be complex. Let's examine the game from the perspective of the raping and pillaging record company and find out just why they're so mean. I suggest that if you are not familiar with the differences between a label and a distributor that you read "Understanding Distribution," page 55; "Record Companies," page 34; and "Distribution Companies," page 46.

⊛ The Distribution Vig

The word "vig" is short for vigorish—the difference in percentage between the cost of business and the net reward. It's often used to describe the commission paid to a bookmaker in sports betting.

The crux of why anybody is stingy usually boils down to one thing—how much money is it costing them to do business, or what is their vig? Why, when a CD costs $18, does the artist only get about a buck and the producer about 30 cents? Where does the rest of the money go? In this chapter we will answer that question.

The first cut in the pie is the distributor. The distributor sells new releases of mainstream artists to the large record chains for between $10 and $12 per CD album. The record store marks it up to $16.95 or $17.95 and eventually, if the record is not selling, will mark it back down to $13.95 or $10.95 to get it out the door.[1]

If distributors sell the record to retail stores for $12, what are they paying for it?

It depends. If the label that created the record is distributing itself (like Warner Bros. Records being distributed by WMG), they don't pay anything per se. But if it comes from one of their "indie" labels then they will pay Rhino about $9.60 per record on bona fide sales.[2]

The distributor marks up the record $2.40, about 20% of their wholesale price of $12.

Why would a small label let a Big Four distribute them and let them make that extra $2.40 if they could just take the records to the store themselves or make a deal with one of the digital retailers? The answer is because the smaller label stands a better chance of getting paid by the brick-and-mortar retail store if they are affiliated with a Big Four distributor (and as far as digital distribution is concerned, they will still need to go through a new type of middleman called an "aggregator" to get on those services. See page 47.)[3] However, the sacrifice can be costly, because it brings the profit margin down.

Regardless of who produces the record, $12 is about the going rate for what a retail store will pay.[4] The point being made here is if a parent label like Warner sells records produced by one of the labels it wholly owns (like Atlantic Records or Elektra), they make all $12; if they distribute records on behalf of one of their one-deep labels they keep only the difference between what they agree to pay the label (about $9.60) and the $12 they sell it for, or a net of about $2.40. This is the vig: what the middleman tacks on to make a profit. Every time you put another middleman between the label and the store, you can count on an additional vig of about 5%. So if you're a two-deep label, the vig is a bit higher (25%), and if you're a three-deep label, a bit higher still (30%). The farther away from the trunk of the tree you move, the wider the spread between what you make as a label and what the record sells for in the store.

❷ Deductions

Once the distributor passes the $9.60 on to the label (or in the case of non-subscription-based digital distribution, about 66% of the purchase price), the label will try to keep its overhead down in order to increase its profit margin. But there are some deductions that it has no control over.

[1] In the world of digital downloads a major label licenses a catalog directly to the digital retailer. The retailer, like iTunes, takes a set amount per sale, usually about 33%. In a subscription-based model like Yahoo, a pooling system is applied, much like ASCAP and BMI, to tally royalties.

[2] Note: They do not pay on records shipped, only sold. The distributor will then apply the same reserve and return clauses to the labels it distributes that those labels apply to their artists. See "Returns, Reserves, and Cutouts," page 73.

[3] Retail stores can be just as sleazy as anyone else. Sometimes they don't pay their bills. However, they dare not screw with a Big Four distributor, lest they not receive the big artists that sell millions of units. See "The P&D Deal," page 131.

Aggregation Fees

For those labels using digital rights aggregators, sometimes called Digital Distributors, they will first have to pay whatever they contracted for—usually between 15% and 25% of the total amount of money collected for their downloads (or streams). So if you sold a single through iTunes for 99 cents, iTunes charges a fee of 33%, or 32 cents, leaving 67 cents. The aggregator then charges their vig. Figure 15%, leaving 56 cents for the label. For the rest of this chapter, however, to make things a bit easier conceptually, we are going to presume that you are a label selling CDs and albums the traditional way, through brick-and-mortar retail. However, I've included a chart of costs for digital distribution in Egghead Box #4.

To the Writers

In the previous publishing chapter, we looked at mechanical licenses and the compulsory rate of 9.1 cents per song that's paid to the writers. Here is where it comes back to haunt the record company.

The law requires you, the label, to pay this fee to the owners of the copyrights you're reproducing. But what if the artist you sign turns in a master with 20 songs that are all 30 seconds long? Will you then be required to pay .091 x 20 songs, or $1.82 in licensing fees per album? Well, fortunately, although the law says you have to pay this fee, it doesn't say exactly when or that the author can't give up the right to receive the fee.

Usually the record company will ask the writer/artist to do a 3/4 rate of the 9.1 cents, or 6.8 cents, and also to keep the royalty applicable to only ten songs.[5]

If the artist on the record is not the writer of the songs, then the record company will have little leverage in asking for a 3/4 rate and will have to pay the full rate of 9.1 cents per song. This would increase their deduction from 68 cents to 91 cents— a 23-cent difference. This may seem trivial, but it adds up to a lot when you have a record that sold several million copies. Based on this, it's easy to see why labels prefer artists who write their own material.[6]

And what about the artist who samples other people's records? Should you, the label, be asked to pay those licensing fees as well? If you agreed to this, then your artist could just turn in a record with no original material and the label would have to pick up the bill. To act as a deterrent to this, labels of late have been adding up any additional licensing fees that need to be paid to copyright owners other than the artist and deducting them from their all-in licensing fee.[7]

The 3/4 rate for a package of ten songs brings the total deduction to 68 cents, leaving $8.79.

---

[4] (From previous page) In the 2003 Universal Music (UMD) announced they were lowering the wholesale price of CDs to $10. It didn't affect the retail price at all. Some retailers lowered prices anyway, not because they were making more margin, but because the large discount outlets (Wal-Mart, Best Buy) began using CDs as a "loss leader" item—selling them at cost ($10.99) to get people in the stores. After the Christmas rush UMD raised it back to $12.

[5] This means that even if there are 11 songs on the record, the writer/artist will only be paid for ten.

[6] See "Publishing Deals," page 81.

[7] See "Sample Rights," page 84.

To the Artist

Eventually, the label will have to pay the artist his or her 86 cents and the producer his or her 28 cents,[8] but only on 90% of sales,[9] which brings us down to $7.65.

[8] See "Recoupable Financing," page 65, for a complete breakdown of this.

To the Musicians

There is a fund established by the Musicians' Union, the AFM (American Federation of Musicians), on behalf of all musicians who play on records. They take a small percentage of retail,[10] or about 8.5 cents, bringing the record company's share down to $7.56. This fund is important for two reasons: (1) it supposedly gets distributed to the musicians who perform on the sessions;[11] (2) if they don't pay into this fund, then as per their agreement with the union, the record company is not supposed to be able to register the title with the RIAA for Gold and Platinum certification.[12]

[9] Unless it's a two-deep indie, in which case the current industry norm is 100% of sales.

[10] This calculation is very rounded. The real calculation is rather complex and based on the amount of units sold and at what price. It also doesn't kick in until at least 33,000 units are sold, making most indie releases exempt.

Giveaways, Returns, and Special Programs

Without freebies and giveaways, the new artist doesn't stand a chance. Even though the record company takes this into account when they only pay on 90% of bona fide sales, it still comes out to more than that for them. About 18% of all new-artist records sold will be deducted as giveaways; this amounts to about $1.80 per record, bringing the bottom line down to $5.76. In reality the record company makes money on only about 50% of the records they manufacture, even on the artists that sell well.

[11] See "The AFM," page 42.

Packaging and Manufacturing

Finally, remember the cost that the record company charges the artist, at about $4.50 per unit, called the container charge? Well, if you have a friend that has ever released an album out of their garage, they can tell you that the real unit cost of manufacturing the CD is about $2.50, and that's without pressing tens of thousands of units. At the level that Big Four distributors reproduce CDs and tapes, the real cost is somewhere between 40 cents and $1.00. Using the high number of $1.00, our total distribution vig nets out to $4.76. Please refer to Egghead Box #4.

[12] Although there are ways around this, too; see "How To Get Even," page 286. And since the RIAA is far more interested in pleasing the record company than the union (since the record companies are the ones keeping the RIAA's lights on), this becomes an unenforced provision.

Now let's re-examine the record deal from the label's point of view. From the profit displayed in the chart above, the record company will have to pay its salaries and rent. A biggie like Warner Bros. Records, which carries overhead in the hundreds of millions of dollars per year, must sell tens of millions of records just to break even.[18] However, the label pays the artist/writer a royalty of 84 cents based on the full *retail price* of the record and another 68 cents for the songs. That's a total of $1.52 going to the artist/writer. The artist nets almost 30% of what the label nets, yet the artist puts up zero dollars for the production and promotion, and their overhead is infinitesimally small compared to that of the record company. From the label's point of view, this must seem outrageously generous of them. Think about it. I go into business with you. I start a corporation, hire hundreds of people, put up 100% of the capital, incur 100% of the risk (and records are plenty risky), and you get 30% of the profit for playing in night clubs and hanging out in recording studios. Not a bad deal. Add to this the fact that 70% of what I, as the label, invest in will fail to sell enough records to warrant me investing in a second record with the same artist. So, one successful artist has to compensate for all the losers on the roster. This reality forces labels to adopt a rationale that dictates many of their decisions:

> [18] As a generalization, major labels' payrolls tend to run into the millions per month. Smaller major labels are in the ballpark of $750,000 per year, and the two-deep baby labels are typically about $200,000 to $500,000 per year.

It's more profitable to have one artist that sells millions of records than to have several that sell hundreds of thousands.

The reason for this should be fairly clear. Once you have a proven formula, it's easy to repeat. Each new band comes with new idiosyncrasies, new risks, and new marketing decisions. With that in mind, we turn our attention next to the marketing department and its point of view.

❷ Image Molding

Did you ever notice that a band that you know from the club scene looks drastically different after they have signed with a major label? This is due to the marketing department and its recommendations for the band's image. The marketing department will assign an image consultant to turn the five kids who look like they might mug you into five kids that look like they could mug you but can afford not to. All this is done in the name of trying to sell more records by making the band look more hip, cool, or whatever to the public. What the producer is to the band's music, the image consultant is to the band's look.

It has been my experience that record company philosophy leans toward the opinion that music purchases are largely impulse/tactile buying decisions where people see a record in the store, and if they like the packaging, they grab it. (An impulse buy, in other words.) This feeling is substantiated by the rise in sales following the release of promotional material such as videos. The visual imagery of the band and its logo or images that are in the video touch a nerve, the buyer reaches for the record, and a sale is made.

14 Writer/artists and producers used to be able to look forward to getting paid full rate and given larger percentages of sales on smaller "indie" label deals. However, this trend is pretty much gone to the consolidation of labels. A full description is given in "Publishing and Royalties," page 136.

15 However, since the direct distribution label is wholly owned by the Big Four distributor, it keeps the $2.40 for which it sells the record to the store, so its profit is really $6.83. The $2.40 vig is recorded as profit for the distribution branch, however, not the label branch.

16 The differential in price is due to the assumption that majors have a slightly better deal with iTunes than most "indies." iTunes claimed in 2004 to have a favored-nations deal with all majors, but majors and indies I've spoken to say otherwise.

Standard CD Sales

Where does all the money go? A breakdown of costs to the label and an analysis of unit-sales profit margins for new artists.

In-Store (Brick-and-Mortar) Distribution

	Direct distribution	One-deep distribution	Two-deep distribution
Big Four distributor's price to retail	$12	$12	$12
AFM's piece of the action	$ .085	$ .085	**Exempt** usually due to low volume (under 33,000 units sold)
Wholesale (distribution) vig	$2.40	$3.00	$3.60
Mechanical license (to songwriters)	$0.68 (3/4 rate)	$0.68	$0.63[14]
Artist's royalty	$0.86	$0.86	$0.86
Producer's royalty	$0.28	$0.28	$0.28
Giveaways (free goods)	$1.80	$1.80	$1.80
Duplication/packaging cost	$0.75	$1.10	$1.10
Gross profit to labels before overhead	$4.40[15]	$4.21	$3.70
Gross profit to labels before overhead in 2nd Edition 2001	$4.92	$4.32	$3.60
Gross profit to labels since 1st Edition 1998	$4.37	$3.92	$3.20

The figures taken from the previous editions of *Confessions* demonstrate that larger record companyies profit margins have dipped substantially in the last five years due to the rising cost of paying songwriters and artists, even though the cost of manufacturing has gone down. Add to this their exorbitant salaries for executives and fluctuating dips and rises in unit sales and you get a rather bleak picture for the future of the major-label CD album.

Smaller labels, although they sell far fewer units, have seen a wider margin between unit costs and unit profits. Combine this with the fact that two-deeps or "indies" pay their people about a quarter of what the majors pay—and since they do not trade as much on "mainstream" artists, they have not been hit as hard by the file-sharing phenomenon—and it's clear that they have, overall, done far better than their major label counterparts and will continue to produce in this area.

Digital downloading adds another dynamic to the bigger picture. Look at the costs to both large label and small.

Digital Distribution

A sale on a service like iTunes might look like this.
(Although several assumptions below might be premature.)

	Direct distribution	Indie going through an aggregator *(similar to a one-deep deal)*
Sale of a single on iTunes	**68 cents**	**60 cents**[16]
AFM's piece of the action	**one half of 1% of wholesale price** *(too little to bother calculating)*	**Exempt, usually due to low volume** *(under 10,000 units sold)*
Aggregation fees (15%)	—-	**10 cents**
Mechanical license (to songwriters)	**6.8 cents**	**6.8 cents**
Artist's royalty	**(9%) 0.07 cents**[17]	**(12%) 0.07 cents**[18]
Producer's royalty	**(3%) 0.025 cents**[17]	**(3%) 0.01 cents**[18]
Giveaways (free goods)	*N/A*	*N/A*
Duplication/packaging cost	*N/A*	*N/A*
Gross profit to labels before overhead-	**52.3 cents**	**36.8 cents**

As is plainly obvious, the major label makes substantially more margin on these sales than does the one-deep or indie. Combine this with an end to "returns and reserves," and it seems like a perfect world for a label. Unfortunately there are two factors to be considered.

Very few people have the technology to use digital distribution compared to the amount of people who buy CDs, DVDs, and Dual Disks worldwide. And this will not likely change substantially until about 2010.

Most digital services are moving to a subscription-based model where the customer pays about $15 a month for "all-you-can-burn" subscription. How these models translate into unit costs is impossible to determine. Since labels work off of unit sales as a key factor in doing quarterly reports, this model makes just about everyone involved extremely nervous. However, a probable outline is in the sidebar "Subscription Models in Digital Distribution," next page.

[17] This presumes that the label does not make packaging and free goods deductions to the artist's royalties. On most majors, the equation is the wholesale price (68 cents) times 130% (which equals 88 cents) and then the base royalty (12% all-in: 9% artists; 3% producer) applied. (130% is a holdover from the days of figuring out a royalty based on wholesale CD sales. In today's paradigm it's a meaningless and arbitrary "standard" number that is still used so that labels don't have to redesign all their accounting software.)

[18] Indie deals are structured a bit differently than majors. They tend not to have the 130%-of-wholesale calculation (see previous footnote); instead they create a royalty base equal to the net of 60 cents minus all the deductions and then apply the base royalty (15%). However, the base royalty is usually higher than majors by a point or two.

Nobody can argue that the band's looks will not play a role in a buying decision. Unfortunately, the band, left to their own devices, will rarely have the marketing savvy to design their own wardrobe. In fact, they usually reject such ideas as a sellout.

A Bit of History

This practice of "dressing up the act" is nothing new. In fact it goes back to the dawn of the pop/rock music industry in the early 1950s, when record companies wanted to sell rhythm and blues, a form of African-American ghetto music, to the record-buying masses, which were largely white suburban kids between the ages of 15 and 21.

The institutional racism of that time was unfavorable to African-Americans, and

SUBSCRIPTION MODELS IN DIGITAL DISTRIBUTION

Unlike iTunes and some other digital retailers, many services are switching over to a "subscription-based" model. In this model the consumer pays a flat fee per month (usually about $10–$15) for a sort of "all-you-can-eat" buffet of music. The subscriber typically gets an unlimited number of downloads, which only remain playable on the subscriber's device as long as the subscription is current. Each time a subscriber streams a tune or listens to one he has downloaded, it constitutes a "play-event"—a new phrase you need to learn if you're going to keep up.

If figuring out what you're supposed to get as an artist wasn't complicated enough, it just got tougher, because now the money received by your record company for your recordings is pooled[19] along with everyone else on your label. (See "ASCAP vs. BMI," "What's that floating in the pool" for why this is something to be concerned about, page 257.)

The majors all have their own deals with each service—Yahoo, Microsoft, AOL, etc.—and it would be too confusing to list each of them here. Below is a basic model of how they work:

Let's say that you're an artist called the Postmen Apostles on Pacific Records, which is part of a fictitious Big Four distributor called Galactic Music and Video Group (GMVG).

GMVG makes a deal with say, Yahoo, that in exchange for licensing all the master catalogs for all the labels they distribute, Yahoo is going to make to them one lump payment each month, as follows:

19 That's because receipts are then divided by number of play events—unless, of course, the penny-per-play-event surpasses the bulk rate.

record company executives knew that parents would never let their sons and daughters have LPs in the house with pictures of black people on the cover. So they went about trying to market rhythm and blues to the white market. The result was artists like Elvis Presley and Jerry Lee Lewis, some of whose tunes were written by black artists; these were sped up a bit and called "rock 'n' roll."

Over time, rhythm and blues separated itself from rock 'n' roll and became known as R&B (industry slang for "black music"). Jazz and bebop, originally called "jungle music" by many a white parent in the 1950s, has not only found acceptance in the mainstream market but is now considered a national treasure.

Almost all American pop music started out as "black music" (a more polite term

---

1) A penny-a-play-event *or*,

2) 40% of *each* subscriber's fee (so, if it's $10 a month, then $4)

3) Whichever of 1 and 2 is higher, BUT,

4) never to be less than $3 per subscriber.

Now to keep things simple, let's say that the amount that Yahoo owes GMVG for a given month is $100,000 (a very low number, but good for now to keep the math simple).

Yahoo also supplies GMVG with a complete list of every play-event for all their masters for that month and cuts them a check for $100,000.

Let's say that the number of Postmen Apostles play-events for that month is 10,000 tracks. And the total number of play-events for the entire GMVG catalog is 10,000,000 tracks. That means that the Postmen Apostles make up 1/1,000 of the play-events. If the total revenue collected for that month for the catalog is $100,000, then the Postmen Apostles' share of the pool is $100.

The label then applies an integer to that number. If you're a time-honored artist you'll likely get 50% of your share, or $50. If you're a new artist you'll likely get about 15%, or $15.

Proponents of the system argue that in this way artist can make money off their fans each and every month as they continue to renew their subscriptions, instead of just once or twice when they buy a new resale once every 1.5 years or so.

Audits, however, will be *nightmarish*. Also, it's still untested as to whether or not people will want to "rent" a record collection. (For much more on this see my book *Million Dollar Mistakes*.)

than some that were used in the early days) and was supported by African-American audiences before becoming economically viable for big record companies to invest in. Once they did, singers changed color, as did the backup bands. Another example of this is disco, which was funk gentrified for the mass market, and hip-hop, which is rap combined with R&B for the masses.

POP QUIZ

On the left are some names of pop singers you've probably heard of. On the right are their real names. See if you can match them up.

Gen X & Millenniums

Shania Twain	Florian Cloud de Bounevialle Armstrong
Tupac Shakur	Eithne Ní Bhraonáin
Dido	Eilleen Regina Edwards
Enya	Lesane Parish Crooks

Baby Boomers & Before

Alice Cooper	Roberta Joan Anderson
Elton John	McKinley Morganfield
Chaka Khan	Declan Patrick McManus
Joni Mitchell	Vincent Furnier
Bo Diddley	Ellas Bates
Sting	Louis Firbank
Muddy Waters	Reginald Kenneth Dwight
Elvis Costello	Yvette Marie Stevens
Lou Reed	Gordon Sumner

Answers to Pop Quiz "Gen X & Millenniums": Shania Twain = Eilleen Regina Edwards, Tupac Shakur = Lesane Parish Crooks, Dido = Florian Cloud de Bounevialle Armstrong, Enya = Eithne Ní Bhraonáin

Answers to Pop Quiz "Baby Boomers & Before": Alice Cooper = Vincent Furnier, Elton John = Reginald Kenneth Dwight, Chaka Khan = Yvette Marie Stevens, Joni Mitchell = Roberta Joan Anderson, Bo Diddley = Ellas Bates, Sting = Gordon Sumner, Muddy Waters = McKinley Morganfield, Elvis Costello = Declan Patrick McManus, Lou Reed = Louis Firbank.

IS IT A TAPAS OR AN APPETIZER?

Latin rocker Ritchie Valens's most famous hit, "La Bamba," was the first song recorded in Spanish to enter the Top Ten. Interestingly enough, Ritchie's real name was changed by the record company from Richard Stephen Valenzuela, and he didn't speak a word of Spanish.

Rap and hip-hop, the most recent example of the above, needed to be marketed with a crossover audience in mind before the genre could gain widespread acceptance. Producers of the megastars New Kids on the Block must have been in tune with this reality. Groups like Color Me Badd were directly influenced by black groups like Guy, and many critics called the Beastie Boys a white version of Run DMC, among others.[20]

Anyone who has been listening carefully and critically to music for more than ten years can easily see how the pattern of recycling and reusing old formats of music works. What makes the recycling process possible is how the music is marketed each time around. This, more than anything, is probably why the over-35

[20] This not to imply that the race of the band made the music of any less quality. (I'm a big Beastie Boys fan.) The point I'm making is that the music was *no different*, only the packaging, and that the repackaging radically affected sales.

AGE BEFORE DUTY

Youth plays an important role in the artist's commercial viability, so many artists misrepresent their ages in order to keep their youthful appeal. Perpetually 30-something Madonna is the classic example. Another example is LaToya Jackson, whose press releases claimed that she is in her thirties as recently as 2003. She's hoping we'll all forget that she is Michael's older sister (born in 1955).

In researching this section I sent my assistant to the library to confirm some facts. She scanned through *The Unauthorized Autobiography of Michael Jackson* looking for some info on LaToya. To her surprise the several pages that mention LaToya's name were torn out.

Trips and phone calls to other libraries yielded the same results. In several public libraries across America, the same set of pages had been torn out.

Could Michael be trying to hide something? Certainly he has the resources to have someone go around and do this. Or perhaps it's just a jealous fan.

generation tends to think that the new music sucks. It's because they've heard it before in a purer form, ten or 15 years ago.

Don't think that bands are not in touch with this process as well. Super groups could not continue to make smash records without understanding the formula for why their music works. Those who understand the realities of how the public perceives the artist usually profit greatly. Those who refuse to accept this reality rarely profit at all.

⊜ Sponsors

Speaking of reality, you may have noticed that lately superstar artists have become synonymous with certain brand names of soda, liquor, and long-distance telephone services. Wow—we've come a long way since artists refused to allow their music to be associated with something as benign as a shoe company for fear that they used third-world labor to make their product.

These days it seems that unless you can find a corporate sugar daddy to slip a few million in your liner notes, marketing your record on network TV is a pipe dream. Companies like Procter & Gamble, Johnson & Johnson, Coke, Nike, and phone giants Cingular, Sprint, and MCI basically own the airwaves when it comes to network TV advertising—which is still, even after 40 years of cable TV penetration, the most effective form of marketing.

TECH ME TO THE RIVER

One example of image molding that I was witness to occurred when I was working on a rave album.

Techno was just starting to fly in 1991, and this fellow, whom I'll call Barfly, approached me to do a record with him. We recorded it in my home studio, and Barfly got some money from a label with a one-deep distribution deal with MCA, selling them with the story that the record was produced by a Czech DJ in his basement studio in Prague. They bit.

When the record came out, my recording studio was not credited, nor was I listed as a cowriter or producer. Instead, the studio and all other credits reflected a production that originated in Prague.

Barfly said to me, "Kids don't buy techno records made by two over-30 guys who live in Queens." I was a bit ticked off at first. Then the next year I witnessed a fistfight that had broken out at a music business seminar about whether "true" rave music had come from Cleveland or Europe.[21] Barfly, if you're out there, you were right.

[21] Where did rave come from? One reader sent me this: "It is Europe in 1959. It was originally used as background noise for films."

A 30-second spot on network prime time is so costly even major labels, who spend millions on radio spots, don't go near the little screen. Instead, they look to slip in the back door by partnering up with some of these corporate giants and get the artists to do endorsement deals. The labels do not get the sponsorship money, but they enjoy a benefit, because every time a grungy rock tune by your favorite alternative band underscores a quirky Cingular or HP commercial, it translates into record sales. Many, many of them. So to the label it's free advertising. The artist gets millions from this type of exposure with no down side (except for the possibility that in the next life they might come back as an ad executive).

In the near future you can count on more co-op sponsorship deals, especially now that the Big Four are doing everything they can to recapture the perceived value of their product—the $18 CD. Soon CDs will be bundled and "given away" as part of promotions for things like BMWs. When this becomes an important consideration, not only will an artist's image play a significant role in their signability, but so will their willingness to play a direct, proactive role in selling products with their music, or *bundle-ability!*

CHAPTER NINE

⊚The Single

T he use of the word "single" has changed dramatically over the years. Throughout the '60s, records were sold in two forms: the 12-inch 33⅓ rpm LP[1] (usually containing eight or ten songs) and the 7-inch 45 rpm single (which had only one song on each side). A record company would introduce a new artist by releasing a single. If this did well, a second single would follow, then an LP that contained both singles and several other new songs put together on one disc.

Today, the 7-inch record is almost defunct. Record companies tried to adapt the concept to CD singles, but they were too pricey and defeated the concept of a random-access medium. Cassette singles were the prevailing source of singles sales in the 1980s, but they have all but completely died. Only some college stations still consider 7-inch vinyl cool—and even this diehard trend will have its limits. So what is a single today?

Even though A&R still uses the phrase "put out a single," this rarely refers to a separate CD or 7-inch that has one song on it. "Single," in today's A&R parlance, means the one song that will be used to promote/launch the artist or their new album. It is the one song that they will push to radio and, in most cases, the one that will be made into a video for MTV and the other video networks.

[1] rpm: revolutions per minute. LP: long-playing record. An LP plays for a total of about 40 minutes. This may seem silly now that CDs can hold over an hour, but this was a marked improvement over the 78 rpm record, which only played for about 10 minutes.

Then there is the obvious observation to anyone with a computer: "A single is the song you can most easily get online." True, the down side to marketing singles is that the public focuses only on the "one good song," and since sending one song through the web is not very time- (or memory-) consuming, "singles" have become the targets of people using P2P (peer-to-peer) file-sharing networks to help others steal music. However, the use of "free" distribution of singles has proven to be a good way to get the public interested in a new release.

So, when industry people say, "I don't hear a single," they are saying that not one song in the artist's repertoire will be usable as a marketing tool. This is not said lightly, and it's a bad sign for an artist.

❷ Who Picks the Single

Wars have been fought over the crucial decision of what song from an album will be the single. Artists often feel that they are best qualified to choose how the public will first perceive them. Record companies usually disagree. Marketing a song is the most expensive part of promoting an artist for a record company.

I've seen both sides of this argument struggle to the bitter end. If the artist wins, the label will oblige them and promote the artist's choice, but rarely with the same enthusiasm that they would have if they were promoting their own choice. If the label wins, they end up with a less-than-enthusiastic artist playing an encore that they will in time grow to hate. Perhaps this is because the label's choice for the single is often the song that the artist feels *least* represents what they are about.[2]

[2] For a frightening account of how this can end up, see the sidebar "Extreme Measures," page 202.

As a decision maker at a record company, you should try to never let an artist dictate how you market your catalogue. This sounds a bit callous, but consider the alternative: How would it be if actors decided on their own hair, makeup, and wardrobe in a film (some do. . .), or if news reporters got to decide what the front page would look like? Perhaps you are the sort of individual who thinks artists should make these decisions. You are certainly entitled to your opinion, but I wouldn't recommend advertising this belief if you intend to raise money to start a record label.[3]

[3] Somebody, please prove me wrong!

❷ The Hit Parade Charts and the "Hit Single"

To the average person, a "hit single" usually means that the record is on the *Billboard* Hot 100 chart in one of the top ten positions. Most people assume that the chart is compiled by tallying up the record sales for that week or is based on the amount of airplay that the song has received. I think it would shock the average person to learn that until 1991 the *Billboard* chart had nothing to do with actual record sales or even airplay! Behold. . . .

Billboard or Bullboard?

"The charts," as they are called, are another form of advertising for the artist (and thus for the label). The prevailing industry attitude has been, if the song is on the charts, it might persuade people to buy the record. To the layperson I know this must seem like the tail is wagging the dog, but if you've been following this book, you'd know that things tend to work a bit cockeyed in this industry.

Now, *Billboard* has always professed to be about album sales, and, in its defense, the magazine has reported the charts as accurately as it can. The inaccuracy comes from two weak links in the "chain of truth." First, until recently *Billboard* had no way of tracking actual record sales at the retail end. It used to rely on the shipping invoices of record companies and retail stores to determine which records were selling the most. As we have seen in other chapters, many records are returned from the retail stores, so shipping receipts are a very misleading yardstick to use.

The second problem with *Billboard* is who reports the sales information to them. Knowing that shipping is an unreliable yardstick, *Billboard* will call various record stores and speak directly to a shipping clerk or manager about what's selling that week. Unfortunately, these clerks can be easily corrupted. Rumors are rampant in the industry of how record company promotion departments offered concert tick-

LOOSE AS A BRUCE

The most blatant example of how misleading *Billboard* charts can be was the 1986 triple live *Bruce Springsteen* album, which opened up, in its first week of release, at No. 1 on the *Billboard* 200 chart of top albums. The retail stores reported an initial order of over two million units—instant double-platinum status right out of the gate. You can imagine the publicity that Bruce gathered because of this rare occurrence.

Unfortunately, many of those records shipped back several months later, unsold. *Billboard* has no chart that gives you that information.

4 Something that
never ceased to
amaze me was
that even though
most record
executives in the
1980s would
admit that the
charts were
manipulated, they
would still use
them to make "in-
formed decisions."

5 The company has
since been pur-
chased by Nielsen,
the same company
that tabulates TV
viewers' viewing
habits and gener-
ates the famous
"Nielsen ratings."

6 Broadcast Data
Systems uses digi-
tal sampling tech-
nology to "sample
the airwaves" in
order to determine
which songs are
most frequently
played by radio
stations. It too is
now owned by
Nielsen.

7 So is the Sound-
Scan system. See
"Billboard or Bull-
board?," page 117.

ets, promotional gifts, and outright bribes to stock personnel for "exaggerating" a bit to *Billboard*'s researchers.

If all this sounds like a big joke, it's no joke to artists whose careers depend on the perception of their record. Record companies use these charts to make important decisions about trends, which artists to keep, and which ones to drop.[4]

SoundScan

In 1991 a small company called SoundScan perfected software that can read and tabulate the bar coding on the backs of CDs and keep fairly accurate records as to how many records are selling.[5] *Billboard* charts now use the SoundScan system in connection with another tracking system called BDS (Broadcast Data Systems)[6] for determining which records are No. 1, No. 2, and so on. SoundScan also issues reports with (somewhat) exact numbers as to the sales of each record on the top 200 selling records of that week. This report is available to anyone who subscribes to it. It is not a perfect system, in that it does not get complete information from small mom-and-pop stores (which can make up over a third of the sales on a major and half the sales on an indie release), but it's vastly better than the old system, which was vulnerable to systemic graft.[7]

In recent years the Big Four have made direct-sales deals with some of the larger chains. These sales—which offer substantial discounts in exchange for large orders—have all but destroyed the mom-and-pop record store. So now, everyone goes to places like Best Buy and K Mart to buy their CDs because they have the best price in town. The bad news is that this consolidation destroys the regionalism of a music community. No more "local record store" where the proprietor knew everything about the records he was *carrying* and could make recommendations because he actually listened to them. He's retired. The good news for labels and artists is all the big stores are on SoundScan, so the sales numbers are far more accurate than ever before. Unfortunately for SoundScan this may be a double-edged sword, as majors may not be interested in using them once they only have to consult a small number of stores to get a full report. Case in point, in 2005 UMVD announced they will be turning away from Soundscan for reporting data.[8]

Other Types of Charts

Billboard is not the only authority in the music industry, although it is the most prominent. Since the college alternative stations, satellite radio, P2P file-sharing services and digital online record stores have become more prevalent, other organizations with their own charts have cropped up. One of these is the *College Music Journal* (CMJ) chart. This follows the college radio stations and uses SoundScan's figures to determine its chart placement. Because it is more of a grassroots publication, it services mainly the indie labels. But many A&R people at the majors consider it a more accurate source for what's selling on the street level. When an act rises into the Top 40 on the CMJ chart, you can be sure that a major label will take some interest in that artist.

Other charts are more exclusive, like the R&R chart, published only in *R&R* (*Radio & Records*) magazine. *R&R* is the No. 1 "insider's" information source, generally subscribed to only by VPs and higher A&R staff at major labels. If you've got a hit on the radio already and want to keep track of your record's progress on stations across the country, this is for you. It's very expensive and, unlike *Billboard*, is not likely to be available at your local newsstand. (Although you can scan it online at http://www.radioandrecords.com/) *Gavin* allegedly had the most trustworthy reporting regarding what's getting spun. Record execs loved it, because unlike other

---

RADIO: THE SUPERMARKET OF THE MUSIC WORLD

The selling of any item where there is limited shelf space usually involves graft. My friend Shlomo managed a supermarket and told me that product manufacturers pay the supermarket a fee to have them put their brand at eye level on a shelf. They know that the average person will see their product first, and that the placement substantially increases the odds of outselling their competitors. Think this is dumb? Maybe this will sober you up: The fee for a major product in a major chain can run as high as $200,000 per month!

The shelf space in the record biz is *airplay*, which gives the public their "free sample" of the goods. The eye-level shelf space is pop radio, the format with the largest listenership. The only difference is that to pay a program director a private fee to put a song on the air is illegal. This doesn't seem consistent when you consider the supermarket example. Supermarkets are not required to inform the public that Procter & Gamble paid $200,000 to be at eye level on the shelf. [9]

[8] (From previous page) There are several reasons for this but one might be a process, which I call sound-scam, that has cashiers being paid to run CDs over the scanner two or three times for each legitimate sale. The computer doesn't catch the error until the sales reports are already published in *Billboard*. SoundScan claims this is not possible, and I have not been able as yet to verify the accuracy of this report, but if this method doesn't work, trust me, someone, somewhere will figure out something else that will. For more on this see "SoundScan Tells All," page 248.

[9] I'll give you the real answer, but it won't leave you satisfied. It's because the radio uses the airwaves. The airwaves technically belong to the public, and therefore the radio is considered a "public trust." Are you laughing?

10 "Crossover hit" refers to a song that has been entered into the regular play list on more than one type of radio station (or market), like an R&B song that "crosses over" to pop. Example: Run DMC's rap tune "Walk This Way" (which featured its original authors, Aerosmith) made a dent in both rap and rock charts.

charts, *Gavin* tracks "crossover" hits.[10] But they folded in 2003. *Hits* includes an interesting chart not featured in the ones above: "Requests," a chart based on calls from radio listeners. *Hits* also features charts that are crossbred between radio airplay and retail sales. They have been facing some financial trouble in the past few years. They make most of their money off the ads that record companies place to inform buyers for record stores about new releases. Now that record companies have large arm's-length deals with the bigger outlets, they spend far less on advertising in "trades" than they used to.

So what's left? In place of all these more "old school" charts we now have "media tracking services" like Big Champagne, which claims a technology that accurately tracks singles traded through both legal and illegal Internet file-sharing networks. While this doesn't directly reflect sales, companies like this are positioning themselves as the new way of thinking about "charts." If your song is being traded 10,000 times a day—even if it's being done so illegally—it hopefully should be generating money somewhere or is at least worthy of A&R interest. We'll see if this theory pans out by the next edition of *Confessions*. (You can see their charts at http://www.bigchampagne.com/) iTunes and other digital retailers also have a "most downloaded" chart on their websites. These have the added value of being super-accurate and almost agenda-free. Along these lines, some of the new "Digital PROs" also have charts that reflect from which records they are earning the most direct licensing money. (See "Performing Rights Organizations," page 37.)

"THIS RECORD HAS SUCH A SOUND, IT'S THE SOUND OF MONEY"

There is an old story from the days of 12-inch vinyl records that tells of an exchange between a promoter and a station manager (SM). The promoter would give the SM a recent release and ask him to play it next week in a prime slot. The SM would hold the album sleeve up to his ear and move it back and forth. If he heard an envelope sliding around inside the sleeve, he would reply, "This sounds like a great record!"

➲ Airplay & Webcasting

When you watch a video on MTV, or on a website while waiting for the page to load, it probably doesn't occur to you that you are watching a commercial for a record. Likewise, when you listen to the radio you believe that this has been designed for your enjoyment. Record companies, however, see it as for *their* enjoyment. The airwaves are the most effective way to advertise their product—the artist.

When a radio station or television station plays a song or a video, they are required by law to pay the songwriter a royalty of several cents per play. Isn't it curious then that the media has to pay an artist for helping them sell their song? How do they stay in business? Well, the answer is that, aside from charging advertisers to put their commercials on the air, they also charge the record company large fees to put their songs on the air. The pay-for-play fees can be much higher than the performance fees they are required to pay by law.

Isn't that illegal or unethical or something like that? The only fair answer is "yes and no." Accepting a covert fee in direct exchange for playing a song is considered bribery. The under-the-table money given to the radio station's program director is called payola.

A little history on the subject will explain a lot about what you hear when you listen to your favorite station.

Promoters and Payola

Since the dawn of rock 'n' roll in the '50s, record companies have known that radio is what breaks the record to the public. In the '60s, many stations consolidated, thereby creating a situation where there were fewer stations and thus less airtime. As with all supply-and-demand situations, competition (in this case the fight to get a song on the air) became intense, and the battle was fought with the major players' sharpest wits.

To outgun their competition, record companies hire independent promoters to "push" certain artists to the radio stations for a good position in the station's rotation (i.e., the list of songs currently being played). Why a station would cooperate with this system is simple to understand. It makes most of its money off advertising—selling products between the songs. In order to charge a lot of money for advertising, a station must have a large listenership. In order to have a large listenership, it has to play the most popular songs. But how can a radio station know that a new artist is going to be popular? It can't, but it can figure out how much exposure a new artist will get by the amount the record label is willing to spend on the artist's promotion.

Hiring an independent promoter used to cost as much as $250,000 per song for the label. For this fee the record label was assured that the song would be played on several top stations in a given territory. This guarantee was a lock because the promoter would bribe the station manager to put the song in the rotation for a week, or a month, or whatever he thought he could negotiate. If the label wanted national airplay, they would have to pay the same fee to a promoter in each region of the United States. This got very expensive. But that was all right with the labels; keeping the service expensive made it inaccessible to their main competition—the small indie labels.

The practice of using independent promoters is hard for artists to accept. They work for years to develop their sound and songs, and whether they become famous or have to go back to working in a warehouse all depends on some wise guy in loud clothing, chomping on a huge cigar, greasing a program director with a bribe. No wonder so many artists take drugs!

The irony of the whole thing is that after the labels have spent this ungodly amount of money, they don't even receive any royalty for the airplay. The only people who receive a performance royalty from airplay are the writer and publisher of the song.[11]

While the record company is spending hundreds of thousands to get the song on the radio to sell the record, the artist/writer gets about a hundred thousand dollars in performance royalties per song.

The indie promoter schmooze has not died out of late. But is has taken on new forms. In the old days the major indie promoters (not to be confused with indie record labels) were, for the most part, tied to the Mob. As the Mob's interest in the record business thinned out in the late '80s (due to government shakedowns and sales to multinational conglomerates) and as competition from new, more legitimate promotion companies sprang up, these grifters of radio promotion found new marks.[12]

Labels were slapped with large fines and now, as a result, let the artists hire the independent promoters themselves. Even though it means more work for the artist, it also means that the artist has a bit more control over his or her career and expenses. In lieu of spending the big bucks on promoters, record companies are now free to come up with clever legal ways to promote records.[13]

What has been happening in the past few years is this: A promotion company would seduce station managers with concert tickets and prizes. These are charged back to the artist's recoupment fund as promotional expenses. It has to be done in the form of a rebate on merchandising, but make no mistake—it's a bribe. I remember one campaign for the '80s group EMF where the record company sent a promo

11 See "When the Producer Wants Publishing," page 96.

12 The book *Hit Men* by Fredric Dannen tells some of the most intriguing stories in print about this corrupt era in the music industry, as does *Stiffed*, by William Knoedelseder.

13 The new concept in artist promotion is for record companies to buy blocks of airtime to promote a new release. This would function just like an infomercial. This is not only legal, but it takes the guesswork out of radio promotion, and it's much cheaper. This was the technique used to launch the band Limp Bizkit in 2000. It worked quite well.

tape around to every program director for their consideration. The tape came presented in a top-of-the-line Sony Walkman worth about $150, with the cassette inside the machine cued up to the single called "Unbelievable." The Walkman was considered packaging for a promotional demo. Uh-huh.[14]

The reason for all this nastiness in getting songs on the radio is the hope that by pure repetition on the air, people will "learn to like the record," generating a sale. There is plenty of marketing data to confirm that this can work, but here is a bit of solace for you purists out there. Although record companies tend to be very secretive about which promotion scams work and which ones don't, I believe in the Abe Lincoln philosophy, which goes, and I'm paraphrasing, "You can make most of the people buy a crappy record some of the time, and you can make some of the people buy a crappy record most of the time, but you can't make most of the people buy a crappy record most of the time."

Basically, you can't make enough people buy a record they hate no matter how much money you throw at it. Although it seems that major labels sure do try.

For those of you who have ever wondered why mainstream radio doesn't play your favorite underground or indie band, you should now understand: it's because their label doesn't allocate the money to bribe the right people to play it. So the next time one of your relatives tells you that you should be a singer because your voice is so much better than "the junk on the radio," you can now explain to Aunt Sophie that it isn't that simple.

Net-Hype

Now that the Internet seems like the hip way to promote singles, record companies have become very clever: they are hiring scores of college students to "assist with promotion" by entering chat rooms and hyping up a new artist. They're not the only one doing this. Unsigned artists commonly bulk e-mail incentives to people to go to an online record company and "vote" or click on their single in hopes of inflating their apparent appeal. They know that A&R people watch these statistics to see who is getting attention. It seems to work. In the past two years, several large deals were "discovered" this way by major labels.

⊘ Satellite & Internet Radio

Since the last edition of this book over 6,000,000 people have each spent about $200 and then $10 a month on a box that receives a digital satellite signal and

[14] Soon we'll see iPods packaged with the same concept. Oh, wait, U2 did that already.

IS THE INTERNET REALLY "FREE"?

How is it that at a time when media companies keep such close guard of their copyrights, a company called Napster, started by a teenager, managed to hold every major record company at bay and let millions of people make legal copies of popular songs for free? Napster allows two parties to share each other's files by streaming them through the Internet. But isn't that just a high-tech version of making pirated tapes in your basement?

The answers come from a glitch in the Copyright Act of 1976, which defines a "copy" as a duplication on a "fixed" medium. Radio stations do not pay fees for "making a copy," because causing a song to wisp though the air is not considered "making a copy."[15] Similarly, neither is "streaming"—moving data though the Internet pipeline. Streaming is not considered "making a copy" as defined in the 1976 Act. The person at the other end might be "making a copy" by storing it on his computer, but even this is arguable. And even if storing a song on your hard drive were considered "making a copy," the file-sharing service is not doing the actual copy-making—it's only providing the means for two parties to communicate.

As of this writing, file-sharing remains active, although Napster was required by a Federal judge to do everything in their power to try to prevent people from pirating music via their service. But there are many other similar services that will be harder to discourage. New legislation will plug the hole in the old Copyright Act, but this, too, will not be without challenge since the Internet is international and a company can always set up shop "offshore." Until all of this is hashed out, file-sharing sites—despite their obviously unethical behavior—are operating within the boundaries of the law.

[15] Radio stations pay performance fees to performing rights organizations, like ASCAP, BMI, and SESAC. See "Performing Rights Organizations," page 37.

provides over 100 additional stations of programming. It's the cable TV of radio, called "satellite"—the relative opposite of "terrestrial radio."

Terrestrial radio uses a series of towers to transmit an analog signal that can be received by a device (radio) that catches the signal and, using a dial, allows you to "tune in" a particular frequency or station. In satellite radio, the multi-band signal originates from a satellite that is in geosynchronous orbit around the Earth. Like terrestrial radio it makes use of the airwaves to transport its signal, but the beam consists of digital bits and bytes that can carry far more information than terrestrial radio's analog signal.

Because of satellite radio's novelty and its abundance of subscribers in so short a period of time, many experts have readily predicted the end of terrestrial radio. They cite as their reason the presumption that people will flock to satellite because of the lack of commercials and its hipper programming. This claim would mean more chances for indie artists to get exposure. And who doesn't want that? To the untrained music business "expert," this might make sense and be a cause for celebration. I mean, isn't 6 million subscribers in five years enough to convince you? No. Not in this "expert's view." Here's why:

It took almost 15 years before cable TV (a business model very similar to satellite radio) became thought of as a "utility" in the American home. And it had many more than 6 million subscribers. During that time the average cable-ready home paid about $11 per month (in 1977) for the service. Cable teetered on profitability for almost a decade and had no direct competitors until Dish in the mid-1990s. Satellite has the same uphill battle while facing several strong competitors.

It would be nice for satellite radio if car manufacturers were accommodating and simply put a satellite receiver in every car they make. But this is not the case. Detroit moves slower than Congress. For example: CD players came into the market in 1980, but it took about 20 years before they became standard in cars below the mid-price range. Then there are the iPods, whose portability has given them a head start in capturing the car market. And let's not forget traditional (terrestrial) radio, which is FREE.

Just as cable didn't destroy network TV, neither will satellite radio destroy terrestrial radio.

The primary factor determining why terrestrial radio will survive even in the wake of new radio formats is simple economics. It's still far cheaper to run a terrestrial/analog radio station than a digital one, mainly because terrestrial doesn't have to pay for the music licenses. Satellite and Internet radio collectively pay over $300,000,000 a year just for their music licenses.

Add to this the fact that satellite radio's format is moving closer and closer to a commercial radio's. Already there are frequencies that are owned outright by labels who use it as an exclusive platform for their artists.

Then there are those who argue that satellite will be better because the FCC doesn't regulate it. These people are simply wrong. The *inevitable* consolidation of satellite's two giants, XM and Sirius, will result in FCC "influence" that will likely go into effect on satellite radio by 2010—as they have on cable TV already. Yes, it's true. It is a commonly repeated misconception that the FCC has no influence over cable TV. It does.[16]

So why would the public pay extra to get the same old gas? They won't. Or, I should say, most won't. Sure, there will be enough to keep the platform moving forward (even though as of this writing it's not yet profitable), but it will in time find its way among all radio formats, like cable did with network TV—co-existing side-by-side, each with its share of the market.

Will any of this mean that indie music will have a better shot at mainstream radio? It's unlikely that developments will alter the status quo, for a couple of reasons. Most satellite music playlists are already or will in time be controlled by major labels' agendas. In fact, terrestrial radio is a more likely place to develop "alternative" programming, since it doesn't have to pay for music licenses, and terrestrial radio might wish to compete with digital radio the same way that network TV became "hotter" with sexier programming to compete with cable. Already one radio conglomerate, which owns over 1,000 stations, is developing an upgraded version of terrestrial radio that will allow you to buy songs as you hear them, Live. If it pans out, this will dramatically change the way record companies market their catalogues.

Then again, satellite might look toward indie artists for "free" content because if those artists are not signed to an RIAA-affiliated label (and therefore not part of the SoundExchange society), they can waive "performance fees."

[16] The Supreme Court affirmed the Commission's jurisdiction over cable in United States v. Southwestern Cable Co., 392 U.S. 157 (1968). Each state regulates cable TV and sets "decency standards" in its own way. For more on this see http://www.fcc.gov/mb/facts/csgen.html and http://www.uweb.ucsb.edu/~colleen-oconnor/]

CHAPTER TEN

>The Independent Record Deal

The Birth of the New Indie

U p through the 1970s, record companies were entities that exploited their product largely through the leverage of their relationships with labor unions and radio conglomerates. Without a multinational company behind them, smaller companies were squeezed out of the pop music game. As we've seen in other chapters, the cost of promotion would escalate beyond a small company's ability to turn a profit, and the distribution channels that a small record company would use were owned by their primary competition—the major labels. In addition to this, the main source of advertising for a new record—radio airplay—was locked up by major label marketing scams, which included expensive promotional gifts to station directors.

Ultimately, an indie's catalogue would be bought out by a major label, if they were lucky. If they weren't lucky, the label, its groups, and its catalogue would disappear into obscurity.

But things have changed in the last ten years. The information age has caught up with the notorious informality of the music industry and has made it far more difficult for major labels to hide a mediocre product behind a tidal wave of publicity and payola.

For the first time, any person who desires can have actual sales figures by subscribing to a plethora of sources. Lo and behold, the revelation of this has shown the industry that the major genre of music selling today is adult contemporary, of which country music makes up a large part. (And all this time they wanted us to think that people over 30 didn't buy records.) Pulling in at a close second for the record buyers' attention is rap, proving its ability to cross over into several markets. Rock and what's now called alternative rock are third place in the national market for the time being. This is up substantially from the mid-'80s, when you were hard-pressed to find even two rock songs on the pop charts at the same time.

According to *Pollstar* (an industry trade mag), in 2004 there were about 2,151 active artists being distributed and promoted by major labels and/or their one-deep and two-deep labels.[1] This same magazine lists the total number of artists, both on majors and "indies," active in the U.S. record business at a staggering 8,008 acts. A standard formula for success in the record business is 5%, meaning that less than 5% of these acts make money for their companies.[2] This means that the record sales industry, an eight-billion-dollar-a-year industry in the United States, is being floated by 400 acts! But if 400 acts are splitting $8 billion, each of these is yielding an average of $20,000,000 a year to their respective labels. This is highly unlikely.

A more likely figure is about two-thirds of this, or about $13.2 million. Assuming for the moment that this is true, it means that 5% of the balance, almost 393 acts, are generating $3.8 billion, which is going into the hands of non-major label affiliates, which I consider true indie labels. That's $3.8 billion going into about 1,000 labels, which crunches out to approximately $3.8 million per year per label on record sales alone.[3]

In terms of catching the crumbs that fall off the plates of the big players, this is real money. As hundreds of acts get dropped from major label rosters because they're not cost-effective, indies are cleaning up, not only by keeping their overhead down but by homing in on the local market that made the band worth signing in the first place. In addition to this, lateral, outside-the-box marketing people hired by artists *independently of their labels* have created new avenues for CD sales. And we're not just talking a few thousand units. In 2004 we saw the following platinum records awarded to artists for non-traditional sales: Ray Charles, 2 million copies via Starbucks coffee chain; James Taylor, 1 million Christmas CDs via Hallmark (without his CD even being available at retail).

Like a large ocean liner turning in the sea, major labels have been slow to respond to the iceberg visible on the horizon. Although they have tried to control the

1 Down from 6,500 in 2001.

2 Although labels claim that this 5% number is real, it is not. Even if not every artist turns out to be a superstar, the economics of major label deals are such that the label recoups their initial investment in far more than 5% of their acts. So while they may not make a bundle on each gamble they don't lose too much either. You can't fly the CEO around the world in a Lear jet on 5% success ratios.

3 This doesn't include the so-called "bedroom labels," obviously. And, in addition, these labels' sales are not tracked by the RIAA. See "The RIAA" on page 50.

so-called indie market by employing the same "promotional" techniques with the college stations, and cramming chat rooms with promotion shills, they have been unsuccessful. The indie market refuses to subscribe to the pay-for-play attitude, and because of this the major labels have had a tougher time controlling this market the way they have pop radio for so many years.[4]

The main reason is that the parameters of each market change from city to city, and the radio personnel and website editors change with each new college semester. These uncertainties have forced major labels to all but get out of the artist development end of the business, leaving it to the indies, much the way the smaller independent production companies have produced nonunion films for half the money of a big studio.

Naturally, there are many exceptions to this. Major record labels still take enormous risks on new artists, but by and large they look to the indies the same way that the NFL and NBA look to the colleges for new talent. Today, more than 75% of the deals done with major labels are simple P&D (pressing and distribution) deals, in which the major takes a substantially smaller percentage than they would on artist development (P&D deals are covered in the next chapter).

This is the best service that their clout and power has left to offer the modern rock 'n' roll act, most of whom are looking for a bit more than a large advance from a label that eventually will drop them from the roster when they don't sell half a million records right out of the box.

[4] This became abundantly evident when, in late 2000, labels almost lost control of the Internet as a distribution system. See the sidebar "Is the Internet Really 'Free'?" on page 124.

CHAPTER ELEVEN

❯ The Independent Record Deal
from the Point of View of the Record Company

❯ The P&D Deal

Most smaller, true independent labels are actually production companies that have what is called a P&D deal with one of the independent distributors. P&D means "pressing and distribution." The distributing label actually presses and ships the records to the stores and charges the indie label a 25% commission. Unfortunately, the contracts for these arrangements are somewhat precarious. Indie labels often change distributors every couple of years. Sometimes it's for positive reasons: maybe the label has grown and is seeking wider placement. Other times it's because the relationship between the label and the distributor has collapsed in a sea of audits and accusations.

Even the stability of the distribution contract doesn't change the frightening costs that face the label taking risks on new talent. Considering the amount of money and person power it takes to sell a record, the indie label had better be very sure that it moves at least 25,000 units of a new title, or it will quickly become cost-ineffective to keep its doors open. In this respect, indie labels function very much like artists: when dealing with their distributors, they have to compete with the other labels that are being shipped by that distributor.

That's why it's important for the band and their manager to be aware of what is called the "hot sheet."[1]

[1] Although we are discussing independent labels, this same competitive dynamic exists for one-deep and two-deep labels on Big Four distributors.

⊜ How Records Get to the Store: The Hot Sheets

While browsing through a record store, did you ever wonder how Best Buy, HMV, or any record store knows what records to buy and put on their shelves?

One would think it's done in a logical manner—the store has a buyer for each department, and he or she is in touch with record labels. The label sends them all their new releases, and the store puts them on the shelf. When a title sells out, the buyer orders more.

If only it were that simple.

You see, record stores don't want to buy and stock thousands of records that don't sell quickly and abundantly. The way to make money is to stock only records that sell. Well, this fairly obvious statement leads to the not-so-obvious query, "How do they know which records are going to sell?" Of course, artists like 50 Cent and the Rolling Stones come with a certain guarantee, but what about new artists? How does the buyer for the record store know which new artists to pick up on and which to ignore? I'm glad you asked.

Record stores follow the same logic as radio program directors.[2] They know that launching a new artist is very expensive. If the label wants the artist to reach a certain number of record sales, then they're going to have to spend a good amount of promotion money on the act. So a buyer for a record store, like the radio program director, will sit back and wait to see how much publicity and resources the label will allocate to a new artist. Using that as a yardstick, they judge what the label really thinks of the act. If they're putting a lot of money into them, the buyer will take a shot. After all, if it flops, he won't look bad in front of the boss.

[2] See "Airplay & Webcasting," page 121.

The buyers for record stores receive things called "one sheets". These are one-page posters that are ads for new records. The ads are not cheap and appear in magazines like *Hits*. So if an indie label has taken the time to do one in, say, full color, it sends a clear message to buyers and program directors that they'd better get their orders in early or be embarrassed when it's a hit and they're out of the loop.

But it doesn't stop there. The promotion department of the label and the distributor will also call up the buyers and sell them on the act. They might offer them premiums and kickbacks to take a shot on a new artist (see "Marketing Mishigas," page 277). This is why the artist only gets paid on 75–85% of sales: the distributor will give away a lot of records to make the deal smooth with the retailer. The give-aways will register as sales on the books, but the label will not get any money for them because they were freebies. Even though the label doesn't get money for give-aways, many indie contracts require the label to pay the artist on 100% of sales. This is clearly unfair to the label, but you'll be hard-pressed to find people with a sympathetic ear for record labels' problems. The perception is that *all* labels big or small make fishnets full of money from unreported sales, so whatever the artist can get away with is okay.[3]

An indie distributor will handle anywhere from 30 labels to well over 100 at a time. Clearly they do not have the hours in a given week or the personnel to individually promote the five or six acts on each label they distribute. So each week they pick several acts that they will concentrate on. The sheet that has the names of these chosen acts is called the hot sheet. And, as an artist, you want to be on the hot sheet frequently.

How does an act get on the hot sheet? This is where the manager earns his 20%. The manager calls the label and the distributor every day and bugs the shit out of them until they include his act on it. Often it's as simple as that.

Buzz is the name of the game in the record biz. The strong buzz, the word on the street, is what sells the act. Generating a mystery and aura around the artist and their music is the yeast that raises the dough. With that in mind, here is yet another bit of record industry Talmud:

The best label for the band is the one that will be the most excited about putting out their record.

Here is where an indie can really excel over a major label. In a major label deal, the promotion department is responsible for pushing the record to the stores. A&R people are virtually useless for this part of the game. The promotion department of a label quite often does not want to deal with the A&R department's dogma about which act they should be pushing that week. It's a twist on the cliché, "Don't let the right hand know what the left hand is doing." Here the right hand knows, it just doesn't care. Meaning: it does a band no good if the A&R department of a major label signs the act and then the promotion department decides that it isn't cost-effective to push them. Or if the marketing department doesn't see how to get the act off the ground, they recommend dropping the act (see "Speed Trends," page 138).

[3] See "Clears, Cleans, and Fake Masters," page 197, and "Getting 'Cutout' of Royalties," page 72. Also, the reality of this has changed somewhat in the past few years. Recent consolidation has forced smaller labels in the food chain to form alliances with the bigger fish (safety in numbers). These deals come with a major caveat: they must accept the "structure" of the Big Four's contract, which almost never pays on 100% of sales for a new artist.

In an indie deal, the promotion department and the marketing department and even the A&R department all have intermingled personnel, because people at indies usually wear several hats at a time. This knocks out a lot of red tape and makes the machinery work more efficiently. Remember, if a record on a major label sells 60,000, it's a flop. If a record sells 30,000 on an indie, it's a smash!

Majors can afford to sign an act, spend $500,000, and then drop it like a bad habit. Indies have to be more choosy. Because they need to be more selective about their investments, they tend to have more loyalty to them. As you'll see in the next chapter, an artist on an indie can oftentimes have the opportunity to make more money than on a major.

CHAPTER TWELVE

The Independent Record Deal

from the Point of View of the Artist

The indie deal contract will read more or less exactly the same as the major label contract, except there will be about 50 fewer pages and less up-front money. Both of these, however, can be a good thing. Most indie advances are between $5,000 on the low end and $75,000 on the high end. Taking the high end into our recoupment equation, we see that the artist is completely recouped after fewer than 100,000 units.

EGGHEAD BOX #5

Artist break-even equation

Artist & producer's share		Aggregate sum		Producer's share
$1.10x	=	$75,000	+	.28x
$ .86x	=	$75,000		

x = 87,209 divided by .9 [90% of sales] = 96.899

If the band is a hardworking act and plays out several times a month, they can actually see some royalty money before they are eligible for Social Security. I have known many situations where the indie band starts to see money long before the major label band because of this exact situation.

Also, the indie labels and two-deep labels tend to let the artist have more artistic control over the recording.[1] Despite the financial constraints, an indie is often the best place for a new act with a strong regional following.

> Publishing and Royalties

If you refer to the breakdown chart on page 106, you'll notice that the mechanical royalties paid to the artist/writer are somewhat higher on two-deep labels. On the surface this seems like a good thing for the talent, but there are a few pitfalls that you should be aware of.

A lot of indies entice artists to sign publishing agreements along with recording agreements by offering to pay "full rate" on the compulsory license (8.5 cents per song or 85 cents for the full album). In exchange for the full rate, the smaller label may pressure the artist to cross-collateralize the mechanical license with the album royalties. This is a bad move, but artists' lawyers allow their clients to do it every day.[2]

This means the writer(s) of the songs on the albums (almost always the artist on an indie record deal) will potentially make about 20 cents more per record. There is just one problem with this: Even though indie labels may agree to it contractually, they often don't pay artists mechanical royalties, and since they are rarely affiliated with the Harry Fox Agency, they are not ever going to come under audit, unless the artist him/herself initiates the audit.[3]

How can they get away with this? Simple. Follow this logic: An indie gives you, the artist, $5,000. You spend it on making a record. It sells about 25,000 units (a big number for an indie). This means you're entitled to receive, after deducting the $5,000 advance, $15,000 for your mechanical royalties. You ask them for it, and they say, "Be patient, we're having some cash flow problems." Instead, they offer you $10,000 for your next record. What do you do? They're offering to let you make another record and giving you $5,000 less than they owe you. Can you take the $10,000 for your next record and still insist they pay for the $15,000? Sure, but you won't be making any more records with that label. You could sue, but the cost of suing will eat up half of what they owe you. Most artists, in my experience, take the $10,000 and count their blessings.[4]

1 Often this is because the label can't force the artist to hire a high-priced producer on the pittance of the advance they give them.

2 See "Cross-Collateralization," page 75, and "Publishing Deals," page 81.

3 I'm not suggesting that this happens frequently, but it does often enough. An important note is that so-called "online" record companies that offer cheap distribution often make the artist waive any mechanical royalty payments. See "The Harry Fox Agency," page 49.

The above also holds true for record royalties. If they don't pay your royalties, there is little you can do about it. What's agreed to in the recording contract seems to be more a list of suggestions or an indication of good intentions than a set of hard-and-fast rules. Only if the artist gets tough or gets huge will the label hold up their end of the bargain.

However, this is a worst-case scenario. Reputable indie labels pay their royalties eventually, even if it's not every six months as most contracts require. They do this, if for no other reason, because most have hopes of someday attaining the prestige of being distributed by one of the Big Four.[5]

In order to achieve this, the indie label can't have acts on their roster suing them. Granted, this is not foolproof protection, but it does create some balance of power for the artist.

❷ Indie in Disguise

An important point to keep in mind when dealing with an indie is what their future intentions are. Many small labels came about as the result of a carefully thought-out business plan that involves *investors*. These investors may love music, but generally they love money even more. The first question they asked the young upstarts who want their money is, "What is your exit strategy?"

An "exit strategy" is the way that the investor will get to "cash out," taking his money out of the investment and off the table. It's a vital part of closing a deal with investors, since very few people want to invest in something as risky as a record company without knowing that a strategy is in place to get their money safely out.

In most businesses there are several strategies: going public and selling shares of your company in the stock market is a common one. In the record label business there is generally only one exit strategy; selling out to a larger label. This brings in huge amounts of cash quickly. The investors are paid off and the small label gets to join the bigs. But is it the same label after this "buyout"? Generally not. Many acts are dropped at this point in the label's life cycle. New policies are implemented. Often acts that are kept are now forced to conform to the new way of doing things.

So how can you tell if the little indie you're considering signing with has this agenda in mind? Easy. Look at their contract. Major label deals have about 57 key points in them. That's why they are so friggin' long (about 50–75 pages). Your indie deal may only be about 12–35 pages, but it will have many of the same provisions, only worded a bit differently.[6] The reason is that when a major comes knocking, one of

[4] (From previous page) Some artists have sued their record/publishing companies; you read about it from time to time. Sometimes it's to their benefit, but most often it's not. It's damn near impossible to get a deal on another label once you've sued the label that took a shot on you. This is not legal advice; it's just an opinion. Each case is different, and you as an individual must decide which battles are in the best interest of your career.

[5] Not only do Big Four labels tend to have higher (usually about 5% higher) distribution fees and wider distribution, they also pay sooner and with more consistency. In addition to this, presidents of labels distributed by one of the Big Four make a shitload more on salary than they do running the label out of their bedroom.

[6] For a complete comparison of the types of contracts, see my book *Secrets of Negotiating a Record Contract: The Musician's Guide to Understanding and Avoiding Sneaky Lawyer Tricks.*

[7] Note: Any label that claims it has investors but also has no intention of selling out to a bigger entity for the right price is either lying, crazy, or has a serious gambling issue.

the first things they look at when they get ready to make an offer is the talent contracts. They want to see if the indie secured the same type of rights that the major would have. If it turns out that they haven't it will affect the buyout price.[7]

◉ Speed Trends

Aside from the cautionary advice I give above, probably the best reason for doing the indie label thing, if you're an artist in search of a contract, is the speed at which the machinery works. Consider the following fictitious example: Band A, Pavlov's Dogs, is signing with an indie on January 1st. Their friends are in band B, the Impulsives. They held out for a major label deal and got one. They too are signing on January 1st. Both bands have strong local followings.

February: Pavlov's Dogs are in the studio cutting the tracks for the record. By March it's finished, and by April it's on the shelves in a record store. Meanwhile, the Impulsives have just gotten the approval of their budget from the business affairs department and are finalizing the contract with their producer. They're scheduled to go into the studio at the end of April.

July: Pavlov's Dogs have sold several thousand records, have paid back most of their advance, and are planning a second record in December. They're packing the local clubs due to the notoriety of the record and its play on local college stations, and they are seeing decent downloads on iTunes, YMusic, etc. The Impulsives are trying to find a remixer to finish the record. By the end of July, the record is finished and delivered to the A&R department for approval. A&R approves and the marketing department begins making its assessments.

Now it's December. The Dogs are starting their second record and planning a tour down the East Coast. The Impulsives' record hasn't hit the shelves—the marketing department has decided that they shouldn't try to break a new band during their fourth-quarter Christmas season, when most people are buying releases by the more established artists. The release date will not be decided upon until after the holidays.

[8] See "The Hot Sheet," page 132.

By February of the next year, the Impulsives have made the hot sheet[8] and are being released. The label has started the radio promotion, and the stores are starting to stock the record in the front of the store. But the Impulsives have discovered that their pull in the local clubs will need to be rebuilt, because they haven't been around for a while. Meanwhile, Pavlov's Dogs have their second record out and it's selling about 1,000 units per month.

June rolls around. The Impulsives have sold only about 40,000 records and are trying to get on a national tour to help promote the record. The radio play has tapered off, and the record company is thinking about dropping them from the roster. Meanwhile the Dogs have sold about the same number of records between both of their albums, and their record company is enthusiastic. Their single has hit No. 35 on the CMJ chart, and has sold about 10,000 singles on YMusic and iTunes; the label has shopped their contract to one of the Big Four and has gotten some nibbles.

By December, the Dogs' contract is about to expire with their indie and they are speaking to a major about having their next record distributed by the major. The Impulsives have been dropped from the roster but are free to take any unreleased masters with them. They shop a deal to another major and even a few indies for a second release. Of course, they have realized no royalties because they didn't recoup their recording fund.

In January, two years after the initial signing, the Dogs re-sign their contract with the one-deep "indie" with the proviso that the record will be distributed by the parent/Big Four label. A major label has been noticing them climb the CMJ chart, and they're being traded on illegal services at a rate of about 10,000 streams a day. They want to distribute the record. The band is in preproduction on a third album with a producer who believes in them and is working on a small or deferred fee. They now have a manager as well. The Impulsives are thinking about personnel changes within the band and are also looking for new management, because their manager doesn't want to work with little indies. (Words to live by: Bureaucracy busts bands.)

There you have two years in the lives of two typical bands. Of course, I've manipulated the story to make a point, but the situation here is more common than you might think. While the major label is stewing in red tape and procedure, the indie has gotten two records out on the street while the band is fresh, and created a strong buzz. This is no small point. This is the difference between a band that grows and one that comes out with a campaign that is too big for their market. In the Impulsives' case, they sold 40,000 records but flopped. The Dogs sold about the same and came out winners.

> ***Good sales are relative to the point of view
> of the observer.***
> ***—Albert Einstein***
> ***(I changed it a little bit.)***

> Super-Duper Cross-Collateralization

If you're considering signing with a two-deep or three-deep label, there is one major pitfall to watch out for. It's when one label is collateralized "inside" another—for example, the two-deep (or imprint label) collateralized inside the one-deep. To see how this works, let's return to the blackjack tables in the casino that I spoke of at the beginning of the book.

You're watching the table from the sidelines and you start to notice something strange. Big Charlie, who never leaves the table, is the house favorite. He knows everybody and everybody loves him. He has a huge stack of chips, and even though he's playing at the $2 table, he plays $50 at a time. Next to him is his little brother, Little Pete. Little Pete has borrowed $600 from Big Charlie in order to play, but he has a funny angle on the game as well. Instead of playing the one hand that he's dealt, he has found five friends and given each of them $100 to play five different positions at the table and kept $100 for himself to play. He figures that this gives him six chances to win. He's also made a deal with his five friends: they have to give any profit they make back to him. Once they have collectively given Little Pete enough money to pay back Big Charlie the $600 he borrowed, then they can start to take some profit for themselves.

So if player one gives Little Pete back $400 (a 400% return on his money) but the other players lose everything, Little Pete will be unable to pay back his total loan of $600 from Big Charlie. Therefore, player one gets none of his 400% profit, nor do any of the other players get any profit they made. Only if they collectively make enough to pay back Big Charlie do they keep whatever profit they individually earned.

This may, on the surface, sound unfair: Borrow $100 and have to be responsible for how much money the other players pay back before you get anything? But for the players it's not a bad offer: if they lose it all, they won't have to pay back a dime to Little Pete or Big Charlie. It's risk-free money.

What a deal. There's a greater incentive to lose than to win. Where do I sign? The answer is, sign a two-deep or three-deep record deal.

Up until recently, many of these deals were cross-collateralized against the advance from the parent label that was financing the so-called "indie." If the small label didn't pay back its full advance, the parent label would take over all of the contracts and ownership. Like all takeovers, this was usually accompanied by cuts to the roster.

Let's say the fictitious major label used in this book, Pacific Records, has a smaller imprint label that specializes in dance music. This label is called Slam Records. Slam does big business, 50 releases per year. Suddenly they find themselves unable to adequately service their techno/rave market. So they set up a new label, XTC, and the head of A&R for techno/rave music will now become the head of XTC Records. The records put out by this label will carry all three logos: Pacific/Slam/XTC (see "Understanding Distribution," page 55, if you're confused).

The new president is going to get an initial advance of $700,000 to start XTC. This money will be divided up as follows: $200,000 for overhead and salaries, and the remaining $500,000 for the development of ten new acts. That leaves him $50,000 for each act. Remember that this budget has to include promotion for these records.

The first thing the new president will do is hire as many of his friends as he can get away with. The second thing he'll do is go out and find acts desperate enough to sign a deal with a cross-collateralized label. Since most of the acts that he will be talking to are young, inexperienced acts, they will usually accept any terms to get a first record out.

Most artists that have been around the block know and accept that they're going to have to work hard just to get a shot at a second record, but in the deal outlined above they're not getting what they're bargaining for. Study the casino example carefully and apply it to this very real-life scenario. They could work hard and sell thousands of records, but if the other bands on their label don't pull their weight, they could still end up with zilch.

In the event of this occurrence, which I call "indie label implosion," the parent company/major label would step in, trim the fat, and renew the profitable contracts. But what happens if the deal is not just two-deep but three- or even four-deep away from the distributor? If you're the artist on a four-deep deal, you might have to wait a long time before you see any royalties, even if you are selling many records. If you're a vendor for this kind of label, like a side musician or an engineer, you may have to wait months to get paid, if you ever do.

The good news is that most of this type of stuff went on in the '80s. In my experience, these days it only rears its head periodically in oddball indie deals, usually in the R&B, rap, and dance markets, and also on producer/production deals, which we will examine shortly (see "The Artist/Producer Production Deal," page 144).

One other question you might want to ask: What if the two-deep label loses its distribution contract after you are signed to it? It happens—often. If I were an artist

[9] In some states, like New York, a company cannot file for a business license using words like "Associates" and "Partners" in its name unless there are actual associates or partners in the company. Unfortunately, there is no similar requirement in the record business. So, for example, a company called Magnum Records may never have produced or released a record. They could be anything from an accounting firm to a recording studio. Don't be lulled into a sense of security because a company has a prestigious-sounding name.

signing with an indie label that was distributed by a major, I would want to know intimate details about their distribution contract and its stability. If I were the label, I would want to keep it confidential.

The point in each of these cases is that as an artist you should know who you're in bed with and what kind of protection they use. If you are considering doing business with a so-called "major label affiliate," you should understand that anything more removed from the main distribution arm than a two-deep label is, for all intents and purposes, a "production company or a vanity label."[9] And that's the subject of the next chapter.

CHAPTER THIRTEEN

⊘The Baby Record Deal

S ince it is my guess that most of you reading this book are either up-and-coming artists or producers, or a new pro cutting your teeth on such a client, the "baby deal" is the most likely type of deal that you are currently looking at to get your career off the ground. For this reason I've devoted a good deal of space to the ins and outs of such a deal.

No matter what the size of the company, if an artist or group is being asked to sign over rights to its sound recordings or songs, it is a "record deal." The only difference between a baby deal and a major label deal is the ability of the contractor to distribute the recordings. The two most common types of baby deals are:

1. The vanity label: a deal where the label is really a production company with one or two acts on it. They have no direct distribution and little money. Or the label is an extension of the artists themselves.
2. The artist/producer production deal: one where an artist contracts with a producer, without a record label as the intermediary. We have mentioned this type of deal a lot throughout this book, and now we'll look at it close up.

An important note: Rather than break up this chapter into distinct points of view, as I have with the other deals, I've argued both artist and producer/label points of view together on an issue-by-issue basis.

⊘ The Artist/Producer Production Deal

There are three types of production deals between artists and producers. All of them have one thing in common—the artist is not signed to a distributing label. Some artists are savvy to the information in this book and have asked themselves, "Why should I give 88% of my profit to a label when I can make and distribute my own record?" For some of these artists, this is a very realistic question to ask. In fact, many recording artists make a good living distributing their own records off the side of the stage at their performances. These artists form vanity labels and sometimes contract a producer to act as a consultant in the production of their record. (We'll look at the pros and cons of this in the next chapter, "The Vanity Label.")

In this situation, there are three ways that the artist/producer relationship can be structured: (1) the mini-record deal, (2) the joint venture, and (3) as work for hire.

The Mini-Record Deal

The mini-deal is just what it sounds like. Here the producer signs the artist to his or her production company the same way a label signs an artist to their roster. The artist, at this point, is under contract to work for the producer. They show up when and where the producer asks them and do as many takes as the producer requests. The producer pays for everything. In exchange for the artist's services, the producer usually gets the same thing that a record company gets, roughly 85% of the record and a publishing deal with the artist for 50% of the artist's publishing, if the artist is a writer on the album. When the tapes are finished, the producer will shop the master to a major or indie label in hopes of getting distribution for the finished master recording. This can take on three forms:

1. Master buyout: This is where the record label buys the completed master recording and pays a fee about equal to the cost if they had signed and developed the artist themselves (about $25,000 per song). There is also a royalty to the artist and producer—usually 12–14% of the SRLP (suggested retail list price)—the same as if the record label had signed the artist initially.

The advantage here to the record company is that they don't take a blind risk on whether a new artist will deliver a good master (a "deaf risk," actually). They can hear a finished product before they buy. However, it's important to note that even though the label has bought the master, the artist is not signed to the label. They are signed to the producer's production company. The label signs the producer to a deal that is exactly like the one the artist would sign if he were signing directly with the label. The producer is called a "furnisher" in these contracts, because he is "furnishing" (or providing) the artist to the label. To ensure that the artist cooperates with this deal, the artist signs what's called a side chain letter or "inducement letter." This letter states that the artist will perform exclusively for the label that the producer now has a deal with, even though they are contracted only to the producer. It's a bit confusing, but it makes sense when you get used to it. Perhaps the diagram below will make it clearer.

2. Master licensing deal: Same as above except that the record label doesn't own the master, they just own the license to distribute the master for a period of time. It's sort of like a trial basis or a lease with an option to buy. The money for these

Side Chain Letters
Flow of Performance Commitments

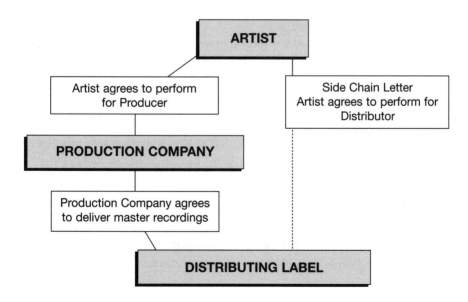

ARTIST

Artist agrees to perform for Producer

Side Chain Letter
Artist agrees to perform for Distributor

PRODUCTION COMPANY

Production Company agrees to deliver master recordings

DISTRIBUTING LABEL

deals is substantially lower, usually a licensing fee paid to the producer/production company of $5,000-25,000 per song and 12% of SRLP.

3. P&D deal: As discussed earlier. Here the producer is trying to take his production company up a peg into the realm of record company and will have a major or indie label just distribute the master.

The Joint Venture

The joint venture goes by several different names. I have seen cases where it is simply called a "production deal" or a "producer/artist deal," but this is too easily confused with what's described above, so for the sake of clarity I'm calling a joint venture any agreement where the artist and producer are on equal footing. In this scenario, the producer and the artist agree to share the finances and the responsibilities equally until the partnership is dissolved.[1]

A typical joint venture is one where the artist puts up the money to do the recording and pays the producer a minuscule amount (usually $300 or $400 per song as an arranging fee or producing/engineering fee) and 5% on the back end. The producer brings his or her expertise in producing records and industry connections to finish a master and get a record deal once the master is finished. A typical budget for something like this is about the same as an indie record deal—anywhere from $5,000 to $40,000.

Joint ventures are my favorite type of deals of the three mentioned here. The artist and producer have more clearly defined roles and are working together, not as adversaries, as in the artist/producer production deal and the work-for-hire deal, below.

The Work-for-Hire Deal

This takes the opposite approach from the mini-record deal. Here the artist hires the producer, usually for a solid fee of $2,000 to $3,000 per song, to produce the recordings that the artist writes. Everything the producer does is at the artist's request and is owned by the artist. When the production is finished, the producer walks away with his or her money and has no claim on the master recordings other than perhaps a small percentage (3% to 5%) on the back end. Here the artist has the upper hand in paying the royalties to the producer. In my experience they will claim endless amounts of expenses before recoupment, just like the labels do to them.[2]

[1] The dissolving of the partnership is usually done at the insistence of a major record company wanting to sign the artist and not retain the producer for the record. See "Buyouts," page 158; and "Overrides," page 157.

[2] For the intimate details of the mechanics of this deal, see "The Vanity Label," page 151.

WATCH OUT!

I t is not that uncommon that an artist who is signed to a production deal with a producer and has signed a side chain (or inducement) letter with a major label and has a good-selling record still makes little to no money.

The label isn't required, under their contract, to give the artist anything—they pay only the "furnisher," who is the producer. The producer's company collects the entire artist/producer royalty (usually 12%–15%) and pays the artist their 9%. The record company also makes the producer pay a flat annual fee (usually about $13,000) to the artist. If the contract is a standard one, the producer will only have to pay out anything above the $13,000 to the artist after the producer has recouped his out-of-pocket expenses incurred in recording and promoting the recording. The producer could continue to claim forever that he hasn't yet recouped for producing the master, and so can't give the artist any additional money. This is how you hear about top artists who sell millions of records but get only a few grand for their efforts.

The artist's only recourse is to audit the production company. Not only will this destroy the relationship that exists between the artist and the producer, but just try and do it. Producers are not like record companies. They don't occupy huge offices. They are very small and mobile, and their money is easily converted into other entities. If you get my meaning.

By telling you this, I'm not suggesting that the mini-deal isn't a legitimate way to get a foot in the door—it is. If you're the artist, have your lawyer mention a letter of direction in the contract. This letter will instruct the record company to pay the artist their 9% royalty directly, bypassing the producer. If you are the artist, you should bring this point up to the producer when negotiating your production deal with him or her. If you're the producer, don't mention it at all. If it comes up, hope it goes away. If it doesn't go away, decide how badly you want this artist. Here's why: Some labels won't accept letters of direction. They hate it because it makes them liable for payments to both parties. (See "Letters of Direction," page 164. This is important; don't skip it!)

⊘ End-Zoning—
Cutting Out the Producer

It may seem from everything above that the producer has the lion's share of power when the artist signs a mini-record deal, but in fact the producer has several Achilles' heels. The act of cutting someone out of your deal involves a strategy called "end-zoning," named from the play in football where the fullback runs around the end to score a touchdown, bypassing the other players. Once the producer's work is finished, their contribution is the hardest to protect.[3] In many cases artists try to eliminate the producer after they get a deal on a major label. The customary way to handle this is with "go-away money," a fee paid to the producer to take a walk, after which the artist will record their major label debut with a new producer.

[3] See "Screwing the Producer," page 161.

This power play is rarely met with enthusiasm by the producer. Producers often develop attachments to the artists they discover. They didn't develop the act and incur financial risk just to take a walk before getting the chance to produce a major label recording. Producers may start to rationalize that their replacement is not right for "their" act. Or that the label itself is not the right label. They may even be correct. But right or wrong, if the producer is stubborn and doesn't want the go-away money, they will often kill the deal. Hopefully they will be successful in getting a better one, because the artist will have no say in this decision. In a production deal the artist is under the thumb of the producer for the life of the contract.

Informal Agreements

Sometimes artists can be very suspicious of producers who try to pin them down with exclusive agreements. If the producer believes strongly in the act, to ease their paranoia he or she may agree to produce and shop them without a formal agreement—sort of a handshake deal. I have seen many cases where once the label takes an interest in the artist, the artist then decides to dump the producer for a more prominent one. In this way artists are also capable of deception.

It is almost impossible for the producer to protect himself from this (see "Contraceptive Contracts," page 149). However, it should be noted that if the A&R man really wants the original producer, he will try all his powers of persuasion to make the band see that they should stick with what they've got. If he is unsuccessful at that, he will then turn to plan B, which consists of giving the band a list of producers that the label is comfortable working with. They will be allowed to interview and choose one of these or go back to the original producer. This seems fair, except that the A&R man has usually stacked the deck with inappropriate choices or ones he knows the band will hate for one reason or another.[4]

This bit of skullduggery will usually result in the band doing one of two things: sticking with what they've got, or picking one of the stragglers from the list. Neither will make the band happy, and the net result is usually an album that lacks a certain luster. When the band is not happy, they don't perform well—it's that simple.

Contraceptive Contracts

Producers over the years have tried to write clauses into their contracts that protect them from the above effect.

Things like "finder's fees" have been tried in contracts to insure that the producer at least gets something out of the introduction he makes for the band. Unfortunately, in the state of New York there is a little snag in the law that makes it easy for lawyers to throw this clause out. The acquiring of a recording contract is considered the gaining of employment. The only people who are allowed to collect a commission from someone else's gaining employment are licensed employment agencies and business managers. Producers are neither.

To be an employment agency, many states require a person to incorporate and put up a bond of $50,000 to get a license. This is somewhat impractical for the start-up producer. This is why many attorneys of producers sometimes try to persuade their clients to have the band sign to a management contract with their client. You need no license to be a business manager, therefore anyone is eligible.[5]

But crafty lawyers try to protect their artist/clients by putting a small clause in the agreement that points out the producer/manager's limitations under the law. If you look closely at many management agreements and production agreements, you'll find a line that reads something like, "The manager is not a licensed employment agency, and the artist will not look to the manager for the purposes of employment."

This one line is the legal trapdoor that tries to cancel out any finder's fees that the producer/manager might try to enforce.

Because the lawyers have gotten too clever on this issue, producers have tried other things to somehow marry themselves to the deal. Most of them have been unsuccessful. State laws are too mellow to deal with the standards and practices of the music business. Therefore, the best defense the producer has against being cut out is to maintain a good relationship with the artist. Or they could just hold on to the masters.[6]

[4] For a real expansion on this subject see my latest book, *Million Dollar Mistakes: Steering Your Music Career Clear of Lies, Cons, Catastrophies, and Landmines.*

[5] Also, there is an exception carved into California's labor law that allows anyone to be a broker for a recording contract. For this reason (and others) we see many production deals based on California law.

[6] See "Holding the Masters," page 159.

CHAPTER FOURTEEN

⊘The Vanity Label

U ntil the mid-'80s, the vanity label was a bit of a joke. Usually it was associated with a trust fund kid living a rock 'n' roll fantasy or a bad pop act desperate to put out their own record. Today the vanity label has evolved into a serious force in the new music industry.

In the late '70s, vanities first showed their power by putting out the punk records that the majors thought were trash. While majors search for the "perfect" recording star, the little indies, with their ear to the street, are making cheap records and selling them through the mom-and-pop stores. Rap, in the mid-'80s, proved to be the next genre that had a life outside of the mainstream. Rap producers would make super-cheap records and distribute hundreds of thousands of them literally out of the backs of cars all over urban areas.

In many cases these start-ups are run out of people's bedrooms until they gain some recognition. But don't let that fool you. Def Jam was operated out of a college dorm room. Below are a few rinky-dink vanity labels that have become contenders in the industry, and the releases that put them on the map.

Artist	Label
Mike Oldfield	Virgin
Superchunk	Merge
Discord	Minor Threat
Enigma	Charisma
Heavy D and the Boyz	Downtown
Tsunami	Simple Machine
Veruca Salt	Minty Fresh (debatable)
Suddenly, Tammy!	SpinART

The up-and-coming producer is the type likely to be attracted to this sort of label. Perhaps they have several good credits either in the songwriting or the engineering department. Or perhaps they were the "good ears" of a known act. Sometimes they are studio owners or house engineers with a flair for producing.

The budgets in deals like this are so small that there is usually little or no producer's fee. Instead, the producer's compensation is derived exclusively on the back end and contingent on the hope of attracting a Big Four label to the act. The producer will be working hard, calling in favors and using all of his or her ingenuity, and probably his own studio, to pull off the small miracle of getting a record completed for the measly $5,000 or $15,000 that they will have to work with.

As you will see, after pulling off this magic act, their reward is that they are the first person to be sacrificed if a big label does come knocking at the door.

Without a doubt the most common type of deal that the new producer or artist is likely to come in contact with these days is the vanity label deal. Earlier we saw how the artist, the producer, and the record company make up a triad of chicanery, each with their own agenda. (See Chapters Five, Seven, and Eight.) But in vanity deals, the artist and the record company are usually one and the same, thus creating only a two-sided conflict. This being the case, I am going to focus mostly on the producer's perspective here because it is the producer who is the most vulnerable.

❯ The Virtual Budget and the Virtual Producer's Fee

Generally the producer will be asked by the artist, the artist's manager, or the production company/vanity label to prepare the budget for the recording. The artist rarely wants to bother with these details, plus the producer can probably get better deals on tape and studio time because he or she has ongoing relationships with the vendors. Still, there are many artists who insist on doing these administrative matters themselves. Some are afraid of kickbacks, and rightfully so.[1]

[1] See "Kickbacks," page 95.

Because the producer is putting his reputation on the line, if he's smart, he will want all the money for the project up front to make sure that the vendors (recording studios, rental companies, sideplayers, etc.) get paid. If they don't, he can kiss them good-bye as business connections.

There is one other reason why producers like to keep things "all-in" on these small production deals: their so-called fee is contingent on what they don't spend. If anything is left over, they get to keep it, much as with the all-in deal on a major label.

There is an interesting psychology that kicks in when the artist is negotiating with the producer. It usually goes down like this:

The producer will ask for a $3,000 fee and $7,000 for the recording budget (a typical example), making a total of $10,000 for the cost of making the record. The artist, thinking he or she is a savvy negotiator, will say, "Can't you come down on your fee?" Sometimes the artist will offer a bigger back-end royalty in exchange. Here is where the producer's business head comes into play more than his musical head. The crafty producer will offer a compromise: "Okay, I'll do it for $2,000, and we'll put $8,000 into the recording."

The artist will usually agree to this, thinking that he or she is getting more for their money. But, as you might quickly figure out, all that's happening is that the producer has found a way to scam $1,000 off the budget into his pocket and get his fee of $3,000 anyway. The artist, even if they are looking for this, will probably not be able to catch the experienced producer. Try as they may, the producer's receipts will always balance out at the end of the day.

Study the breakdowns of the two album budgets in the sidebar on the next page, "Indie Recording Budget."

On the surface it seems that the artist is getting ripped off by the funny numbers in these two budgets, but consider these three rationalizations on the part of the producer:

INDIE RECORDING BUDGET

Below are two sets of numbers for two projects that were done in the late 1990s. On the left is the budget the producer submitted to the production company/artist. On the right is the real budget that the producer kept to himself.

Budget #1

This is for a $10,000 album. The rhythm section is to be recorded in a large studio live onto a small-format ADAT 8-track. Overdubs are to be recorded in a smaller studio and then mixed back at the big studio. Note: There is no stated producer's fee. (Special thanks to Dave "Bee Boy" for this contribution.)

SUBMITTED BUDGET		PRODUCER'S PRIVATE BUDGET	
Basic tracks		**Basic tracks**	
Large studio at $1,000 per day for 3 days of basic tracks	$3,000.00	Large studio for 3 days	$2,750.00
Engineer at $300 per day for 3 days	$900.00	Rentals, outboard gear	$555.00
Rentals, outboard gear for 3 days	$1,000.00	**Overdubbing**	
Overdubbing		Studio + engineer, home studio 8-track	$700.00
Studio—smaller overdub room at $500 per day for 3 days	$1,500.00	Rentals, outboard gear	$880.00
Engineer for 12 hours per day for 3 days at $20 per hour	$720.00	**Mixing**	
Mixing		Studio + engineer	$930.00
2 days at large studio at $1,000 per day	$2,000.00	**Mastering**	$750.00
Materials/tape	$180.00	**Miscellaneous**	
Miscellaneous		Food	$232.00
Food, cabs, cartage, etc.	$800.00	Transportation, etc.	$95.00
		Supplies	
		Drum heads, strings, pens, sharpies, etc.	$50.00
		Tape	$360.00
Total	**$10,100.00**	**Total**	**$7,302.00**

This leaves the producer with a surplus of $2,798. Here, the secret to the virtual producer's fee is in the kickback given to him from the engineer of the overdub studio and the owner of the larger basic-tracks studio. Both have long-standing relationships with the producer and agree to do whatever is necessary to make the deal look good on paper.

Budget #2

Traditional 24-track recording with an "all-in" budget of $25,000; two-deep indie; small producer's fee. (Special thanks to R.C. for this one.)

SUBMITTED BUDGET

Basic tracks
Rehearsals for 1 week
  in rehearsal room $600.00
Lockout for studio, 7 days $4,000.00
Tape (10 reels of 2-inch at
  $150 per reel) $1,500.00
1 day in smaller studio................$700.00

Overdubs
1 week in smaller
owner/operator studio..............$2,500.00

Mix
11 days at mix studio $10,000.00
Tape (5 reels 996, $50 per reel) ..$250.00
Rentals $1,000.00
DATs $60.00

Postproduction mastering
Digital editing, 32 hours $1,200.00
Sequence premastering,
  4 hours at $40 per hour $200.00
Mastering, 4 hours at
  $175 per hour..........................$700.00

Engineer/producer fee $3,000.00

Total $25,710.00

PRODUCER'S ACTUAL BUDGET

Basic tracks
Rehearsal in studio....................$560.00
1-week lockout in large studio $4,000.00
Tape..$1,720.00
Tips...$50.00
Assistant.....................................$140.00

Overdubs
2 weeks at smaller studio $2,600.00
Assistant $1,400.00
Maintenance fee...........................$40.00

Mix
11 days at studio $5,000.00
8 reels ½" tape at $50 + shipping......$400.00
Rentals $450.00
DATs $88.00
Travel $200.00
Miscellaneous.............................$200.00
Mix engineer $1,000.00
Phone $100.00

Postproduction
Digital editing, 32 hours
  at $40 per hour $1,280.00
Sequencing/premastering
  at $40 per hour.......................$200.00
Mastering, 4 hours
  at $175 per hour.....................$700.00

Engineering/producing fee....$4,000.00

Total $24,128.00
Rebate from tape return $1,112.00
Adjusted total $23,016.00

Here the producer has managed to skim an additional $2,694 by doing two things. The first is the standard kickback arrangement we saw in the previous budget. The second is quite clever: The tape rebate is this producer's way of hiding additional profit. This is recording tape that was unused and was returned to the supplier for a credit. This credit will never be reported or passed back to the label as it should be. Artists and small companies rarely kept track of how much tape was used on a project. In the next budget to the next client, this producer would overcharge them tape costs as well, and again return the unused reels. Over time, the producer can build up quite a hefty reserve at the tape supplier. This reserve is eventually converted to equipment or cash.

Today the tape rebate scam is obsolete because most of us use hard drives to record. But think of how much easier this makes the scam. That hard drive in the corner of the studio, the one you're being billed an extra daily rate for, the one that is a "10 terabyte drive"-How does anyone know how much memory it really contains?

1. The artist has no clue how much work the producer will have to put into the project in terms of his or her time or how much it costs to actually get things done. Therefore it is arrogant for the artist to assume that the producer is asking too high a fee in the first place. And although it might seem that a healthy chunk of money goes in the producer's pocket, when divided by the time it takes to produce something of quality, it still averages out to very little.

2. The producer promised to deliver a master for $10,000. So what difference does it make how much of that ends up in his or her pocket? The bottom line is, does the producer deliver a good master on budget?

3. The producer will probably never get the back-end royalty promised by the artist/production company. Why? A diligent production company is supposed to remit accounting statements and receipts showing how many copies of the master were run off and sold. But they often "forget" or misplace the paperwork. And because the artist has no intention of hiring a business manager to keep track of the producer's royalty, who is really ripping off whom?

In addition to the above reasoning, the producer has expenses that the artist or production company will never want to hear about, such as their attorney (who will eat into much of the surplus profit), their general daily overhead, phone, stationery, equipment, and other things that he or she will be asked to "throw in" to make the deal viable.

❯ Producer's Compensation Package

Since there is little or no up-front money on a vanity project, the incentive for a producer taking on a new artist on spec is the hope that he or she will be retained to produce the second album on the major label for a much higher fee. Artists generally agree to this in the beginning, but often wish they hadn't after the record is successful. Money-making masters are rare, and now that they have one, they don't want to be beholden to a particular person. Since the producer is aware that they are likely to be ditched like a dress after prom night, they tend to ask for a slightly overreaching compensation package. Let's check it out.

5% Royalty

The indie producer shouldn't be afraid to ask for a little more than the usual 3% of the SRLP. Five percent of the SRLP has always seemed fair to me, the logic being that in a standard record deal the artist is getting 9% and the producer 3%, or one-third of what the artist gets. Since the artist/label will be selling the record themselves and keeping over 60% of the net profit, 5% seems more than fair. And since the producer is not getting an advance of any real size, I also feel that it is fair to ask for payment of this royalty to start from the sale of record one (instead of waiting for the artist to recoup their expenses, as in a major label deal).

Overrides

In the initial agreement with the artist, the producer should ask for an overriding percentage of the artist's second record (hopefully being produced on a major label) and sometimes the third as well, even if he or she doesn't get to produce it. The override is usually 1% (1 point).

From the artist's point of view, this is burdensome. Once the artist is on a major label, the all-in royalty package will be 12 points, with 3 going to the next producer. Now, the artist will have to find a producer who will take 1 point less; otherwise the artist will have to dig into their 9 points to give the next producer the 3 points that he or she will want. This will cut down their money substantially.[2]

Why does the producer feel justified in inconveniencing the artist in this way? Is it just because he feels he can bully them into it? No. Here's why.

In many such start-up cases, the producer is bringing more credibility to the project than the artist, especially if it is a production deal or if the producer has several platinum albums to their credit. But no matter how good the record comes out, the fact is that it probably won't sell more than 100,000 even if the band is extremely lucky. New artists on major labels rarely sell more than 60,000 units on their first record. That means it will lose money from the artist's and producer's point of view.[3]

However, even with low sales, the major label is likely to give the artist a second shot with a new record and probably a new producer. This record will have more of everything: more money for production and more money to promote the record. Simply by the law of averages it will probably do better than the first record. The second producer will make more than the first simply because of their position in the game. The producer of the third record will make even more, and so on until the popularity of the band starts to diminish.

But what of the first producer? They tend to feel that the first record is the launch point usually forgotten about by the third album (where most pop acts start to break

[2] Sometimes the record label will give up the point from their side if they feel the situation warrants it. But they don't have to.

[3] See "The Major Label Deal from the Artist's Point of View," page 63.

the Top 40 barrier). This is why the first producer will feel justified in asking for the override on the second album if they do not get to produce it themselves.

Buyouts, or the "Screw You" Clause

Sitting right next to the override clause in most contracts is the "buyout" clause. This comes into play when the artist doesn't want to continue working with the producer under any circumstances. Instead the producer is given an amount of money to take a walk. This is often called "screw you money" or "go-away money." Despite the harsh terminology, it is a welcome friend to both sides.

"Go-Away" in a Production Deal

A production deal, however, has a different dynamic. Here the producer is bringing the act to the record company and is contractually tied to the artist for the life of the deal. But sometimes the label may want to sign the artist with the intention of bringing in another producer with a better track record. The "go-away" fee in these deals takes the form of the producer/production company selling off the artist's contract.

❥ The Producer as a Virtual Partner

After all the above, the artist will undoubtedly think of the producer as a thief—asking for 5%, or a nonrecoupable advance, or a record-one payment, or an override on the second album whether they produce it or not, or a percentage of publishing. But remember, the odds of the producer collecting anything on the back end are slim to none—and as you will see in the chapter Who Earned What, of the three parties we're examining here, the producer makes the least off a successful record.

Artists love to bitch about how the producer drove a hard bargain and asked for more than he should have. What they are forgetting is that a producer is not a partner in the act's profits, even though the artist's manager might try to imply otherwise. The producer doing work for hire is an employee of the artist. In trying to get the producer to "be reasonable," the artist usually makes him feel he is part of a team with lines like, "If it hits, we'll all be rich."

If that were true, then the producer would receive an equal share in everything—as in a joint venture. "Everything" means publishing, any and all advances, merchandising, and so on. But just try to actually ask for this as the producer, and you will soon find yourself looking for a new client. It's a double standard that seems impossible to shake.

The fact is that if the artist's record hits, the producer makes the least money, because he won't share in any money made from personal appearances, publishing, or any subsequent records (unless he has an override). So if you are a new producer and unless you need the practice producing an act, get a good deal up front. Don't let vanity labels or artists guilt you with sob stories and bullshit about "industry standards." I'll bet most vanity labels learned about industry standards by skimming through a 1992 edition of *This Business of Music* that they forgot to return to the public library for the past decade or so.

● Where's My Contract?

It's not uncommon for small recording projects to start and sometimes even be finished before a contract is signed. This is bad for all parties, but it happens a lot. The reason it happens is because contracts are expensive and neither side wants to pay for one until they hear some positive results. One could spend $2,000 negotiating a production agreement only to find out that the producer and the artist can't work together. In major label deals, these things tend not to be issues, because producers have track records and the artist is usually happy to get someone with good credentials to work with them. But in the indie world and particularly the vanity label world, the norm is for all parties to be new at this stuff.

The net result is that everyone works on good faith with a handshake or a memo agreement binding the deal. When the project is halfway done and it is proving to be fruitful, then the investment in a contract is justified. Vanity labels have been known to wait until after there's an offer from a label before finalizing the deal between themselves, the artist, and the producer. This leaves the artist and the producer floating out in "legal limbo" until the lawyers sort it all out.

● Holding the Masters

Invariably it's the producer who stands to lose from the informality described above. In order to keep the deal rolling along smoothly, he has "gone along with the good faith vibe." Especially if everyone involved is a drinking buddy. Rarely do people set out to con anyone, but somehow when the dust settles, the producer, who's the most vulnerable, is usually left out in the cold. There is one sure way for the producer to protect him- or herself: holding the master recordings. It's my advice to new producers to retain the master recordings and all the finished mixed master tapes until a formal and final contract is signed between the producer, the artist, and the vanity. Whoever has the masters controls the destiny of the project.

The vanity and the artist will bitch and moan about this and once again turn to dogma about "industry standards." The producer should articulate that it's a good and ethical business standard to have a written and signed contract before you start work. Therefore, it is not an unreasonable request to hold on to the masters as collateral; this is the only bargaining chip that the producer will have in ensuring that the vanity keeps its word.

➲ What You Don't Know *Will* Hurt You

One bit of power that the smart producer has in his arsenal is the fact that most artists and small vanities are not very familiar with the copyright law and how it protects authors. While everyone is busy arguing about publishing and points, they are completely ignoring a common legal opinion—that the producer is also an author, an author of the sound recording. This is accepted as true whether he's given up the masters or not.[4]

[4] Authorship of the recording should not be confused with the authorship of the songs themselves. See "Sound-Alikes" and "Sample-Alikes," pages 192 and 195.

This is no small point. I have seen many deals where the vanity or the artist tried to cut out the producer by never forwarding his contract to him. They believe that by not formalizing the agreement they could leave the producer stuck in a "he said, she said" kind of argument. What they are not understanding is that without the producer's signature on a release, no one is free to exploit the master in any way—including making copies for shopping a deal.

The Copyright Act implies that three people control the authorship rights of a master recording: (1) the artist, (2) the party that puts up the money (record label), and (3) the producer of the recording, unless the producer has signed a work-for-hire agreement with the entity that paid for the recording.

In any standard licensing agreement or master buyout, there is an indemnification clause. This means that the person who is selling the master to the label is warranting that the master is free of any claim of rights by any third parties. If the scamming artist in our example tries to cut out the producer and license the master to a label, the producer can prohibit its use unless they get him to "sign off" on his portion of the rights. If the producer has not given up his rights expressly, then any artist licensing the master behind the producer's back is committing fraud.

This doesn't stop them from trying. I know of numerous deals that have gone south because the vanity label sold the master and then a producer came forward demanding compensation in exchange for his or her signature. This is why it is best for both sides to get a finished contract with all the signatures on it before the deal starts to get too big and people get too greedy. As much sense as this makes, many vanities and artists just don't think about it or don't care. They figure they'll find a way to end-zone the producer later.

❷ Screwing the Producer, or the Re-Record

The most common type of end-zone tactic used to remove a producer who has control of the masters is the re-record.

A standard contract states that if the producer's tapes are used on the record, then he must be paid. If the artist or production company wants to get around this,

HAVING "BIG FUN"

Several years ago I was asked by a vanity label to produce, on spec, an unknown band we'll call Big Fun. Big Fun's manager was putting up the money and started this thumbnail-sized vanity label to front the whole project. He couldn't pay me anything and so promised me 5% on the back end in exchange for an investment of over 100 hours of my time. There was no contract; we just shook hands on the deal with the understanding that I would keep all the masters as collateral on our agreement until he sent me a contract.

I produced the record. After it was completed, the vanity label shopped Big Fun to every major label in the industry. Everyone passed.

One afternoon, about a year later, I got a phone call from a new two-deep label. They were interested in buying Big Fun. They wanted me now to turn over the master tapes for pressing. I told them that I would love to, except that I had never been given a contract (even though I had asked the vanity label for it time and again).

Well, now it was time for the vanity label to settle up and put into writing my 5%.

What I did not know (and later found out) was that the vanity, desperate to make a sale and wash their hands of Big Fun (and pay back the seed money borrowed from the Irish mob), settled with the two-deep label for only 15 points. Nine went contractually to the band, and five were previously promised to me, leaving the vanity label only *one point*.

They informed me that I was to settle for 3% so they would have more for themselves. If I refused, they threatened to have the band re-record the album, which would leave me completely out of the deal.

I called their bluff. I knew re-recording the record would not guarantee that the new master would pass muster with the label. They had a sale; why blow it?

The vanity finally settled with me, but I was cast as the bad guy, damaging my relationship with the band. To this day I'm not sure the trade-off was worth my principles.

all they have to do is simply re-record the songs with the exact arrangements that they did with the producer. They could even hire the same engineer and the same recording studio. The producer will be powerless. Since the musical arrangement of a song is an idea (and therefore not copyrightable), the artist is not violating the copyright law. The producer is not an author of the new master and is completely removed from the loop.

However, there are attorneys who will argue otherwise. Some producers have tried to sue on the basis of a "sound recording copyright infringement," but it's a difficult and expensive case to prove. Nor does the sometimes-tried "derivative work lawsuit," wherein the producer will contend that the new master is a derivative work of the old one and therefore ownership must be acknowledged. The problem here is that since Congress, at present, hasn't established a statutory rate for sound recording authors, it's very hard to prove what the producer's share is worth.[5] (See the sidebar "Who Is the Songwriter in Rap Music?" on page 21.)

Situations like my experience with Big Fun (see the sidebar) are quite sad and, more often than not, are brought on by both sides being too stubborn about a settlement. The bad karma of the litigation usually destroys the vibe and the buzz of the project, the record flops, and both sides lose. I can't help but put some of the blame on the pros. Lawyers tend to polarize the sides and make a settlement harder, boiling the entire experience down to one of mutual exploitation between the artist and the producer.

Because of this, the savvy producer should want to deal with the vanity label as little as necessary. If this is how they behave when there is no money on the table, imagine how they get when it comes time to pay the royalties! Indeed, the only way a producer can hope to get paid in these situations is to get a major or indie label to distribute and promote the master. Then theoretically the producer won't have to deal with the small vanity label. Or will he?

As we saw in the section on the artist/producer agreement, the major label signs not the artist but the vanity label/production company. This means all producer royalty money travels through the production company. So how can the producer make sure that the production company/artist pays him if they get a distribution deal with a major? The answer is with a letter of direction.

Pay attention—this is no small point.

[5] Recently the copyright office introduced an SR (sound recording) performance royalty that will be implemented for downloading and streaming off the Internet and other "digital" sources. This new royalty will probably find its way into several lawsuits by producers who can now claim damages for the theft of their arrangements.

⊘ Letters of Direction (LODs)

This may be the most important section in this book. Here you will learn to ask for what most people don't even know exists: the only paper trail you can create to insure that you, the producer or the artist, get paid—the letter of direction.

In this chapter I use a lot of terminology from the sections on vanity labels (page 151), artist/producer production deals (page 144), and the major label deal from the artist's and producer's points of view (pages 63 and 87). You may want to scan those before going on.

We're going to learn about LODs by way of the example we've been constructing in this chapter. A producer is being hired by a vanity label/production company to produce an artist signed to the vanity label. It's a spec deal with a back-end percentage of 5% for the producer. Since the producer isn't getting any advance money, he argues reasonably that he shouldn't have to wait to recoup anything, but should get paid from the first record sold (typically called a "payment from record one"). Sounds fair, right?

The producer is taking a big risk in terms of an investment of time here. A vanity label is a production company or record company that has no specific deal to distribute its records. Once the project is finished, the vanity label shops and gets a deal with a bigger, more established major label that will market and distribute the artist. The major gives the vanity label an "all-in" royalty of 20% (20 points) for furnishing the talent, meaning that the vanity label pays all the vendors (the artist and producer are vendors here) from their 20%. The agreement that the vanity label has with the artist typically requires them to give the artist 9 of those 20 points. The producer gets 5 points, leaving the vanity label with 6 of the 20 points.

It can take as much as a year and a half for the vanity label to collect the first money from the distributor. What happens if, during that period, the vanity label goes out of business or files for Chapter 11 bankruptcy? How do the artist and producer collect their money? The answer is—they don't.

This entire dilemma can be solved with a letter of direction. This is a letter attached to the producer's contract with the vanity label stating that if the vanity label is successful in placing the artist with a major label, the producer's royalty is to be paid from the major label directly to the producer, bypassing the vanity label (see diagram on the next page). The logic here is that the major label is likely to be a more stable and rooted company than the vanity label, so the producer won't have to chase anyone down the street for his or her 5%. The major label, or one-deep label, signing the artist will do all the accounting and write the checks.

This seems fair to all concerned, doesn't it? The vanity label doesn't have to worry about paying the producer, which means less accounting for them to do, and furthermore they are not liable for any errors in the royalty payments. Everyone is happy, right? Wrong.

Production company/vanity labels that have been around the block know that most labels will raise objections to letters of direction regarding the producer (or the artist, for that matter), for two reasons:

1. For the very same reason that it excuses the vanity label from doing the accounting, it is a liability to the major label.

2. It means more money has to come out of the major label's pocket sooner. Since the producer's agreement stipulates that they are to be paid from record one before recoupment, they must pay him or her first.

For both of these reasons, the major label will usually reject the artist who presents an LOD as part of the contract, unless they want the act real bad.

If the vanity label didn't realize that this would be a problem when they made the agreement with the producer, they will now be between a rock and a hard place

Letter of Direction Money Flow

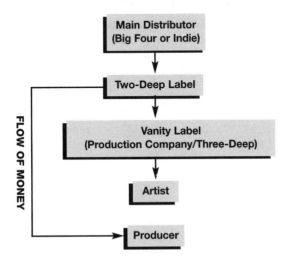

NOTICE THAT THE PRODUCER IS PAID BEFORE THE ARTIST.

since the LOD must be part of the deal, and therefore the vanity label will be bound to find a major label who will honor such a condition.

For this reason, artists' managers and vanity labels fight not to give in to the producer on this point. If you're the producer, my advice is to hold out; without an LOD you're not likely to ever get paid, and if they want you bad enough, the vanity label will cave on this.

However, the producer must be prepared to compromise come the day that a major label wants the act. When this happens, all parties will be asked to give up a little of what they were promised to make the deal work. For this reason the producer might want to ask for more points than is customary on a standard deal; he or she will probably have to give one of them back as an act of good faith.

❷ Artist's LOD

An interesting point that is often overlooked is that an artist rarely knows to ask for a letter of direction instructing the label to pay the artist's royalties directly to them and not through the vanity label. As we saw above, the producer will not hesitate to ask for this, but artists usually don't. Not having this letter means that they stand the risk of never seeing their money should the vanity label/production company get into financial trouble. Without the letter of direction, the artist cannot go to the distributor and ask them for money or advances of any kind.

Lately, however, indie labels are more accepting of LODs from artists. It's my guess that within the next few years, as many producers and artists become more aware of the mechanics of the business, almost every artist/producer production agreement and vanity label deal will have at least one LOD attached.[6]

[6] For more goop on this subject, see "Letters of Misdirection," page 223.

CHAPTER FIFTEEN

❯Wrap-Up—
Who Earned
What?

Using all the information from the previous chapters, let's see how each party—the artist/writer, the producer, and the record label—fares in a typical successful record deal. This is designed as an exercise only. All of the numbers below are approximate, and don't take into account an individual's tax bracket, deductions, and other variables.

Let's assume we have a four-member band where all the members share writing credit, and that they have written all the songs on all their records. They've signed a four-album deal where all of the records are cross-collateralized but no publishing is cross-collateralized. The first record sells 100,000 copies, the second record sells 250,000, the third record sells 1,000,000, and the fourth record sells 2,000,000. The combined recoupable recording advances and promotion costs for each record amount to $500,000 for the first record, $500,000 for the second record, $750,000 for the third, and $2,000,000 for the fourth (which includes a $1,000,000 bonus for being profitable enough to deserve a fourth record). The artist/writer has a typical 50/50 publishing deal in which the publisher gets 50% of the publisher's share (a 75/25 split in the writer's favor, for those who skipped Chapter Six. Here's the breakdown:

 Artist

When examining the numbers below, keep in mind that these are the dollars earned for a very successful artist during what will probably be the five most successful years of his recording-artist career. Much like athletes, artists have a shelf life. In the recording business that shelf life is about five years.

Artist/Writer Record Royalties

| 1st record | $.86 x 100,000 units = $86,000.00 |
| | subtracted from $500,000.00 = ...–$414,000.00 |

| 2nd record | $.86 x 350,000 units = $301,000.00 |
| | subtracted from $1,000,000.00 = ...–$699,000.00 |

| 3rd record | $.86 x 1,350,000 units = $1,161,000.00 |
| | subtracted from $1,750,000.00 = ...–$589,000.00 |

| 4th record | $.86 x 3,350,000 units = $2,881,000 |
| | subtracted from $3,750,000.00 = ...–$869,000.00 |

That's right—after selling more than 3.75 million records, the band is still almost a million dollars in debt to the label. It's a good thing they have other income from the sources below.

Recording Advances

This chart shows an estimated surplus in the recording budget, which is kept by the artists. This is the only money they will see that is directly related to "sales" of the master recording, since they are still in debt to the label. It is based on normal costs for record production.

Advance

1st record	$250,000.00	surplus $96,000.00
2nd record	$250,000.00	surplus $96,000.00
3rd record	$375,000.00	surplus $125,000.00
4th record	$650,000.00	surplus $1,170,000.00

| Total | | $1,487,000.00 |

Publishing 1: Mechanical Royalties

This is money earned by the songwriter (whom we are assuming is also the artist in this example) for the licensing of material on a record. The formula for calculating this on a typical major label deal is as follows: (10 x the statutory rate of $.085) x (75%) = $0.68 per record sold.

1st record .... 100,000 units $68,000.00
2nd record....................... 250,000 units $170,000.00
3rd record .... 1,000,000 units........................... $680,000.00
4th record .... 2,000,000 units...................... $1,360,000.00

Total mechanical license revenue for artist	**$2,278,000.00**
Harry Fox auditing adjustment of about 5%	**−$113,900.00**
Adjusted total	**$2,164,100.00**

Publishing 2: Radio Play

An average royalty for a hit single for one year is about $150,000 when collected and passed on to publishers by ASCAP, BMI, or SESAC.[1] We'll assume the band will have one hit on each of their first four albums (they should only be so lucky).

$150,000.00 x 4 albums = $600,000.00

Publishing total:	
Mechanicals	**$2,164,100.00**
Radio	**$600,000.00**
Total	**$2,764,100.00**
Minus 10% administration for publisher	**−$276,410.00**
Subtotal	**$2,487,690.00**
Minus publisher's cut (25%/75% split)	**−$621,922.50**
Total	**$1,865,767.50**

[1] The formulas are mind-bogglingly complicated, but basically boil down to this: about 450,000 plays at a mean average of 3 cents a play.

Touring

If the artist is a superstar they can multiply these numbers by ten, but suffice it to say that a band with moderate endorsements and a song on rotation at several stations could expect to net about $15,000 per show for the second two album tours.

$15,000.00 x 4 shows per week =..$60,000.00

$60,000.00 x 15 weeks (average tour)=.............................. $900,000.00

$900,000.00 x 2 album tours =.. $1,800,000.00

Sponsors

Any successful band generally has a sycophantic sneaker company or Jägermeister wannabe hanging around wanting them to sell their soul for an extra few bucks. So let's tack on another $500,000 in sponsors and endorsements for the last two tours. Total income from this: $1,000,000.

Which Adds Up to...

Here's how the band's financial picture looks over this four-album period:

Record royalties of –$969,500.00 (forgiven debt) $0.00

Surplus from recording advances $1,487,000.00

Publishing $1,865,767.50

Touring $1,800,000.00

Sponsors $1,000,000.00

Total $6,152,767.50

Minus 15% manager's commission....................................–$922,915.12

Minus business manager's/professional fees of 5% ....–$307,608.37

Adjusted gross $4,922,244.01

Minus 40% for income taxes (including Social Security)... –$1,968,897.60

Total $2,953,346.41

Divided by five years [2] ....$590,669.28 per year

Divided by four group members (if equal split) $147,667.32

Compared to 2001 Edition ....$142,053.90 per year

[2] It is divided by five years and not four years, because four albums on a major label generally take about five years to be realized, sometimes more.

❂ Producer

In all likelihood the same producer would not work on all four of a single artist's records, so I've broken it down by four records of comparable success. Also, keep in mind that a producer works on several records of different budgets each year. So the calculations below are difficult to apply to the same structure as the artist above.

1st record	$0.28 x 100,000 units	$28,000.00
2nd record	$0.28 x 250,000 units	$70,000.00
3rd record	$0.28 x 1,000,000 units	$280,000.00
4th record	$0.28 x 2,000,000 units	$560,000.00

Total gross earnings...$938,000.00
Minus 15% manager's commission ....-$ 140,700
Adjusted gross...$797,300.00
Minus 40% tax ....-$318,920.00

Adjusted gross...$478,380.00
Divided by four albums $119,595.00

Compared to 2001 Edition $135,675.00

From this, the producer must pay his overhead. But as you can see, the construct does not hold up, because any producer selling this many records is probably netting far more than $119,595 a year. A fairer guess would put a producer of this caliber closer to $500,000 a year, after expenses.

❂ Record Company

Album	Units Sold	One-Deep $4.21	Major Label $6.80
1st record	100,000	$421,000.00	$680,000.00
2nd record	250,000	$1,952,500.00	$1,700,000.00
3rd record	1,000,000	$4,210,000.00	$6,800,000.00
4th record	2,000,000	$8,420,000.00	$13,600,000.00

Total record company earnings...$15,003,500.00 ....$22,780,000.00

Advances & non-recoupable

promotion costs

(all four records) ....$0.00 ....$6,000,000.00
(flowed through to major)

Adjusted gross..............................$15,003,500.00 ....$16,780,000.00

40% taxes......................................$5,252,800.00 ....$6,712,000

Gross earnings before overhead.........$9,750,700 ....$10,068,000.00

Compared to 2001 2nd Edition .....$8,683,200.00 ....$11,113,200.00

Compared to 1998 1st Edition.......$6,432,000.00 ....$8,802,000.00

Percentage variance from 2001 ....+12.3% ....–9.4%

There are as many variables to the above conclusions as there are artists, producers, and labels, but this will give you a good starting template. Also, you have to keep in mind that the above is based on a band that sells almost 4,000,000 records. Acording to the RIAA, less than 5% of all artists signed by major labels go to this level. Actual circumstances may vary; record companies may make more on the publishing if they have a publishing division, and artists may make substantially less if they don't write their own songs, or substantially more if their music gets licensed into a big Hollywood movie.

The final score is artist $2,953,346.41,[3] producer $478,380.00, the major label roughly $10,068,000.00, and the indie or two-deep label roughly $9.7 million. This has increased by about 26% since the late 1990s for Big Fours and about 35% for one-deep labels (during which time labels have justified massive layoffs by saying they can't make enough to pay their employees). However, since 2001 the income from record sales has seen a huge slip of about 10% for majors.[4]

The numbers above show that it's more cost effective to keep labels small and boutique-like, rather than the old style of label with big offices and glamorous boardrooms. It would not surprise me if this conclusion forces Big Fours to consolidate further and push all artist development onto the smaller one-deep and two-deep labels—in other words, imprints and vanity labels.[5]

Between 1998 and 2001 artists saw a significantly better increase, about 50%—but this number can be misleading, as it applies only to major stars. From 2001 to 2005 they saw a 30% increase. Also, it should be noted that between 1998 and 2001 artists were earning more not because they had succeeded in getting a larger piece of the record-sales pie, but rather because of alliances with advertisers, like Britney Spears with Pepsi. However, this margin changed from 2001 to 2005,

[3] Approximately 33% of that ($1,074,502.22, after taxes and commissions) is just from songwriting.

[4] It's important to keep in mind that these numbers reflect only *record sales* and do not include things like "master licensing," which represents far more income, percentage-wise, to labels.

[5] This is as I wrote it in the 2001 edition. I left it in because this is exactly what did happen in 2004.

with artists now earning more because of rises in statutory rates and retail sales prices of records.

Count on seeing more of this in the future as well. For the average recording artist and producer, the increase has been about 12%. Unfortunately, this has barely kept pace with inflation, so it is not a well-realized gain. To add to this, artists and producers with less clout don't always get their record sales money, for various reasons that we'll explore later, so their actual earnings need to be adjusted further. But the distributor always gets paid. Always.[6]

So now you know how you earn your money and how much you have the potential to make. You are in a unique position. Most people entering this business have no idea how to gauge their success.

Now that you know how much you should make, in the next part of this book we are going to explore all the ways that folks will try to cheat you out of it.

[6] For an in-depth look at the mechanics of this, see my 2nd book to *Confessions: Secrets of Negotiating a Record Contract.*

PART TWO

Scams and Shams

Successful and fortunate crime is called virtue.

—Seneca

➲Watching Your Back

Did you ever notice that as you gain more experience in things, you find out that nothing is exactly the way it first seemed or the way you were taught it should be? It appears that nothing in nature looks the same when you examine it closely. In fact, the record industry has a direct parallel in nature: it's the observable comparison between the physical or Newtonian world and the subatomic world.

Huh?

Quantum physics teaches us that when you look really, really closely at the molecules and particles that make up the world we live in, you notice that nothing acts the way it seems to work to the naked eye. For example: Gravity is something we all experience and can observe. Isaac Newton wrote laws of gravity that work well as long as you only apply them to the macroscopic (directly observable) world. But when Albert Einstein wrote the theory of relativity, he suggested that gravity is not a force that pulls everything down, but merely an illusion, that things only appear to "fall down" because that's the perspective from which we observe them moving. Quantum mechanics later proved that subatomic particles, when observed closely, appear to "fall" in all directions and even move backward in time.

What the hell am I talking about? Well, the above example may sound a bit confusing, but it's worth taking the time to understand it. Quantum physics can teach us an important lesson about business in general—namely, that nothing moves in the direction or at the speed that we think it does. This is doubly true in the record industry.

This section talks about the devious things I've either been witness to or heard about through the grapevine. Let's take a look.

CHAPTER SIXTEEN

❯The Myth of Copyright Protection,
or "Hey, They Stole My Song!"

I f you've ever asked a lawyer about how you can protect your song, he or she will probably give the stock answer—register it on a PA (Performing Art) or SR (Sound Recording) form with the Library of Congress. Others might say that all you have to do is mail it to yourself and never open the envelope that it is in—the postmark will document the date of your copyright. Others will tell you simply to notarize the lyric sheets—the notary stamp always has a date on it. The best yet is the poor man's copyright, which is a manipulation and loose interpretation of the Copyright Act; that is, you don't have to do anything, because the minute a piece of music is recorded, it is automatically copyrighted.[1]

But in practical terms, all of the foregoing are equally useless. The plain truth is that there is only one way to protect yourself from having another writer steal your song, and that's to make the song famous before anyone else does.

Right now there are about a thousand lawyers out there squirming as they read this, about to write me a nasty letter. But they know it's true. Here's the scoop.

Let's say that you wrote a song and did all the necessary procedures to register the copyright. Let's say you even wrote out the lead sheet (something most

[1] Whether the postmark or the notary stamp would stand up in court is debatable. It's true that you own the copyright of a piece of music that you record even if you do nothing to *register* the copyright, but if you ever find yourself facing a legal challenge, your lawyer will tell you that before you can go to federal court you must have registered the work with the Library of Congress.

songwriters never do) and registered that with the Library of Congress as well. So now you've copyrighted the song, the arrangement, and the sound recording of the song.[2] You've covered your ass, and so you confidently go about shopping your demo to record companies or publishing companies.

One day you're sitting in a restaurant on a hot date. You're warming up to each other, thinking about later in the evening back at your place, when suddenly over the restaurant sound system you hear something that's distracting you. It sounds awfully familiar. It's your song!

Your date is befuddled as you start to explain in a panicked voice, "That's my song we're listening to. I wrote it about a year ago. The same lyrics and melody—everything." There are a couple of arrangement changes, but it's still yours. They've stolen your tune. "Those sons-of-bitches!" you scream. Now you're gonna make them

[2] You should by now understand the difference. If not, review "Publishing Deals," page 81; and "When the Producer Wants Publishing," page 96.

WHAT EXACTLY IS A COPYRIGHT?

We've all heard of the word, seen it in print. Maybe you have a friend who is an author and you've heard them talk about protecting their copyrights. But how many of us really know what the word really means?

As obvious as it might seem, the meaning of the word "copyright" is literally the "right to make a copy." Just as with the right to freedom of speech, the laws of this country protect the right of an author to decide when, where, and how to have his or her creations copied—that is, duplicated. Whether it's a story or a song, the minute you write it on a piece of paper or record it on tape you become that work's author, and the law says that, at that very moment, you have rights. Your main right is the decision to have that work copied or not copied. It's your choice as the author; no one else's. This is how authors make money: by controlling that right. If you then assign the right to make commercial copies to another party, like a book publishing house or a record company, you're giving them the right to make copies for sales to book or record stores. In all cases you must be paid money for this right, just as if real property were changing hands. It's the law. It's called "giving consideration." If you give someone your copy-

pay! Well, we'll see. Maybe yes, maybe no. In this chapter we're going to examine the ins and outs of suing stars and several cases of those who tried.

⊜ Suing Stars

You're hopping mad that someone has stolen your precious hit song. The first thing you do is go back to your lawyer friend, the one who told you to fill out a PA form and you'd be fine. You ask him to sue the bastard. (We'll call the culprit Johnny Rock Star.) But your lawyer doesn't sue people, he just does contracts. You need a litigator. So he refers you to someone else. The someone else he refers you to is not a slick wheeler-dealer type of attorney like yours was. This guy is a bit starchy, very down-to-earth, and serious. He's not going to tell you fairy tales, because un-

right and they don't pay you for it, then there has been "no consideration" and a court of law could find that the contract is not valid. Just as when you're selling a house or a car, you must be paid, even if it's only a dollar.

Have you ever seen a funny cartoon and made a Xerox for your refrigerator? Or how many times have you seen an article on something that may be of interest to a friend and made a copy? Most of us have. I copied an Al Capp cartoon for my seven-year-old niece once. She laughed for ten minutes and kept repeating the joke all weekend. I'll bet you didn't know that when you made that copy, you were breaking the law. It's true. Every time you make a copy of something without the permission of the copyright owner (often, but not always, the author) and pass the copy on to a friend, you're breaking the law.[3] When I made the copy of the Al Capp cartoon and gave it to my niece, by strict interpretation, I broke the law.

Now don't worry; no one's going to court over this. You're protected by a legal doctrine that goes by the fancy Latin name De minimis non curat lex, which translates to: "The law does not concern itself with trifles." Another legal principle that you're more likely to have heard about is "fair use" (see the next sidebar in this section). The Copyright Act includes certain exceptions under which you are allowed to make copies of other people's work without their permission or payment to them: teachers in a public school can make copies from a book and pass them out to their students, for example.

[3] If you buy a CD and burn a copy of it to listen to in your car, the Supreme Court has said that you're not violating the rights of the copyright owner. But if you give the CD to a friend, you've broken the law. It's called piracy.

like your music attorney, this guy generally works on commission. That means he doesn't take a case unless he thinks he can win and win big.

You start to tell him about the PA form and how you wrote to the Library of Congress and requested Johnny Rock Star's PA form. Johnny's form was dated later than yours. That means you have proof that your song came first. You've got him!

Well, not exactly. That only proves that the two of you wrote the same or similar song and that you filed your form first.

AVAST THERE, MATEY. PUT UP YER HANDS AN' THROW THE CDS TO THE DECK.

Are you a pirate? Use this excerpt from the Copyright Act as a guideline.

§107. Limitations on exclusive rights: Fair Use

Notwithstanding the provisions of sections 106 and 106A, the fair use of a copyrighted work, including such use by reproduction in copies or phonorecords or by any other means specified by that section, for purposes such as criticism, comment, news reporting, teaching (including multiple copies for classroom use), scholarship, or research, is not an infringement of copyright. In determining whether the use made of a work in any particular case is a fair use the factors to be considered shall include —

1. the purpose and character of the use, including whether such use is of a commercial nature or is for nonprofit educational purposes; 2. the nature of the copyrighted work; 3. the amount and substantiality of the portion used in relation to the copyrighted work as a whole; and 4. the effect of the use upon the potential market for or value of the copyrighted work.

In plain English, this says that if you're selling (or giving away) copies of a copyrighted work, which will have the effect of reducing the potential money the copyright owner could make, it's not "fair use" and you're a thief. Sometimes fair use is easy to determine, but other times it requires a day in court, as in the case of file-sharing companies that allow people to distribute songs digitally via the Internet. Witness the 2 Live Crew case in the main text of this chapter.

When you accuse someone of breaking a federal law (such as copyright infringement), you must go to a federal prosecutor and file a complaint. Federal prosecutors tend to be career-oriented attorneys who would rather enhance their track record by going after mobsters and inside-trading honchos, not rock stars who rip off a song from some unknown writer. You would be hard-pressed to find a prosecutor who considers the case a good use of taxpayers' money. And that's the good news.

Even if you found a crusading prosecutor willing to pull Johnny Rock Star into court, and even if Johnny were found guilty, intellectual property fraud is punishable by a simple fine and/or one year in jail. (The latter wouldn't happen—the jails are full enough.) In addition to this slap in the face, you would be required to appear in court several times, exposing you to many top industry professionals who would hate you for dragging them into this. And you would receive not one penny for your effort. The fine goes to the state—you've done your civic duty by acting as a witness.

So what about all those big settlements we hear about in the papers about so-and-so being sued for stealing samples and lyrics and so forth?

Those are not criminal suits. They are civil suits—a lawsuit done in civil court, where the plaintiff (that's you in our example) is seeking a money damage award for the theft of their property (in this case, the theft of a copyright of a song).

Since you will claim that you have been robbed of money from the copyright from a song that you wrote, it will not be enough to prove that Johnny Rock Star stole the song. You have to prove that he stole the song from you personally!

In legal terms, this is called "proving access." You have to prove that Johnny had the opportunity to steal your song by being in proximity to you or to a copy of your song. If you can't show access, then the court will in all likelihood be forced to conclude that it is a mere coincidence that you and Johnny wrote the same song around the same time. In this case Johnny may walk away with the copyright and the cash.

Think this is easy? Let's look at several actual cases.

Mick Jagger and "She's the Boss"

This was a case in 1985 involving Mick Jagger of the Rolling Stones and a Jamaican reggae artist, Grand View Alley, who had several small successes in the Virgin Islands. He sued Jagger for stealing a song of his and putting it on Jagger's 1984 first solo record, *She's the Boss*. It was big news at the time, and radio stations played both the reggae version and Jagger's rock version side by side on the air during the trial. To the average listener, they did seem to be the same song with different arrangements.

Before the trial began, lawyers from both sides took statements from all the witnesses that would be brought before the jury. (The statements that witnesses give are called "depositions.") During the taking of the depositions in this case, it was learned by both parties that Jagger's current drummer had played on the original demo of the reggae version of the song. Grand View Alley seemed assured of a favorable outcome at the trial. But when the drummer was called to the witness stand during the trial, he testified he couldn't remember if he had played on that exact demo. This was all the jury needed to find in Jagger's favor.

Michael Bolton and "How Am I Supposed to Live Without You"

This case has similar overtones. Here songwriters Michael Bolton and Doug James and singer Laura Branigan were being sued for stealing the song "How Am I Supposed to Live Without You."

Bolton and James had originally written the song for Laura Branigan's second album in 1983. When the record came out and "How Am I Supposed to Live Without You" was on the radio, it came to the attention of a New Jersey composer named Gary William Friedman.

Friedman was no amateur—he had written several important scores and songs, including the critically acclaimed off-Broadway musical *The Me Nobody Knows*. He noticed that "How Am I" bore a striking resemblance to a song that he had written some years earlier called "Promise Me." But unlike the situation in the Grand View Alley case, Friedman would have no problem proving access. He had had a previous relationship with Laura Branigan.

Like most singers, before she got her major label record deal, Laura Branigan sang on numerous demos to make a meager living. Friedman had employed her many times to record rough versions of his songs before sending them to his publisher.

When Friedman first heard "How Am I" on the radio, the similarity was so close that he thought Branigan had actually honored him by recording the song. Upon closer examination he realized a grim truth. The melody was all too familiar to him, and some of the lyrics were altered.

He looked on the record and found that the writer credit had gone to Michael Bolton (who at the time was not a household name) and Doug James, the very person who had played piano on Friedman's original demo of "Promise Me."

Armed with a stream of witnesses and a paper trail, Friedman sought justice in a New York federal court. But even after Friedman presented the court with the canceled checks that he had paid Branigan and James for their services, under oath both claimed that they simply couldn't remember if they had performed "Promise Me."

Friedman lost the case, was stuck with massive legal bills, and did not receive one penny in royalties or recognition for the song. In the end a jury seemed more impressed with the lineup of celebrities testifying on behalf of the defendants than with the paper trail, the similarities between the two songs, and Friedman's indisputable associations with Branigan and James.

Bolton and James' attorneys offered Friedman a measly few thousand dollars to waive his right to appeal. Devastated by the crushing verdict, he took the five g's.

"How Am I Supposed to Live Without You" has grossed over $2 million for Michael Bolton and Doug James.

New Kids on the Block and "I'll Be Your Everything"

Even if your song is a hit, you may not be protected.

In 1992, teen heartthrob Tommy Page was sued by George Soule for stealing the hit song "I'll Be Your Everything." Page penned a song with several members of New Kids on the Block, and somehow they managed to give it the same title, a similar opening lyric, and an almost identical opening melody as Soule's song.

The original "I'll Be Your Everything" was made famous by legendary R&B singer Percy Sledge and reached No. 15 on the Billboard R&B charts in 1975, just five years after Tommy Page was born.

Can two people write the same or a similar song, with the same title, and yet have no knowledge of each other even when one version is an American classic still played on hundreds of radio stations? A jury thought so. They found in favor of Page. The defense went so far as to have Page up on the witness stand with a synthesizer to demonstrate how he came up with the melody. When his attorney asked him what the inspiration for the song was, he replied, "God."

2 Live Crew and "Pretty Woman"

In the above cases, the writers who filed the lawsuits probably felt that the jury was biased toward the stars. Certainly many attorneys have argued in recent years that juries are just ordinary people who often get bedazzled by faces that they've seen 40 feet high on the sides of buildings. In hindsight many songwriters who've sued have felt that they should have opted to have their case heard by a judge. Well, that's no guarantee either.

Enter the 2 Live Crew case. Here the rap group took the song "Oh Pretty Woman" by Roy Orbison and turned it into a rap tune with a much peppier title, "Pretty Woman." The lyrics of the song were almost identical as well. They even took the famous guitar riff, and yet they got clean off the hook. (Pardon the pun.)

"PRETTY WOMAN"
AS RECORDED BY 2 LIVE CREW

Pretty Woman, walking down the street,
Pretty Woman, girl you look so sweet,
Pretty Woman, you bring me down to that knee,
Pretty Woman, you make me wanna beg please,
Oh, Pretty Woman

Big hairy woman, you need to shave that stuff,
Big hairy woman, you know I bet it's tough
Big hairy woman, all that hair ain't legit,
'Cause you look like Cousin It
Big hairy woman

Bald headed woman, girl your hair won't grow,
Bald headed woman, you got a teeny weeny afro
Bald headed woman, you know your hair could look nice,
Bald headed woman, first you got to roll it with rice
Bald headed woman here, let me get this hunk of biz for ya,
Ya know what I'm saying,
You look better than Rice-a-Roni
Oh, bald headed woman

Big hairy woman, come on in,
And don't forget your bald headed friend
Hey Pretty Woman, let the boys jump in
Two timin' woman, girl you know it ain't right,
Two timin' woman, you's out with my boy last night
Two timin' woman, that takes a load off my mind,
Two timin' woman, now I know the baby ain't mine
Oh, two timin' woman
Oh, Pretty Woman.

They argued that since a part of the Copyright Act contains a section called "fair use" and that this provision opens up the possibility for "spoofs" that parody the original to be exploited royalty-free, 2 Live Crew did not owe Orbison's estate a dime because their version was commenting on the original. (WARNING: See the footnote.)[4]

The "parody defense" is intended to apply to comedy versions of things, like what you might find on *Saturday Night Live*, and has roots going back to when popular songs were rewritten with new lyrics to be used for political campaigns. Many argue that it was never intended to be used to create completely independent master recordings that would become commercial hits.

To prevail under the "parody defense," 2 Live Crew would have to prove that their song "pays homage" to the Orbison hit, and was not used simply because 2 Live Crew wanted to create a rip-off version.

In a decision that stunned many attorneys, 2 Live Crew persuaded a judge that indeed this was the case. To make matters more interesting, the ruling was handed down in a court in Nashville, known to many as the city of songwriters.[5] The plaintiffs appealed and the decision was overturned. 2 Live Crew appealed the appeal, taking the case all the way up the ladder to the Supreme Court, who remanded the case with a ruling that was tantamount to a favorable decision to 2 Live Crew. In the final settlement, 2 Live Crew did not have to pay anything for infringement, but they agreed to pay a royalty to Roy Orbison's publisher going forward.

The original judge (who, I can promise you, was not star-struck by these brash young men) decided in their favor because he felt that the 2 Live Crew version lived up to the fair use standard because it had contained "social criticism of the original."

The law works in mysterious ways, so please see the previous sidebar for your daily dose of social criticism.

George Harrison and "He's So Fine"

Once in a while, the writer does prevail. One significant case was a suit against ex-Beatle George Harrison. Harrison was sued by the author of the 1963 hit "He's So Fine." He claimed that Harrison's 1970 song "My Sweet Lord" was a direct clone with different lyrics. A court agreed. When asked to comment on what had happened, Harrison was quoted by reporters as saying, "Well, sometimes a tune gets caught in your head and you can't remember where it comes from."

The court held that Harrison did not consciously copy the earlier song, but it was still an infringement to copy it unconsciously. Harrison was not alone in his caper. Veteran record producer Phil Spector produced the hit that got Harrison in Dutch. Which only proves that a selective memory is contagious when working on potential heavyweight hits.

[4] Don't try this at home, kids. Creating parodies and claiming that they are fair use is the stuff that major lawsuits are made of. To prevail, your parody must contain social commentary or criticism of the original. Only a court can determine if a parody is fair use. It is very risky, so consult a qualified entertainment attorney before distributing any spoof recordings.

[5] In fact, Orbison wrote and recorded "Oh Pretty Woman" in Nashville.

⊘ When Band Members Sue Each Other

Sade

In the mid 1980s the musicians in Sade's band were already playing for several other hip British bands. But together they produced demos for Sade, one of which was the song that would become a mega-hit, "Smooth Operator." The record company, however, was interested only in Sade as an artist, and she signed a solo contract, dismissing her band. At the time the band members thumbed their noses at her and moved on. After all, they were already thought to be the strength in the deal anyway. She didn't write, and her voice, unique as it was, had its limits. They didn't count on the record company releasing the demo *as is*. No one did that back then. When the song became a hit, some band members filed suit to collect royalties. But by British law too much time had passed and they would only be allowed to collect money the song earned *after* the time they filed suit. By then the record was in the cut-out bin. Moral here: If you're going to sue, do it right away.

Duran Duran

Andy Wicket was the original keyboard player in the '80s sensation Duran Duran. He wrote and produced the original demos for "Girls on Film" and a song that would later become the hit "Rio." But Andy gets nothing today for his efforts. Just weeks before the band was signed to EMI, he left the group over "creative differences." They asked Andy to sign a one-paragraph "release" that gave up all rights to Duran Duran for today's equivalent of about $1,200. Andy's lawyer (who was a real estate lawyer by trade) advised him to do it, as this would create a clear paper trail from him to the band. Bad advice. After the songs became hits Andy tried to sue in British court. But the paper he had signed held up. "Girls on Film" has earned millions in royalties for Duran Druan.

Both of these stories are explored in greater detail in my new book *Million Dollar Mistakes*.

⊘ More Problems with Suing Stars

The worst part of getting yourself embroiled in a case like those above is that the litigator, the lawyer whom you are trying to convince to sue Johnny Rock Star, has more reasons to not help you than to help you, even if he or she thinks that you have a good case. If the attorney is trying to attract the very type of client that the disgruntled songwriter wants to sue, they may be fearful of industry blackballing. For this reason many copyright theft cases never get to the courtroom.

If you hear your song on the radio and you yourself have no clout, you will find it almost impossible to collect anything unless the star you plan to sue has a policy that favors paying off "chasers" (people who try to sue stars for copyright theft).

Some stars get sued so often that they find it cheaper to settle with the plaintiffs than go through the process of litigation. This is not necessarily an admission of guilt but simply more economical. Many times a settlement of $100,000 will pacify a suing songwriter. The lawyer for the plaintiff will explain that they should take the settlement because if they go to court they will probably lose, as such cases are notoriously hard to prove. The plaintiff usually gives in and takes the cash, the song remains the property of the star, and the negative publicity is zip. The only exception to this scenario would be if the star felt that they had a particularly strong case and chose to fight. Or if, for some reason, a lot of publicity came to surround the case. In these cases the star will fight tooth and nail to win the case. They usually do.

Other stars feel that they have a reputation to protect and have a policy of not giving in to anyone no matter what. Either they have the money to enforce their policy or they are up-and-coming stars who don't want the negative publicity while they're still gaining the trust of the public. The lawyers who specialize in copyright suits know which stars are less prone to pay and try to avoid confrontations with them. They fear that a frivolous chaser suit will be met with a "we dare you to sue us" memo. The artists that have these policies tend to be the biggest of the big stars. They are the hardest to sue. They never go down without a fight, and they usually win because they can financially outdraw the chaser.

❯ Collecting Your Money

Sometimes the stars do lose, and when they lose they lose big. You might think that once that has happened, they simply cut a check to the winning party and that's that. Sorry. Winning a lawsuit doesn't guarantee that you will collect the money. How you collect is up to you to figure out. The court will try to enforce the judgment, but in many cases their hands are tied. If the star is good at hiding his or her money, they can delay payment for years.[6]

So years later, after the star is considered a deadbeat, the songwriter can get a court order and then the performing rights agencies will stop paying the star's account. I am told the average collection on cases of this type is around four to six

[6] Most famous example: O.J. Simpson, who was ordered to pay $9 million in damages to the family of Ron Goldman, whom Simpson was accused of killing. The Goldmans have been unable to collect even a dime in over a decade.

years. Oh yeah, remember, a third of any money collected goes to your lawyer.

The bottom line on this subject is to beware when lawyers and people in general speak of your rights and suing for them. Most people haven't been through a lawsuit and don't know what they're talking about. Suing, in all phases of business, is a long and expensive process, and your rights are only worth what you're willing to invest in protecting them. Stars have more money and resources than most people and can afford to have an attorney on retainer to handle these things while they go about their business. You probably can't.

From the above information, we can now understand the meaning of this next piece of Record Industry Talmud:

> ### When people talk about "your rights," they are suggesting that you spend thousands of dollars suing someone.

So if the law won't protect you, what can you do? Here are a few "unofficial" suggestions a lawyer will never make.

⊘ Blockage

In 1986 I worked on an R&B album paid for by a major label. I was only an engineer, but I was doing a lot of producing on the project as well. When the project was finished, I submitted the last of my invoices, totaling about $3,500 that the production company owed me. They told me that they were expecting the last installment from the record company soon and that I should please be patient. I was patient for about six months, after which time I decided to do something covert to get my money. A friend who worked in the publishing department at EMI told me a little trick that she knew worked for a writer friend. It went like this:

Knowing that the record was due out in another four months gave me a little time to put the plan she called blockage into action. First, I found out if the artist was on BMI or ASCAP. This is not hard; I just called the record company and got the information from a secretary. In this case it was BMI, which I was already a member of.

Next I filled out a PA form for all the songs on the record that I worked on as an engineer and sent it in to Washington with my name and the name of the artist listed as the two authors of the songs. This was sent return receipt requested, which means that when the Library of Congress receives the PA forms, they must sign a receipt for it. Even though it will take several weeks for the PA forms to go through their computer, the receipt will act as a sort of "patent pending" for the songs. That means that until anyone says otherwise, this artist and I cowrote the songs.

Then I registered all the songs with BMI, listing myself and the artist as the cowriters. Now, one would think that BMI would do a computer check to see if the same songs were registered once before with different writers. They didn't, and last I checked (about three months before this book's first edition was written), they still hadn't. If, in fact, the song never earns any money, both conflicting forms will remain on the BMI computer forever. But the minute a royalty has to be paid out, the computer will recognize the conflict and freeze the account until all parties can settle on who the actual authors are.

Almost a year later, that's what happened. The song charted and the artist was anxious to collect his money. If you've read the previous chapters, you know how badly he needed it at this time. BMI, however, would not pay the artist a dime until they settled with me. BMI does not discriminate. They simply say, "You guys work it out and call us when you do."

When the artist's lawyer called me to settle, I told him that I had patiently waited over a year to be paid on my invoice and was not going to wait any longer. They immediately paid me the $3,500 plus interest, and I relinquished my copyright claim.

Both BMI and ASCAP frown on this sort of activity. They claim that they will excommunicate those who make false claims, but they probably would never kick out a member who has a hit. Besides, they don't seem to mind holding on to the money at 4 or 5% interest while the two parties resolve the problem.

❯ Name Blockage

Once a manager friend of mine was dumped by his artist right after they got a deal with a major label. Because he had only a handshake agreement, it was not hard for the band to dismiss him once he had gotten them in the door of the label. As you can imagine, he was fuming from the betrayal.

Over a drink I suggested to him that he plan a little legal revenge. I told my friend to check with the county clerk to see if the band had incorporated their name and logo or had a trademark license established for them. The odds were that they did not, and sure enough, that was the case. All my friend had to do was file a DBA (Doing Business As) with the state county clerk's office and sit back. The damage was done.

He waited patiently for almost a year. During that time the label issued advances to the band that he never got a commission for. They began recording an album, and the label started doing press for the upcoming release. Just when the record was about to come out, the label did the same name search that my friend had done a year earlier. You can imagine what they found.

Outraged, the band now had little choice but to make an offer to buy the name from my friend. (Their only other option was to change their name, but few bands want to do that after going through the trouble of gaining a reputation.) My friend was merciless and unforgiving, selling the name to them at a price more than double what his commission would have been.

Revenge is a dish best served cold.

❷ Sound-Alikes

You'd think that after you go through all the B.S. it takes to get a hit record that you can sit pretty. Well, maybe. Now that you have an important copyright, it's up to you to protect it. If you can, that is. Enter the sound-alike. This is another form of copyright abuse.

When a movie or TV show wants to use a popular song in their production, they must obtain the permission of several sources before they can do it. Each source will charge a fee.

The first of these fees is the synchronization license for the song. That's a license

YOU BETTAH, YOU BETTAH, YOU BETTE

Several years ago, Bette Midler won a landmark case in California against an ad company for using a celebrity impersonator in a radio spot. Even though the ad specified that a Bette "sound-alike" was used, Midler's attorneys found grounds to sue because her signature sound was being misrepresented. The impersonation of her recognizable "style" implied that she herself endorsed the advertised product. A court agreed, based on California's "right to publicity" statute. Since there are many celebrities in Los Angeles, there is a special law that protects advertisers from hiring look-alikes or sound-alikes for endorsements.

This might open up the door to make sound-alikes more difficult to pull off. In all likelihood it will always be legal, but through performance rights clearances it can be made so expensive that producers may as well pay for the real thing.

to take the song and synchronize it to a moving picture like a movie or a TV show. This license usually sells for about $2,000 and is obtainable through the song's publisher.

Next is the Musicians' Union, who will require the show's producer to pay a performance reuse fee to the authors of the sound recording (i.e., the performer or artist who recorded the song). Tack on another $1,000 for that.

Last but not least is the record company that owns the sound recording of the song. For a typical use of the master in a film or TV show, the money will usually add up to about $30,000, but it can be much steeper or lower depending on the flexibility of the label. I have heard of situations where a master was licensed for up to $1,000,000 for a single use in a film, millions if it is used in a commercial. (By the way, none of this money necessarily goes to the artist — it's strictly a record company fee, unless you negotiate otherwise. To learn how see my book *Secrets of Negotiating a Record Contract*.)

Several years ago I was approached by a sleazy TV producer who wanted to use a popular Rolling Stones song in one of his shows. He asked me what I thought it would cost and I described the above payments to him. He melted into his seat, shaking his head and saying, "There must be a better way." There was.

He obtained the sync license from the publisher, saying that it would be for background use only. Somehow he got them down to $1,500. Now came the hard part, how to sidestep the union and the record company. That's where I came in.

He hired me to "compose" and record an exact duplicate of the original recording. I did. I reprogrammed the original arrangement and, using a computer, made it exactly as it was on the original record. I hired a nonunion singer who by coincidence sounded a lot like Mick Jagger for $100 and mixed it with the exact same treatments of reverb and effects. It sounded identical to all but the most scrupulous listeners. Considering it was going to be in the background of a scene with dialogue on top of it and other sound effects, we were home free. No record company, union, or rights organization needed to be paid. I used myself plus one other nonunion musician and charged the producer an all-in fee of $3,000. His total cost was $4,500 instead of $25,000, and the best part was this was completely legal!

To add insult to injury, he proceeded to use the song anywhere and everywhere he wanted to—background and foreground. (Foreground licensing fees are substantially higher.) The TV show aired in Europe, which is not carefully monitored by American PROs like ASCAP and BMI, so he got away with paying next to nothing for a hit song in the foreground of his TV show.

This is now a common occurrence in the broadcast industry, and what makes it legally possible is a Catch-22 in the interpretation of the Copyright Act: that the in-

SIMON SAYS, "NO SAMPLING"

This is how as an engineer I helped one record company "steal" a sample from Paul Simon and get away without paying him a dime. What makes the story especially juicy is that the culprit was a major label, one that certainly could afford to pay for the sample.

This label had recorded, mixed, and mastered a song by a new artist, not realizing that there was a sample loop used in the arrangement that had not been cleared. The producer took the sample off of one of those "beats" records assuming that because it was on a CD of things designed to be sampled, it was precleared. It wasn't.[7] The two-bar loop, already used in a number of rap and R&B records, belonged to a cover of a song originally written by Paul Simon.

While most producers had gotten away with using this sample without consulting Simon, this A&R person decided to "do the right thing" and ask his permission. A fatal move. Simon, at that time, was notorious for being a hard-ass about such things. In this case he asked for 50% of the new song's publishing. Here is where the A&R man and I got smart. My reputation for making sound-alikes was well known. So after a few drinks the A&R person and I decided to make an exact duplicate of the loop. Musicians were contracted, studio time booked, and the "Paul sample" surgically removed and replaced with my bootleg.

But something wasn't quite right. The new sample very subtly changed the feel of the groove, even though it was all but identical. What to do? Go back to the studio? Spend more time and money to make it fit? Instead, the A&R man said to me, "You have everybody's invoice for this fiasco. Then who's to know we didn't actually replace it?"

Gambling that in case of a dispute the record company could give the appearance that they really did replace Simon's sample, they then elected not to. The Paul Simon sample remained. The record went to stores, and no one was the wiser.

It's a shame when big record companies break the very laws they lobby for. There is no honor among thieves, but there is karma: the record was a colossal flop.

[7] In fact, many so-called "beats" CDs do not have cleared samples. With these CDs, you're expected to use the samples for demo purposes only. Before using them on a commercial record, you'll need to get clearance through the original publishers that control the rights. If you're using CDs with newly recorded beat loops intended for sampling, read the fine print on the back cover or insert. Some CDs claim to contain only original, license-free samples. Even then, if you use the beat and it turns out to have been lifted from a copyrighted record, guess who pays.

strumental arrangement of the song, although considered part of the underlying copyright, cannot be protected unless it is deemed "unique." Otherwise it is seen only as an interpretation, or an expression of an idea. Ideas cannot be copyrighted.

But who decides what is original and what is just a ripped-off "idea"? Twelve people who sit in a box, called . . . a jury. And while most artists believe that their sound is unique, the average citizen (or judge, for that matter) is generally less of a connoisseur of bass lines, drum patterns, and synth patches, making "unique" about as hard a standard to prove in a court of law as "obscene" or "pornographic."

Clearly this is a Neanderthal interpretation, and hopefully there are lawyers out there fighting to have the Copyright Act amended by making judges and juries sympathetic to the plight of producers, artists, and arrangers. But change is unlikely; the broadcast industries have powerful attorneys on their side as well, fighting to keep things just the way that they are, and for a good reason. This catch-22/loophole saves them millions a year in sound recording licenses. As digital technology makes it possible to make more and more accurate copies of things for less and less money, this loophole will become a noose tightening around the necks of record companies and artists trying to protect the originality of their sound. But there is hope.

◗ Sample-Alikes

A sample-alike is a close cousin to the sound-alike. To understand what this is you must first understand what the art of sampling is about.

"Samples" are the series of "borrowed" sounds that make up a portion of the main groove of a song (known as a "loop"). Sampling as an art form found its way into modern pop music when the Beatles cut "Revolution #9," which "borrowed" tidbits of British radio broadcasts and intermingled them with the song. In the '50s and '60s, things of this nature were commonly done without regard for the original owners of the recordings from which the sounds were taken. But today, whenever pieces of other recordings are used in a new recording, the authors of the new recording have to "clear" the sample. This process involves getting permission from both the record company that owns the sound recording and the publishing company that owns the rights to the song. It's complicated and can get very expensive, and that's assuming the artist is cooperative.[8]

Often the loop being used is so obvious that the sampled artist feels entitled to ask for up to 50% ownership in the new song's publishing. Many artists and labels have agreed and given in but not with great enthusiasm.

[8] Some artists feel that samples are corrupting the art form of modern music. By way of example, Electric Light Orchestra refused to grant permission for a rock act to use a sample from their hit "Fire on High." Ironically, ELO was widely rumored to be lip-synching at their live stadium concerts in the '70s.

A sample-alike is a re-creation of a sample using the same techniques and based on the same legal principles as the sound-alike discussed above. Thus, the bother of dealing with temperamental artists is avoided as well as the Gestapo tactics taken by labels when they realize that they have something someone needs. See the sidebar "Simon Says, 'No Sampling'" for an eye-opening example of this.

After the incident in the sidebar, I refused to do any more sample-alikes, but they're still quite common. It has become the newest way to screw writers and record companies.[9] As hip-hop and rap (the most sample-dependent form of music today) continue to prove profitable, sample-aliking has become a mini-industry, building the reputations of many engineers willing to assist producers in ripping off their fellow producers and writers. Tsk-tsk.

[9] See "Sample Rights," page 84.

CHAPTER SEVENTEEN

⊜Master Fraud

I n this chapter, heavily expanded for this Third Edition, we're going to get up close and personal with several common ways that business entities prey on the dreams of songwriters and artists. Master fraud is any enterprise that uses deception to get an artist to give up rights to their most valuable possession—the rights to master recordings.

Sometimes the method is obvious, as in a record deal, where you sign over your recording to a company that purports to exploit it and then pay you a royalty. Some are sincere but some are not. We've covered that one extensively in the first part of the book. But there are other scams, far more subtle ones that prey on those who are *not* signed to major labels. They go for the average indie artist and exploit his notion that if he's dealing with a small folksy "independent" company, somehow he's not involved in anything dangerous.

The first examples below show how record companies both large and small can manipulate both the public and their own artists with shaky sales techniques and crafty accounting.

⊜ Clears, Cleans, and Fake Masters

When I was working as an engineer, I mixed a couple of big-selling records with one producer who was very well connected. We became good friends. One afternoon I entered the studio to find him yelling into the phone. He slammed the receiver down, looked at me very perturbed, and said, "They're ripping me off." The argument he was having was a dispute over the quarterly statement reflecting his royalty. His royalty is dependent on the sales of the records, so I asked him how he could know how many records the artist had actually sold.

He said to me, "Well, you can audit them, but don't expect to make any friends that way. You can check SoundScan and that will give you some idea. But the only way to know for sure is to have a friend in the Mafia. They can tell you the exact number, but it will cost you."

I had to assume he meant that you would owe them a favor. He continued, "If the record company says they sold two million records, they probably sold about two and a half million."

CLEAR A SPACE FOR ME

There is only one case that I have heard of where an artist tried to take a record company to court over clears.

Before the digital age, clears were easy to spot. They were pressed using a copy of the master lath. A trained ear could hear the deterioration in quality.

Armed with a crate full of these dirty-sounding LPs and an FBI file that told of the connection between the record company and a famous "family-run" bootlegging organization, this artist sued their record company for $321,000 in royalties they believed they were owed.

The case was dropped after the record company settled out of court, but in the pretrial questioning of a disgruntled record company employee it was alleged that clears were a regular part of this company's policy.

The artist never got their money. The record company was sold and two years later filed for bankruptcy. The artist never recorded another album and was dropped from the roster.

Since CD technology was embraced by the major labels in the late '70s, the situation has grown grimmer. These days, the glass master used to make a CD can be copied an infinite number of times without any deterioration in sound, making a modern clear virtually undetectable.

"But how?" I asked naively. "Don't the bar codes show up whenever a sale is made?"

"If the sale is in America. It's a big world, you know." He was talking about what have been referred to as "clears" and "cleans," both shady ways for big labels to sell records without reporting the sales.

Clears

In a clear, the record company would make a second master lath[1] and give it to a duplication factory that basically does not exist. This plant will make bootlegs of the record, called "clears." The label will supply the "distributor" with the packaging materials and whatever else is needed to make the record look like the genuine article. In fact, there is no difference between it and the normal record except that the duplication house making these records won't show up on any of the record company's invoices.

These "clears" will then be shipped by the private distributor to places unknown, mostly countries that are not in the normal distribution channels. These places don't have sophisticated accounting equipment like bar coding; they just sell the records over the counter and ask no questions. In this manner many record sales fall through

[1] The steel plate used to press melted plastic into millions of 12- and 7-inch records, called "platters" by the pressing plant.

THE KING OF CLEANS

The King of Cleans was a man named John LaMonte. In 1974 he purchased several million damaged records from Capitol Records that were to be brought to a vinyl recycling center. Many of these records were Beatles singles.

Instead of sending the units to the graveyard, LaMonte slipped a plain white cover over the records and resold them for 40 cents apiece to rack jobbers, middlemen who sell to smaller stores. The rack jobbers allegedly knew the records were damaged and that they could return the goods to Capitol for 90 cents each.

No one even noticed something was wrong until Capitol realized that there were more records coming back than there were going to the stores. They tried to have LaMonte arrested, but he hadn't done anything illegal. He bought the records legitimately and sold them legitimately, and there is no law against manufacturing plain white sleeves.

the cracks and avoid showing up in the event of an artist's audit. This is the record company's hedge against their enormous overhead and their slim vig.

Cleans

A close cousin to the clear is the clean. These are records that are given to private vendors with the intention that they will never be passed on to a retail store but instead returned to the label for a refund as if they were a returned consignment item. The name comes from the now-famous tale of the corruption that pervaded MCA Records in the 1980s. Executives inside the company were authorizing the pressing of hundreds of thousands of excess records. An invoice marked "Clean" was code to those vendors in the know that these units could be returned to the record company for cash with no questions asked.[2] They were caught because somebody noticed that more records were returning than were ever manufactured. Oops.

An informer-assisted audit will usually expose cleans and clears. Unfortunately, the informer will get a commission of from 30% to 75% of what's recovered. Add to this the fact that the record company will be eternally antagonistic toward you in the future. This, above all, is what deters many artists and producers from challenging the record company's accounting.

2 See the sidebar "The King of Cleans," page 199, and also "Getting 'Cutout' of Royalties," page 72.

❯ Soundtrack Scams and So-Called CD Samplers

If you've ever signed a registration book for a music seminar, then you ended up on a mailing list. Whether you know it or not, your name, along with those of the thousands of other people who signed with you, ended up in the computers of many companies. At least one will be one of the many sleazy record companies that claim to help you interface with "the industry" through their CD samplers.

These are compilations that take various unsigned acts and put a song from their demo on a compilation record. This record will supposedly be distributed to many radio stations and labels or used for a soundtrack of some bogus movie that has no studio distribution. The idea is to give the act exposure and hopefully get them a recording contract.

These offers sicken me. They prey on the desperation and naiveté of young bands, most of whom are out in the boondocks and think that the industry is inaccessible to them. Many new artists have started out on compilation records, but not the kind that these people offer to do. This is how it really works.

These companies send out advertising to artists through direct mail and hope for a 5% response. They know that there are thousands of acts out there, so all they need are 20 or so responses to go to work. Generally they charge an "all-in" fee for mastering and placement on the CD and on the liner notes. They say that 500 or 1,000 of these CDs will be sent out to "the industry." The fee for the act is generally about $5,000. This is steep by any stretch of the imagination. The fact that people go for it is somewhat depressing to me.

Think: If this company gets 11 responses, that translates into $55,000 in revenue. Mastering costs for the entire CD are about $2,000 tops, and CD duplication for 1,000 units about another $1,500. Add about $2 per unit for shipping (assuming they really send out all 1,000 of them) and you have a total production cost of $5,500.

Net profit—$49,500. Not bad for a couple of months' work.

To add insult to injury, they will always make the artist sign away their rights to their mechanical licenses (see "Publishing Deals," page 81) since they claim that all the CDs are being given away. Plus if the artist wants several copies, they will usually have to pay for any more than five of them.

There is no way to track or audit these fly-by-nights to insure that they are sending anything to anybody. They buy lists of names of unsigned artists from list brokers, who get them from the seminars mentioned above and the Internet, and they're usually located in some state in the Midwest or Florida.

There are a few companies that are performing this type of service legitimately. They have distribution contracts with reputable distribution companies. Ask about distribution contracts as a test to see if the company is on the up-and-up. Also ask for a bio of the people in the organization and who they're affiliated with. If this book has taught you anything, it's taught you that this a business of connections. If this company that wants your $5,000 is truly effective, they should be connected as well. But weigh the cost-versus-return carefully.

If they're hesitant to answer any of your questions, RUN THE OTHER WAY!

❷ 9-to-1 Publishing, or "Why Is There Only One Good Song on the Record?"

If you've ever gone out and bought a CD because you liked the song that you heard on the radio, only to find that it was the only good song on the record, you're not alone.

There are several reasons why this happens. The most typical reason relates to publishing. It is not uncommon after a mercy signing (described in "The Mercy Signing," page 247), or another signing where the label is unsatisfied with the finished record, that they call in a ringer to save the album.

This usually boils down to hiring a songwriter other than the artist to write the song that will be the single off the album. The single is what you'll hear on the radio and is understandably the best song on the album. Sometimes, however, an artist's manager will know that the label will want to use outside material to sell the artist even before the record deal is signed. He or she may know this because they have a gut feeling that their client's material is weak. If they feel this way, they will make sure that the artist's contract states that at least a certain number of songs written by the artist must appear on the record.

The reason for this should be obvious. Remember that the compulsory license is worth about 6 cents per song (after the record company's adjustments). So if the artist writes nine songs on the record and an outside writer writes only one song, but that song is the hit, the artist still gets 54 cents per album and the ringer gets 6 cents.[3]

3 See "Publishing Deals," page 81.

Even though the ringer's song is selling the record, the artist makes the killing, because their nine loser songs are riding the coattails of the one hit. Managers work on commission, so they have a vested interest in how much mechanical licensing

---

EXTREME MEASURES

In 1994 Extreme's sound was very aggressive power pop. But there was one song on their second record, a tender, mellow love song, called "More than Words." The record company chose this song as the single, and if you were anywhere near a radio in the year 1992, you will remember that it was a huge radio hit.

But when people got the record home and realized that "More than Words" was the only song of its kind on the record, many of them promptly tried to return it to the local record stores. The situation got so out of hand that one record store in Atlanta had a sign by the cash register reading, "We don't take back Extreme records."

Although Extreme's career took a nosedive after that album, "More than Words" is still earning bucks on the radio. In the long run, a wrong hit is better than no hit.

money their artist realizes. If you ever hear a manager talk about this "great song that my client wrote" and you think it stinks (even beyond the limits of your personal taste), you can now guess what's on that manager's mind. This example, of course, goes for producers and anyone else who stands to profit from the compulsory license paid to the writers of the songs on the record.

The way to spot the "9-to-1 syndrome" is easy. Look at the liner notes of the record. If all the songs are written by the artist except the single, be skeptical.

The other reason for the "only one good song" phenomenon is a bit more innocent. Even if the artist writes all the songs on the record, sometimes a record company will pick a song that is the least representative of the band's overall sound to use as the single. The best example I can think of was with the band Extreme (see the sidebar on the preceding page).

❷ CD Replicator Scams, or Getting Duped by the Duper

Just days after an emerging artist has weathered the frustrations and joys of finding a producer and finishing an album, he is besieged with competitive offers by CD manufacturers. Some of them sound too good to be true.

1,000 CDs for $400
Guaranteed distribution
Cheap barcodes
Better quality than their competitors through a "special process"
"Fingerprinting" protection

This section dissects some of the more common claims in CD replicator advertising. Don't replicate without it. Also expanded versions of these articles, with real-life examples of places to look to and avoid are posted on www.MosesAvalon.com, under "Scam of the Month."

When a CD Isn't a Real CD

I can think of no greater career horror than finally hooking up with a person who can make a difference in your career, getting them to sit down for ten minutes to listen to your CD, and then putting it in the CD player only to find out . . . it doesn't work. What gives? You made it on your own computer with a high-quality CD burner, yet it's stuttering. Maybe you should have had the copies made by a pro. But consider this:

It's one thing to blame yourself for cutting corners and making a CD on a PC, but it's another thing entirely when a professional manufacturing plant takes your money and does the *exact same thing*. This is called "duplication," and it's different from "replication," which is the technical term for professional mass production of CDs.

"Duplicated" CDs are made from a digital file that can be transferred from any computer onto a consumer CD burner. "Replicated" CDs are made from a glass master with a much more sophisticated transfer process, one that is less prone to glitches. Also, the "replicated" CDs are made through individual injection molding of polycarbonate.

One process costs about ten percent more than the other, yet many houses will charge the same amount for both and won't specify which process is being employed (at least in their advertising). They rely on your assumption that a CD is a CD is a CD, with claims such as "1,000 CDs for $500."

When paying for the professional manufacturing of CDs, always ask if you're getting *replication* or *duplication*. If the answer is vague, run! If they give you a choice, always choose replication with a glass master, and make sure the price doesn't suddenly shift from what was originally advertised.

Guaranteed Distribution

Wow! Get your CDs replicated and distributed all at the same time, adding the hot-button word "guaranteed." Sounds as close to an actual major label deal as this arena can provide. But is it true, and is it "distribution" that you couldn't get on your own? Let's begin with a vocabulary lesson: "Distribution," as defined by the standards of commerce, refers to: *"The marketing, apportioning and placement of a volume of physical product owned or controlled by a distributor into a retail environment rather than directly to the customers."* (See "Distribution Companies," page 46.)

Most of the dupe houses who offer "guaranteed distribution" are giving away "distribution" through e-tailers like CD Baby and Amazon.com. But read the definition above. Shipment from a manufacturer to an e-tailer is *not* really "distribution." These companies offer "fulfillment services." In other words, they only ship units and generally do *no* significant marketing or promotion for their individual artists, unlike the Big Four or actual indie distributors like ADA. (See "Digital Rights 'Aggregators' or Digital Distributors," page 47.)

To bolster the claim, some add "digital distribution through iTunes." But if you ask you'll probably find they have no *direct* relationship with iTunes themselves, but rather have subcontracted with another company (called an "aggregator"—see "Digital Deceptions" in this chapter and "Digital Distributors," page 47) that can only *submit* songs for iTunes' approval. Aggregators take a percentage for this of anywhere from 15% to 50%. You can do this yourself without two middlemen. In addition, some of the iTunes "aggregators" that have partnered with CD replicators require the transfer of *exclusive copyrights*. This is hardly "free," and this is a point often glossed over by replicators pitching this feature.

All things totaled, the "guaranteed distribution" promise should probably be renamed: "Guaranteed shipment to e-tailers and licensing with digital rights aggregators."

Not as sexy, but more accurate.

Cheapie Barcodes

It sounds outrageous: as little as $30 for an item for which one must normally pay $750 and buy from a company called GS1 US (formerly the Uniform Code Council). Sometimes they throw it in for free. Artists have been "educated" to believe that a barcode is required to track sales on SoundScan, the company that supplies much of the information for the *Billboard* charts. But does this cheapie barcode really do the same job as the $750 version?

No. The cheapie barcode given to you by the duper is not an entire, unique UPC. It gives your product only the middle five of the complete ten-digit code. The front digits, *which identify the distributor,* remain the same. This practice is called "subbing" and is against GS1 US policy. Many replicators know it's a no-no, but do it anyway, stating that the company can't do anything to stop them. Is there a sacrifice on your part?

Yes. Each title that gets a UPC needs to have a form filed at SoundScan in order to track sales. (See "SoundScan Tells All," page 248.) But if you let the replicator send that to SoundScan for you, you could get tangled credit information and the credit for the sale might go to the replicator (or "distributor") and not to you as the label or artist.

Replicators usually won't send in the forms for you, and most all of them neglect to inform you to do it yourself.

Jitter, Dither, and Blither-Blather: The 1x vs. 4x Debate

The term "1x" refers to the process of making a glass master CD in "real time," where each one second of music takes one second to transfer from your source files to the master disc. Using "4x" replication speeds the process up to four times faster, so every four seconds of music gets transferred in one second. Or thereabouts.

Most houses use 4x and charge between $100–$300 extra if you want 1x. Some try to discourage you completely from going the 1x route by telling you everything from "it's a waste because it won't sound any better" to "it will actually make your CD sound worse." The truth is decoded by answering the real question at the heart of this issue: Is data corruption likely to occur at the faster transfer speed?

Seems a straightforward enough question, but have you ever tried to get a straight answer about the advantages of 1x over 4x from a replication plant? Don't bother unless you have a degree from MIT.

I once asked a regional sales manager for Sony Manufacturing, who said, "At higher speeds the quality is better. The higher the speed, the less jitter."[4] He added that it's really an "emotional issue" and likened the debate to the one in which silly old-timer music fans argue that analog, vinyl LPs sound "more natural" than CDs. (I'm one of those silly old-timer music fans, by the way.)

From the mastering engineer's side of the debate, we get a different viewpoint and one that jibes with my common sense on the subject. They insist on transfers to glass at 1x. The slower the speed the more reliable the transfer.

So who's telling the truth?

Obviously it takes more time to transfer 50 minutes of music in real time than it does at high speeds. When you're doing about 200 glass masters a day, time literally is money. So it stands to reason that manufacturers are going to favor an opinion that says 1x is unnecessary. And you can bet that they will try to sell this concept to replicators as well. Conversely, those on the mastering side have a vested interest in hanging their work on an esoteric process that only someone with trained ears can appreciate. I've mixed and mastered more records than I care to remember, and I believe that if producers and labels spent as much time obsessing over audio quality as they did about talent we wouldn't even have this debate. Heed this advice:

A 1x transfer is not going to help sell more records if the music sucks. Fact.

If you're really an audiophile with bucks to burn, spend it in the *mastering lab* tweaking your product, not the transfer itself. That's where I believe your money will translate into a perceptible difference.

4 Jitter: subtle stuttering that occurs during the digital-to-analog conversion process. It can only be heard by experts, but the effect can be perceived by anyone as a sort of "nervous" feeling when listening to the music.

In a time when there is huge focus on intellectual property rights and "piracy," one never stops to think that your CD replicator might be pirating in order to provide cheaper service. Or worse yet, helping others pirate your music.

To run a legitimate replication house you have to license the machinery from either Philips or Sony (the co-inventors of the CD). Each time you make a copy you are required to pay about an 8-cent royalty to these companies. When you consider that a replicator only charges about 80 cents per copy to the end user, that royalty cuts into their profits by about 10%. A huge chunk. To be competitive, many unscrupulous ones opt to simply not license the technology and fly under the radar.

While some artists may not care if their CD replicator is paying his licensing fees, there are those who like their product to come to market with "clean hands." How can an artist *know* if the replicator they're using is "authorized," and what could making disks on black-market equipment mean to the quality of the end product?

One question immediately leaps to mind: Does the replicator you're thinking of working with make you sign something that states *you* have the right to make copies of the songs on your record? In other words, does he make sure that *you* are not bootlegging?

If not, then he's probably not doing it for anyone else either, and the potential for bootlegging increases dramatically. How can you spot a pirate replicator? Here are a few clues. Grill your replicator on these questions before you give them your business:

- Do they use a fingerprinting system to ensure that only you are making copies of your music?

- Do they carefully check intellectual property rights forms that are submitted with each order?

- Do they encourage their clients to make sure that songwriters and publishers are paid for any "cover tunes" on their CDs? Songwriters are the forgotten victims in the brave new world of digital media, and I feel, in part, it's the replicator's responsibility to help keep everybody's ethics in check.

If the answer to *any* of the above is "no," you're probably dealing with a company that will be attractive to bootleggers and song thieves. Walk away.

Remember that it's a competitive world we operate in, and sometimes the "nice guy" who makes you feel comfortable with a cool vibe could also be the one cutting corners that could hurt you.

⊘ Digital Deceptions & iTunes Scams

From the dawn of pop music until the mid-1990s, if you had put a recording contract in front of most hungry artists they would probably have signed it without thinking twice. But since the First Edition of *Confessions of a Record Producer* artists have become too savvy to go gaga about getting a boilerplate offer from a record company, and, as a result, music biz hucksters have had to become more creative about getting an artist to sign a contract without looking closely at the fine print.

These days, record companies have given the same old pitch several new names, "digital distribution" being the most common one. It sounds relatively benign. Small record companies who advertise this have a new name as well—"aggregators." Their mission: to expand their catalog of copyrights by collecting specific "digital rights" to an artist's master recordings. Some refer to themselves as "digital distributors," or "multimedia providers," but essentially they are all "aggregators," meaning that they aggregate the digital rights and license the masters to places like iTunes. (See "Digital Rights 'Aggregators' or Digital Distributors," page 47, for more on this.)

Now, aggregators are not bad entities any more than record companies; in fact, they are necessary. But they need to be approached with the same caution as you would any traditional record deal offered by a traditional (analog?) label. The start-up costs for an aggregator are cheap and the demand for access to iTunes is high. This attracts many dodgy fly-by-nights.

Unscrupulous aggregators will entice you with advertising like "Get your music on iTunes for free." It sounds so innocent that you could forget that you're being asked to give up something valuable regarding your music. Meanwhile, unlike the traditional record company, the aggregator gives you no up-front money, incurs no risk, and offers no promotion or even the guarantee of distribution, yet he takes about 15% of all money earned from the sales of your downloads. Not bad work if you can get it.

Why are some of these deals so dangerous for the emerging artist? Several reasons.

Artists desperate to get their music "out there" often don't realize the price that they could be paying for the chance. Digital Distribution at the moment is limited mostly to outlets like iTunes, Yahoo, and their competitors—still a minority in terms of music sales—so it seems as though you're not really giving up an important piece of territory in regard to your copyrights. But in the near future this method of retail will grow to literally cosmic proportions with people receiving music "beamed" into their cell phones, iPods, podcasts, and other personal media devices from a vast variety of sources.[5] Meanwhile, "analog" distribution (as I'm calling it simply for contrast) will quietly fade into the sunset. Here's the skinny:

5 According to some experts, about one in four people on the planet owns a cell phone. Most cell phones will be capable of downloading music by the year 2008.

No legitimate label will ever sign an artist if that artist has already given away the exclusive rights to distribute their music on any mass scale.

These "digital distribution" deals are generally about three years long. Not only is this a lifetime in a recording artist's emerging years, it's a lifetime in the world of digital technology. New avenues for digital transmission are opening up every month: satellite radio, Internet radio, podcasting, streaming into restaurants and arenas, you name it.

I could see why, for some, giving up these rights is not a serious thing, especially if you have no intention of ever getting to the bigs. But don't let your investors (or parents as the case may be) learn that you're giving away important rights willynilly just because you think you don't want to "sell out."

What should you do if you feel the need to sign with one of these companies? "Carve out"—as the lawyers say—the rights you want to keep when signing with an aggregator. For example, limit the aggregation deal to just retail sales on the Internet, or to just one particular Internet retailer like iTunes or Yahoo, or whatever company you're having trouble getting your own deal with. No one says you have to accept their boilerplate contract, which usually asks for *all* digital rights in *all* venues.

This negotiation would be plausible and acceptable but for one thing: in many cases you become affiliated with an aggregator through a non-negotiable "click-to-agree" contract posted on their website. Even though these are vital rights to keep protected, they've made signing them away as easy and as thoughtless as clicking "yes" on the standard licensing agreement for installing everyday software, except you're now saying yes to a legally binding *record deal*. To frustrate you even more, in many cases you can't get them on the phone as they are Internet-based entities. Some don't even list their location in the brick-and-mortar world.

All in all, the world of aggregators is still very new and unregulated. Yet the rights they take are fundamental. Be cautious when signing them over. Even if the company seems down-to-earth, remember that companies change hands often, especially in the world of intellectual property. Keep the contract short and keep the rights you give them very limited. If you *can* get the company you're interested in dealing with to talk to you, here are three primary points to consider reworking.

Exclusivity

Most aggregators offer "excusive deals," meaning that only *they* have the right to distribute the masters "digitally." This mimics a traditional "record deal" in that a label engages an artist "exclusively" to record masters. Ideally, you want a completely non-exclusive deal, but this may be unrealistic considering the job of the aggregator: to get your music into many venues. As you'll see below, having more than one aggregator will ultimately lead to serious confusion about how you get paid from these sales. But, as I wrote above, you can try to limit the scope of their distribution territory. Sometimes those aggregators who *insist* on rights in "perpetuity" (lawyer talk for "everywhere you can think of"—see "Internet Labels and Their 'Nonexclusive Contracts," page 219, for more on this) try easing your apprehension by advertising "non-exclusive" deals. This sounds very appealing until you look carefully at the fine print.

In these contracts, the key to whether or not they own your music *exclusively* depends on how the aggregator defines what "digital rights" are. Each contract does so differently. Look carefully at the clauses that define the words "metadata," "license," "content," and "masters." In nearly every case I've seen, the definitions of these words have been engineered so that the "non-exclusive" rights you get to retain are to the *master recordings* themselves, but the esoteric things like how the metadata is filed and placed on their server is owned by the company *exclusively*. In other words, you get to keep rights to your original recordings but not the "digital file" that people will download off the Internet. Clever.

Make sure when dealing on this point to make it clear that if you terminate the contract (see below) you get to keep what are called ISRC codes. These are the online retail sales "fingerprints" for the masters as they are being downloaded from the Internet. Like a barcode, this is sort of like a Social Security number for your recordings, and it should travel to whatever company you license your music to. Aggregators typically get them from the RIAA the same month you "sign" their contract. Make sure that this ISRC number—and any other data necessary for you to repost your music elsewhere—is yours to keep once the deal is over.

Payment Threshold

If you just sell one or two downloads for 99 cents a month, the aggregator may owe you only about a buck. Aggregators claim that they would go broke if they had to write checks for a dollar to everyone every month, so virtually all of the digital distribution contracts have a "payment threshold." This is a financial goal post that you have to reach in order to trigger a payment. In some cases that threshold can be as high as $200 a month, and this is *after* they take their 15%. That means in most cases you would have to sell about 338 downloads a month. (Not 200 downloads, as you might initially suppose if you are thinking in terms of about $1 a sale. See footnote for the math.)[6]

6 Example: For a 99-cent download on iTunes, about 30 cents goes to Apple, leaving about 70 cents that is passed on to the aggregator. Then the aggregator takes its 15%, leaving 59 cents. 59 cents divided into $200 is about 338.

Since aggregators figure that about 400 sales is far more than the average indie artist sells in a 30-day period (at least as long as physical CDs are still selling), they may never have to pay you unless you can get that threshold down or negotiate a "liquidation period." This is a set time after which, no matter what, you get paid out. Six months seems reasonable. Hopefully your aggregator will still be in business.

Termination and "Opting Out," or See You Later, Aggregator

"Who cares if I sign a bad deal? The contact says I can opt out with 30 days' notice." Does it really? I've examined many of these contracts, and only a couple offer a true "opt out" option. The lawyers I work with agree that most aggregators are rather clever about getting around this promise, using phrases like, "You may terminate this agreement at any time by providing Company with thirty (30) days' written notice of your *intention* to terminate." You might read this and think you simply fire off an email and then you're out of the deal 30 days later, but this is not so. Read it carefully. An *intention* to terminate is not necessarily the same as "opting out" and *actual* termination does not mean that you are free to go elsewhere *at that time*.

Now, this is not necessarily designed to be underhanded. Many of the clauses in an aggregation deal *must* survive your decision to terminate because the aggregator has to now go to every place they licensed your masters (iTunes, Yahoo, MSN, AOL, etc.) and retract your music from all the digital retailers that they licensed it to. This could take months.

Since the advent of "digital distribution," many people have tried "opting out" of old deals in favor of newer, better ones only to find that now there are multiple copies of their same masters on download services months later, each paying different royalty rates. Imagine seeing one of your titles on iTunes three times, and each one is attached to a different aggregator that each pays a different rate to you. Other artists have had their songs posted and sold without *any* compensation because there were multiple aggregators fighting over who should get paid. The net result is that even months after sending an "opt out" letter, these requests will likely go unrealized for many, many months.[7]

7 This could be due to a variety of factors not within the aggregator's control, not the least of which is understaffing for this "retraction" procedure.

In general, "opt outs" are a fallacy. No company can really get you out of the system with 30 days' notice. This might change as the network evolves, but don't expect it anytime soon. I suspect that you'll see mention of this feature start to fade away from legitimate aggregators' advertising, as it cannot really be fulfilled reasonably.

⊘ Independent A&R Services

With all the action happening in New York, L.A., and Nashville, one wonders how songwriters in the sticks get exposure to Big Four artists. Don't worry, there are quite a number of companies out there willing to act as a bridge between "the industry" and writers in Podunk—for a fee, of course.

They call themselves "independent A&R companies." Their pitch: They're plugged into the network and can get your music (provided you pass their "audition process") in the face of big players in the industry. They charge for this service an average of $300 *a year*, plus ancillary costs—a small price to pay if even one of your songs gets placed through their service. Some claim that the money is only an "application fee" to cover the costs of reviewing your material, and if you're rejected you'll get most of it back. Few artists do. Regardless, is it worth the $300-plus even if you are "accepted"? That depends on how you look at it. On the good side:

- You get critiques of your music allegedly by "pros" (for about $5–$10 a song).

- None that I am aware of take any percentages, like a manager might. And you can quit at any time with no strings attached.

- The services are located near big companies, and, let's face it, you're not getting to L.A. or New York on a regular basis these days.

- You get to attend conferences where you can meet other people who are also paying $300 a year, as well as some of the company's "screeners" (more on them below). Many people tell me that they have made great connections at some of these events. You could pay far more than $300 just to go to SXSW[8] without the "A&R service."[9]

- Most of their "successes" are in the movie area, where they submit your music to supervisors to get it placed in films. That kind of real exposure is difficult to get on your own.

On the down side, notwithstanding the annual conferences (which only one such company offers), you will probably never get to meet any of these industry hotshots, even the ones who like your music. And that's the good news. The bad news is that for the most part these services just don't deliver the results that most are hoping they will. Here's why:

8 South By Southwest. A large annual music conference.

9 Actually, this perk is offered only by one of the leading (and oldest) such companies, TAXI.

On the surface, the concept of an independent A&R service sounds appealing and logical. After all, doesn't an agent or publisher do the same or similar thing, and for high commissions or percentages? Yes and no.

If the quality of the material was the primary component determining what song was placed on a major artist's album, then independent A&R companies might have a slam-dunk argument for their services (provided they had the best songwriters as members). But in reality, most songs are placed on pop records because of personal relationships. This relationship is what justifies the percentages taken by a publisher or manager. (See "Managers," page 11, and "Publishing Companies," page 35.)

If you're the manager of a top act or music supervisor for a big studio picture and you need material, you've put the word out and have already received submissions faster than you can hail a cab in New York. You might find yourself (within mere days) sitting behind your desk with towers of compilation CDs from several sources: Warner Chappell, Peer Music, Sony, Bug Music, and other reputable publishing houses. You might also have another 20 or so CDs from personal songwriter connections that you've made through the years.

And then, off to the side, near the radiator, the package that came by U.S. mail, from someone with little to no personalized connection to you, are the compilations from independent A&R companies. Who do you think is going to get your best consideration? Even within the CDs at the top of the pile from some of the top songwriters in the country, the ones with the best chance are those with whom you already have a *strategic alliance*.

For instance, if you're managing an artist signed to Sony Music, writers from a Sony-owned publishing company will likely get first crack. If you're a music supervisor choosing cuts for a movie produced by Universal Pictures, songs by one of the hundreds of Universal artists will have a leg up before the word gets out to independent A&R services, who, not being part of the corporate family, have not pre-agreed to license songs on the same terms as the rest of the industry.[10]

But independent A&R companies argue: Once in a blue moon someone gets lucky. A new writer with a great song slips though and wins the lottery. And true, sometimes this happens through an independent A&R company. But how often?

Now, you'll notice that I don't use the word "scam" to title this section like I do in some others. The reason: What most of these companies do to entice you is *not* illegal or even *misleading*. However, that doesn't mean that giving in to their seductive pitch isn't about as prudent as hoping to win a jackpot for a single bet at a roulette wheel. And guess what? That's not just a random analogy. The odds of success are in the same neighborhood.

10 All publishers in the major label system license songs at the same rate, three-quarters of the current compulsory rate (about 9 cents per copy sold; see page 82.) Licensing a song from outside "the Big Four family" can be considerably more expensive.

Let's do some basic math. Several such companies generally advertise only a handful of major-label placements even after being in business for years. (If there are more successes, then they are rather quiet about it.) During that same time they may have taken fees from about 7,000 members each year. Let's say that if they've been in business for an average of five years, then that is approximately 35,000 members in total. (Granted, a percentage of those are renewed members.) Even if they could advertise 10 major artist placements out of 35,000 over double that time (none have that many, to my knowledge), that's still only 1:350 odds. The roulette wheel is looking like a sure thing compared to this.

You have to decide if, for all the costs involved, those are playable odds. You also have to trust that your music tickles the fancy of their screeners, who are often not really as "highly placed" as advertised. They are generally paid around $40 an hour for their "golden ears"—less than the cost of an experienced recording engineer.

The other main caution to keep in mind concerns the way these companies' service works. Your membership buys you access to a bulletin board (usually online) where "opportunities" are posted.[11] You read them, decide if your music fits one, and send in your songs with a check for each song. In some cases you will be told that your music hit the mark and was passed forward to the "client."

But, according to my sources who have worked as screeners, in the majority of cases the "screener's report" will tell you that your music was not appropriate and was rejected for this particular job. You will probably never learn the name of the screener. And even if the screener thinks your songs are the bomb, the client could still reject it. This is worse than a "no sale," because even if your song was not right for this particular job, the label exec may have still liked your work and wanted to "bookmark" you for another one. Except that because of this system, you never met him or learned his name. If independent A&R services kept such records in a cross-referenced database, giving their members who distinguished themselves a break, I might be inclined to say, "Now that's worth some annual cash." But to my knowledge only one claims to.[12]

But, in the defense of such companies, one has to remember that they are all relatively new to the landscape of the music business. As more consolidation causes the "emerging artist" pyramid to broaden at the base, the opportunities for independent A&R companies may also be increased. But for now, with only a handful of major labels (about 35) and film music supervisors available to market to, it looks to me like these companies are necessary only for those too intimidated to push their own work.

11 Over the past couple of years I have received reports from ex-members of one such company claiming that some of the "opportunities" posted were contrived to get members to send in submissions for additional fees. I have found nothing in my research to substantiate such claims. On the other hand, since no personal information about the "client" is given to the members and since there is no independent oversight on the operations of these companies, it's impossible to verify the legitimacy of posts made by them.

12 TAXI keeps personal libraries and on occasion plays "matchmaker" for former members when a song fits the bill. Their website states that one such case resulted in a top-five hit for two former members from Orange County, California.

Yes, I know that holding down a day job makes it tough to cultivate connections, especially if you're located outside the urban areas. But the Internet has made geography an almost insignificant factor. I have clients in England and Australia who sell songs to Hollywood without any assistance whatsoever from independent A&R companies or from agents. The signature benefit of this: Once you make a connection personally, you get to keep that connection for life, which, in my opinion, is better than just leasing someone else's Rolodex for $300-plus a year. One leading independent A&R company readily admits on their website, "If you're trying to land a record deal, nothing works better than hitting the road, playing hundreds of gigs, and selling thousands of CDs from the trunk of your car."

I agree. If you are a self-starter, save your money for a more productive marketing item. But . . . if you feel that the pressure of marketing your music is too overwhelming to do from your remote location and feel strongly about taking a shot with one of these services, here's what you need to think about and inquire into vigorously:

- Who are their screeners? Most won't want to give up a specific list, but it's quite important since these are the gatekeepers standing between you and the "industry" after you pay your annual fee. You don't need specific names, but a general—*truthful*—description of their backgrounds seems a reasonable request. Also, along these lines, does the company screen the screeners? Ask about what kind of quality control they employ to make sure their screeners are not just jealous music biz has-beens.

- Some independent A&R companies have more solid strategic relationships with majors than others. Make them prove it to you in more than just a vague blurb on their website before you write them a check.

- Read their success stories carefully. They are often very vague in the details and rarely if ever offer the names of the companies they "got a deal" with. Why? Is this privileged information? Puhleeze. Ask for an actual referral. A client's website will do. If the A&R service got this person a real deal on a real label, it will likely be so stated on their site in the form of a "thank you."

- Also, in regard to testimonials, beware of ones that use the phrase, "One of our members got a deal with…" as a header. Such wording is often deliberately designed to help you overlook the fact that the independent A&R company had *nothing* to do with the member getting the deal. A reputable company will be able to prove their track record.

- Find out their lowest rate. Often they advertise one rate but run specials with far lower rates.

- Ask about their refund policy. If they don't offer one, they can't have very much confidence in their service.

To research this yourself type "independent A&R" into your favorite search engine and poke around.

Good luck.

CHAPTER EIGHTEEN

>Sneaky Lawyer Stuff

The University of Colorado has published a study that surveyed various sides of the controversy surrounding the testing of animals in medical laboratories. After collating questionnaires from activists and researchers, the study reached a unanimous conclusion: Instead of rats, labs should use lawyers to perform their various tests on. The study concluded this for two reasons: (1) the lab technicians didn't develop as much of an attachment for the attorneys as they did for the rats, and (2) there were some things that the rats wouldn't do.

We all love to lawyer-bash—even lawyers joke about how devious they can be. Well, it is not so funny if you happen to get your toes stepped on during the attorney minuet. Following are a few dance steps.

Disclaimer: Not all attorneys do these things. Only most of the ones that I've met.

> The "I Forgot to Mark the Contract" Trick

Most lawyer tricks revolve around one main concept—wasting the opposing side's time and money. Every attorney works by the hour. Even if they agree to do a job for a fixed fee, they are figuring how many hours they will put into a project. Once that time threshold is crossed, their enthusiasm and the quality of their work will decline rapidly. The tricky attorney will try to exhaust the other lawyer's time in an attempt to encroach on that threshold.

When an attorney reads a contract for the first time, he or she may take several hours just to go through it and make notes for changes. The industry norm is to underline the changes with a blue or red pencil, making them obvious to the attorney on the other side of the negotiation. Some attorneys, in an attempt to confuse or exhaust the patience of their opponent, will make some of the changes that were requested but "forget to mark the contract." This makes the contract look like a first draft, and it now must be read from scratch, just as if it were a new contract.

Sometimes they will send a cover memo alleging that all the changes were made but in reality keep some of the old provisions. They will "red-pencil" only the changes that they want the other attorney to see.

The hope is that perhaps the other attorney is not as observant as they should be and will not take the time to read the entire contract over again.

Since the advent of word processing software that tracks changes to a document, lawyers have had to become more clever about this technique. "Tracking changes" works by automatically highlighting any alterations to a document. But all one has to do to override this is create a new document with the same name as the old one, and *poof*, you can effortlessly camouflage changes. High tech gives this old trick a villainous twist that exploits our ever-expanding trust of computers.

❷ Virtual Terms

Virtual terms are terms that are only offered when someone is trying to lure you into taking a job—for example, when a producer or label promises someone X, Y, and Z, but when the contract arrives those terms are nowhere to be found.

If you call them on this, the attorney will usually say that a mistake was made or the secretary sent a "standard agreement," not the special one that was for you. The conversation will usually end with the attorney saying that all the original terms of the agreement are still in place and he will forward the contract ASAP.

After some time goes by and it doesn't arrive, you start to worry. You call the attorney. He says (if he comes to the phone) that it must be in the mail and you shouldn't worry about it. He will probably encourage you to start the gig and you'll sign the contract whenever it gets there.

If you persist in wanting to see the agreement before you start working, expect to be fired, or else something will happen where the job is delayed and they will "call you as soon as we work it out." Not surprisingly, you will never hear from them again.

Believe it or not, these people are doing you a favor. They never intended to pay you anyway. Unless there is a contract or at least a signed deal memo—watch out.

❷ Internet Labels and Their "Nonexclusive" Contracts

In the past few years many artists have been attracted to online "independent" labels and their folksy offer to distribute records for little or no cost to the artist. These companies, which have cool animated introductions on their websites, are leveraging the popular theory that millions of people will have access to the record because there are just so many damn people using the Internet. They promise to distribute a record to stores as well as create links from other websites. They rarely reject anybody, so long as the artist pays the small up-front fees for barcodes and administration (usually not more than $100).

This "get signed for a hundred bucks" offer sounds like a dream for many artists who've already produced an album's worth of material and are tired of dealing with major label bullshit. Online indies, as I call them, offer a turnkey record deal. No managers or lawyers to deal with, and no obnoxious A&R comments like, "Well, I don't hear a single." Screw that. You'll show 'em all, put the damn record on the street, and keep all the profits. It's a nice dream, and these online indies attract excellent artists whose music is probably too "niche" (read: too original) for most major label marketing plans. But there is a real danger.

First, understand that some of these online indies are actually shells for larger labels. (To get an idea of who owns what, refer to the family trees on pages 297–302.) But aside from this trickery, here's the real snag: These companies know that no artist will sign over their *exclusive* rights to a virtual company that offers no advance. So, buried within their seemingly benign contract is a nasty loophole that could tie you to these people *forever*.

Most of these contracts start off with a congenial intro that says something like, "You are entering a special place where dreams are fulfilled and hopes grow. In order for it to work we must have an agreement, so here it is!" It will then con you into thinking that you are entering into a one-year contract that will pay you 70% of any money earned from selling your recordings through them and that the licensing of your record to them is "nonexclusive." Which means that you can enter into the same agreement with anyone else.

It's phrased like this: "We agree to provide You throughout the Territory and during the Sales Period with listing of your Recordings in E-Stores during the Term."

Followed by this clause: "You grant to us throughout the Territory and during the Sales Period the rights to use your name(s), professional and/or group name(s), photographs and other images and likeness of You, biographical and/or other information concerning You regarding all of our business activities."

Sounds good. 70%!!! The major labels didn't even offer you that much (more like 12%), and it's only a year contract. How much harm can that be? If you hate them, it's over in a year. Right?

Wrong.

The key lies in how this contract defines the "Sales Period" and the "Territory." At the bottom of the contract the following definitions can be found:

"'Territory' means the Universe."

"'Sales Period' means the time period beginning on the Signing Date and continuing in perpetuity for each of your Recordings in each country of the Territory."

For those new to this business, "perpetuity" is lawyer lingo meaning "forever."

So, an accurate translation of the opening paragraph would be this:

"You grant to us throughout the universe and till the end of time itself, the rights to use all your recordings (even ones you didn't send to us), your name(s), professional and/or group name(s), photographs and other images and likeness of You, biographical and/or other information concerning You in all of our business activities."

Add to this the fact that you have to supply them with the produced CD and press materials. Their investment is about $0.00 and they get to own you completely.

Even though they say the licensing is "nonexclusive," they do this knowing that major label deals are *always* exclusive and will make you swear that you've broken ties with everyone else before they allow you to sign with them. Oops. Can't sell your vital organs to more than one hospital, can you? Well, you can try, but you'd be guilty of fraud. And you can kiss your career good-bye if you're caught playing that game.

You don't have to be a Harvard Law grad to see how this scam works. The virtual record company plays the numbers; they sign thousands of artists a year, waiting for the day when one of them gets an offer from a major label. Needless to say, getting off the old "nonexclusive" deal will be like a Hollywood divorce. Expect pain.

Still think it's worth 100 bucks?

Before you go disconnecting your computer, understand that many companies do this legitimately and want nothing more than to see you succeed. Knowing which type you're getting involved with can be tricky. Pay attention to the contract you are signing. For more on this, see the section in the previous chapter called "Digitial Deceptions," page 208.

⊘ The Little Squeeze

I love this one. Watching it in action is like watching *The Sting* with Robert Redford and Paul Newman. The Little Squeeze, as I call it, is when two or more parties conspire to "squeeze out" someone who is impeding the progress of the deal. Now the sad part is that the someone in question could be impeding the deal for legitimate reasons, or they could just be a pain in the ass. But in either case, everyone else involved wants them out of the way. What makes it hard is that the squeezee is usually placed so well in the game that the squeezers will have to use some finesse to push him aside.

Here's an example that I was party to.

In the mid-'80s I knew an up-and-coming manager who had only one act. He asked me to engineer the demo that he was producing and I did. Afterward I took it to a record company I was doing some work for at the time. They liked the artist but not the production. This was a small record company and they didn't have a lot of money to spend. They knew that I had delivered good masters for them in the past with a small budget, so they said they would put up some money if I produced it rather than the manager.

The manager felt that he should produce it, despite the fact that he could not get a deal with the tape he had made. Even if he had, no label would have let him produce, since he didn't have a track record producing *anything*. This point became a deal-breaker, and although everyone tried to talk sense into him, he wouldn't listen. He was determined to produce, and it was killing the deal; the artist would never get signed, I would lose the investment of my time in the project, and the label that was interested in signing the artist would not get a good act. Everyone was being screwed because of this manager's arrogance—especially his client, the artist, whose career would go down the toilet if he didn't get a deal real soon.

In came the lawyer—my lawyer. He suggested a partnership between the label and a group of us as *general partners*. The label would put up $25,000 and the partners would collectively put up the other $25,000 to make a record, making a total budget of $50,000. The record label and the general partners (GPs) would do a one-off master licensing deal. (See "The Artist/Producer Production Deal," page 144.)

The GPs would consist of myself, the manager/producer, and my lawyer. We would have 50% ownership of the master. The other 50% would belong to the label.

This kind of deal is not uncommon in the indie record world, where no one party has the full amount of money to put up. But here's the catch. The 50% ownership would be divided up equally among the GPs based on the percentage of their participation. So if the total partnership between myself, the manager, and my attorney was worth $25,000, then each of us would have to put up $8,333.33 for it to be an equal partnership. Sounds simple enough, right?

The label, the manager, my lawyer, and of course myself would transfer their share into my production company's account. The checks for the production would be written off my company's checking account, and I would be required to keep all receipts for the end of the project to verify that the money was spent.

Now, what the manager didn't know is that the label and I wanted him out of the production picture, but we needed his participation in order to sign the artist to the deal. The lawyer provided the means by drafting the partnership agreement. We gained the manager's confidence with the partnership concept and then used our money to leverage him out. Here's how:

He couldn't come up with $8,333.33 at the time we needed it. So we agreed that he would only have to put up what he had, and my lawyer and I would make up the rest. He only had $4,000 to invest, so we put up the balance of $21,000 to complete the partnership. This made the manager only a 12.5% owner in the partnership. Seems fair, right? He's only putting up 12.5% of the money. Here's the ballbuster:

In reality, the record company only put $10,000 in my account. My lawyer put in nothing. I put in $2,000 and the manager put in $4,000. That's only $16,000. That's what I made the record on. Except that I made arrangements with the recording studio to supply me with enough invoices (fake ones, of course) to total $50,000. Studios are used to doing shady things like this for producers if the relationship is a good one.[1]

The manager was actually entitled to a 25% interest, but with creative invoicing he became a tiny minority partner. With him in a minority position, it was easy to outvote him with decisions like who would produce, engineer, and so on.

To add insult to injury, I claimed to go *over budget*. In a partnership situation, when costs go over budget all the partners are required to make up the difference.

The manager claimed to be tapped out of money, so the record company paid off his share of—you guessed it—$4,000. This reduced the manager's percentage participation even further. Oh, well.

The moral of the story is:

Lead, follow, or get out of the way.

[1] See the recording budgets in "The Virtual Budget and the Virtual Producer's Fee," page 153.

❂ Letters of Misdirection

This is a name I've given to LODs when they are designed to undermine the deal.[2] It is not uncommon for an artist's or label's lawyer to argue for months over small points, driving the producer's legal bills through the roof, before they finally come to terms, only to draft a letter of direction that circumvents the payment terms. Here's an example:

2 See "Letters of Direction," page 164.

The artist's lawyer will argue that the LOD is a sort of "permission slip" generated by the artist allowing the label to forward the producer's share directly to the producer. But what if the major label refuses to sign the LOD? If an artist has agreed that the producer will be paid via an LOD directly from the major label, then the assumption is that label will do just that. Despite that, many labels are reluctant to sign.

If this occurs, the producer may find himself without a right to audit the label and get his money. In order to make the label sign and honor the LOD, he will have to sue the artist for what's called "performance," meaning that the artist is not performing his or her part of the contract in making the label sign and pay. The only way for the artist to make the label pay is to sue the label. The artist, of course, will never do that.

The telltale sign of letters of misdirection is that they use language like "This letter is a courtesy only; the producer is not a beneficiary of it." Meaning that just because the artist has given the label permission to give the producer money, the label doesn't have to honor it.

The best way to avoid this sort of thing is for the producer's lawyer to draft the LOD himself and have both parties sign it. The producer's lawyer will usually wait for the artist's lawyer to draft it because that's the way it should be—the contractor should generate the first draft of any agreement for the contractee. But it doesn't always work out that way, as you will see.

❂ The First Draft Is the Coldest

Most lawyers will tell you that the person generating the first draft of an agreement is at a disadvantage. It's true. Not only is their hand being exposed first, but the cost of generating the first draft is the hard hit in one's legal bill. Revisions can get just as pricey, but if it's a simple and basic agreement, then the majority of the bill will be for customizing the first draft to the specific job.

Since many contracts happen after the deal is done, the sleazy lawyer will take advantage of this and send a "false first draft." This is a contract that has nothing to do with the deal that you made. Now bear in mind that this does not happen often on standard record deals and production deals, but many up-and-coming artists and producers sign unconventional deals with sleazy vanity labels to get their foot in the door.

Let's say, for example, that an artist and a producer want to develop some songs together. The plan is to record some demos at the producer's studio and then shop them to a label. Pretty basic, right?

There seems no point in doing an expensive contract at this time since it's not even clear if they will like working together, so they proceed on good faith, the way many artists do. After several months, some good work comes out of it, and the artist takes the tape to a lawyer, who gives it to an A&R person at a label. They bite, and the game is afoot. Now a contract must be formalized between the artist and the producer.

Whatever their original verbal agreement was, it will now be thrown out the window by the artist's sneaky lawyer. He will forward a contract that is a production deal, but not one that pertains to the producer as a cowriter or copublisher. Also, the points in the agreement will be ridiculously low compared to the industry standard.

Naturally the producer will respond with some surprise and confront the lawyer and/or the artist. This is where the relationship starts to break down. The label will usually side with the artist and tell both parties to work it out soon or the deal is off. The lawyer for the artist will then say something like, "Well, if you don't like my boilerplate, then you generate your own first draft." This is unethical and downright wrong, but it happens a lot. The producer will now have to spend the money him/herself to generate the contract that the artist should be paying for. Sometimes they will, but sometimes they will just go with the flow so as not to rock the boat and spoil the deal.

This happened to me twice. After the second time, I had two lawyers draft my own customized agreement that I use whenever I feel I'm dealing with a shyster attorney. When the artist's lawyer sees my agreement, they usually get in gear and do the right thing.

➋ "Voted Out"—The Band as a Corporate Entity

When you see four or five members on the cover of a CD, the assumption is that these individuals make up the band. But what is a band?

This seemingly obvious question in fact is more complex than most musicians know. A band that plays in a garage or in some of the clubs around town can be anything. But once the act is signed to a major label, the time comes to decide who really will and will not make up the band as a corporate entity, meaning the band as a business.

Creating a corporation is the process of creating a new entity that will own all the things that the band or artist produces: songs, logos, the images that get printed on T-shirts, endorsements of musical equipment, and so on. Why not just let the artists own everything themselves? The answer given by many lawyers is, in order to protect the band from lawsuits it's simpler if there is only one artist in the group. If the corporation owns the copyright of the songs, then a chaser going after a copyright sues the corporation, not the artist.[3]

PAYING A DRUMMER FOR NOT PLAYING

My friend Jordan was the drummer in Atom (not their real name), a mid-1980s hair band. Although he had been with the group since the beginning, he was asked to be subcontracted after the writing members of the group were offered a deal on A&M. Feeling a bit bitter, he asked for $1,000 a week. Feeling guilty, the band agreed, and the label agreed to cut a weekly check on the band's behalf to Jordan. As you can guess, the $1,000 was charged to the band's account.

Although the band was advanced about $500,000, most of this money went to the producer and the production of the record, a 48-track digital recording, which at the time was very avant-garde. Meanwhile, Jordan collected his check every week.

After a lengthy production and marketing campaign, A&M asked the band to do a tour to promote the record. They agreed. Jordan, still under contract, became the single most expensive member on the road.

The tour was unsuccessful. Record sales didn't budge. The market had been oversaturated with metal bands, and Atom decided to regroup and alter their sound a bit. They let go of every one of the subcontracted players, including Jordan. One problem: Jordan's contract was good as long as A&M didn't drop them from the label. So while a broke and busted Atom auditioned new members and wrote new songs, Jordan stayed home and collected his $1,000-a-week salary.

Think ahead when forming your corporation.

But what if there are two songwriters in the group? Traditionally it's only the writing members that will be stockholders in the corporation. The other members become subcontracted sideplayers. They draw a salary or are paid on a gig-by-gig basis even though they appear everywhere the two main players appear—on album sleeves, at personal appearances, MTV interviews, the works.

The sideplayers often feel cheated by this until they get used to it. Suddenly you are not a team anymore. There are advantages to being a sideplayer, however. You are guaranteed to be paid, usually by letter of direction from the main label. I have known several situations where subcontracted drummers ended up making more than the stockholders in a group (see the sidebar on page 225).

This is where it can get very tricky. Even if all the members of the band are part of the corporation, that is not foolproof protection against one member being ousted. Each band member holds a percentage of stock or ownership in the corporation. Sometimes the stock is divided equally. For example, if the band has four members, then

WHO BUTTERS MARILYN'S BREAD?

In June 1997, Marilyn Manson found himself the subject of a lawsuit by his cowriter Daisy Berkowitz. It seems that Marilyn neglected to pay Daisy (whose real name is Scott Putesky) his share of the royalties from those cool hit tunes they penned together. Daisy trusted Marilyn to be the executor of the copyrights by signing over the administration of his share to a company he thought was equally owned by the entire group.

In his suit, Daisy claimed that the group's attorney intentionally drafted the agreement in Marilyn's favor. He also claimed that Marilyn told him signing the agreement would guarantee that Daisy would be in the band *for life!*

After the record was certified platinum, Daisy asked for some money. Instead, he was fired from the band without a cent. His ten-count lawsuit includes malpractice against the attorney for not making him aware of the inherent conflict of interest in representing both sides.

I'm not holding my breath for a quick outcome on this. I think Daisy will eventually get something, but only after he spends gobs of cash. Word of advice: Before signing anything, always get your *own* counsel.

each member would get 25% of the stock. But sometimes the division is not equitable. Let's say that one member of the group is the clear frontman or -woman. They might get 51% of the stock and the remaining 49% would go to the sideplayers.

The difference between a corporation band and a regular band is that in a corporate environment decisions are made by majority vote. If the one member of the group with 51% chooses to fire everyone else, he or she can get away with it because he or she is the majority stockholder. He or she can fire a person even if that person is a founding member of the band (see the "Marilyn" sidebar).

❷ Legal-ease?

Legalese is the language of lawyers, and anyone who has ever looked at a contract prepared by lawyers can attest to the conundrums they create for the rest of us. Why say, "You can't do that," when you can say, "That action is contraindicated"? Well, the skeptical answer, and one I'm partial to, is that it makes your client more dependent on you.

Revealed below are some of the basics of legalese. These are only a few of the key phrases, but they will get you started. (A complete book of translations would be as large as several dictionaries.)

For simplicity, the examples below are written from the artist's point of view, but they apply to producers, labels, and just about any situation where talent is being contracted.

After this section, go on to the next section, "Decoding of an Actual Warner Bros. Record Contract," and see how some sneaky lawyers took advantage of multitudes of recording artists during the '70s and '80s with an actual slimebag agreement.

Note: Nothing in this book or this section should be construed as legal advice.

WHEN IT SAYS:	IT REALLY MEANS:
Some Easy Ones	
"Audiophile Recording(s)," "LPs," or "Phonorecords"	An antiquated term for a record, CD, or tape.
"Pursuant to the receipt of a financial instrument"	"When money is actually received," as opposed to when the contract *says* you will be paid. There is a distinct difference.

WHEN IT SAYS:	IT REALLY MEANS:
"Commercially satisfactory master"	An album that the record company feels they can easily sell without too much effort.
"In perpetuity throughout the known universe"	Anyplace you can think of and "until the end of time itself." This bit of sci-fi is designed to cover all possible territory in which any money might be made. It almost always pertains to the transfer of rights and is taken to mean that the rights granted are granted forever, just in case someday we find a way to sell the record on the planet Jupiter.

Advanced Legonics: Loophole Creators

"Notwithstanding anything herein contained to the contrary . . ."	"If anything else in the contract contradicts the next half of *this* sentence, then *this* sentence is the *prevailing rule*." This bit of jargon is one of the biggest red flags. Often it is used to construct a trapdoor or "loophole" by creating an exception to what is fundamentally promised in the agreement. The exception created will often be a brutal and costly one.
"Except as otherwise hereinafter set forth . . ."	"Except when the contract says otherwise further on down the page or later in the agreement." Upon seeing this phrase one should carefully scan through the entire contract to find exceptions to what is about to be promised in the second half of the same sentence. Example: "Except as otherwise herein set forth, artist will be paid on 100% of sales." For certain, buried somewhere within the body of the contract there is a phrase that will contradict this. Often it will begin with one of the phrases mentioned in this section.

WHEN IT SAYS:	IT REALLY MEANS:
	Note that where the phrase above this ("Notwithstanding anything . . .") creates a loophole by making specific exceptions to general concepts, this does the opposite: it creates a loophole by making generalities out of things that appear specific.
"Notwithstanding the foregoing . . ."	"What follows is an exception to what was just said a moment ago." This is a first cousin to the two phrases right above it. You will often find that these three seemingly innocent words are being used to carve a loophole in certain obligations that the record company would prefer to dodge. Following it may also be the things they want the artist to do that will be over and above the "normal" duties listed in the agreement.
"Without limiting the generality of the foregoing, the Artist (producer, writer, etc.) hereby . . ."	The words *following* this phrase should be taken to have the *broadest possible interpretation.* This phrase is often used when discussing the transfer of copyrights and is a common strategy of an insecure attorney. Instead of listing every possible situation or grant of rights (and risk leaving something out), the attorney will insert a phrase like this one, which basically means "plus anything else I can't think of right now."

Advanced Legonics II: Confidence Instillers

" . . . shall be completed in a timely fashion."	Whenever the word "timely" appears in a contract, it's time for caution. Contracts that use this phrase are attempting to keep certain time frames nebulous and subjective, often for the benefit of the party offering the contract.

WHEN IT SAYS:	IT REALLY MEANS:
	Example: "The recording of the album shall be completed in a timely fashion." Who decides what "timely" is? Answer: The one who has the checkbook. A fair agreement will usually spell out time frames *precisely*.
"Company shall consult with Artist on . . ."	A meaningless phrase designed to instill false confidence in the artist that the record company is duty-bound to ask the artist's permission on a particular subject. A provision containing this phrase usually refers to cover art or selection of the single. In reality, if the company even says to the artist, "Hey, we already decided this, but what do you think?" they have "consulted." Artists' lawyers and managers use this one to bamboozle their clients into thinking they did a great job negotiating on their behalf. It's a joke.
"Approval from Artist will not unreasonably be withheld."	Living in the same neighborhood as the previous phrase will be this little trickster. It sounds as if the artist has been given power over something, but in fact it's the opposite. This phrase actually prevents the artist from holding out too strongly on any issue that needs to be determined after the contract is written (like cover art, tour support, and marketing decisions). Example: "Artist's approval of cover art not to be unreasonably withheld." Although this seems to protect both parties, in essence it only protects the record company, because they have more leverage in deciding what is and is not "reasonable."

WHEN IT SAYS:	IT REALLY MEANS:
"Prior to the expiration of the applicable period"	"Before time has run out" on whatever issue this phrase is connected to. This would be relatively harmless except that figuring out when the "applicable period" begins and ends in most recording contracts can be confusing. Scan carefully for any sentences using this phrase and see if the "applicable period" is really what you think it is. Lawyers have sneaky ways of extending a two-year contract so that it turns into a three- or four-year contract.
"The invalidity or unenforceability of any provision hereof shall not affect the validity or enforceability of any other provision hereof."	"If one item in the contract is later deemed invalid or illegal, the rest of the contract will still be in effect." This can be a pain, because it gives the label a license to throw all kinds of junk into the contract that they know is unconstitutional. If a judge later determines that one clause is completely enslaving (in legal terms this is called "overreaching"—how demure), then the artist will still be bound to produce and perform for the company.
"Company shall give reasonable notice of . . ."	Usually pertains to the label's legal requirement to send an artist relevant information about the status of their recording agreement. It often refers to royalty statements. In reality, the record company won't give a rat's ass whether they notified the artist or not. If the artist didn't get the notice, the label will assume it must have been lost in the mail, with the mail being "reasonable notice" in the eyes of the record company. Good contracts will insist on "registered mail" as reasonable notice.

❷ Decoding of an Actual Warner Bros. Record Contract

Now we're going to put the above lesson into action. We're going to examine a common fraud in the record industry: It's customary to offer new recording artists a sliding royalty scale for future albums. So if an artist is only getting 12% on album one, the record company might offer an incentive by saying, "But we'll give you 14% on album two and 15% on album three if you turn out to be really good and turn in all your records on time."

"On time" is the linchpin here and the key to the empty promise of higher royalties, as you'll see in a minute.

Below are the first three paragraphs of a major label recording contract. First review the paragraph. Directly beside each you will find the TRANSLATION, broken down line by line in plain English. Then, below that, I restate the clause to show how it might actually be applied in reality. Remember, this is actual language from a Warner Bros. contract that was in common use throughout the '70s and '80s.

4 "Limpidity": legalese for "clearness."

Note: COMPANY refers to the record company, ARTIST refers to the recording artist. Key phrases mentioned in the previous chart are in bold for limpidity.[4]

EXCLUSIVE ARTIST'S RECORDING
AGREEMENT

1. COMPANY hereby engages ARTIST's exclusive personal services as a recording artist in connection with the production of records and ARTIST hereby accepts such engagement and agrees to exclusively render such services for COMPANY during the term hereof and all extensions and renewals.

TRANSLATION: The artist shall make records only for this specific record company, and for no one else for as long as this contract runs.

REALITY: The killer phrase "all extensions and renewals," as you will see, allows the record company to extend this agreement for several years beyond what the artist thinks they are contracting for.

2. The term of this Agreement shall be for a period of one (1) year commencing on the date hereof ("Initial Period"). ARTIST hereby grants to COMPANY four (4) consecutive separate options to extend the term for further periods of one (1) year each ("Option Periods"), each upon the same terms and conditions applicable to the Initial Period, **except as otherwise hereinafter set forth.** The Initial Period and every Option Period for which COMPANY has exercised its option are hereinafter sometimes referred to together as the "Term." Each option shall be exercised, if at all, by notice to ARTIST at any time prior to the date the Term would otherwise expire.

TRANSLATION: The length of this contract is one year starting at the date when the artist signs the contract. This first year is called the "Initial Period." The artist gives the company the right to renew this contract four times, once each year. Each new year in which the contract is extended is called an "Option Period," and all the same conditions and hidden traps from the first year apply to each additional year **unless it specifically says so elsewhere in this contract.** The first year and every other year of this contract will sometimes be called the "Term." (Or it may be called something else.) Each time the company renews its option to keep the artist on the label, they will notify the artist before the end of the year.

REALITY: The length of the contract is five years, but the record company can terminate the agreement at the end of any year. While under contract to the company, the artist can record *for no one else,* including a song on a buddy's film score, making a silly home-recorded birthday announcement, or singing on a friend's demo, without express permission from the label.

A fair agreement would have an exact time frame as to when it would end and not base the end of the term on whenever the record company feels like ending it. However, the company is not without compassion: The last line of the paragraph says that if the artist doesn't hear from the label before the end of the year, they're free to go. Oh boy!

3.(a) During the Initial Period, ARTIST shall jointly perform for the recording of masters the equivalent in playing time of one (1) LP. At COMPANY's election, ARTIST shall jointly perform for the recording of additional masters provided that such additional masters shall not exceed the equivalent in playing time of one (1) LP during the Initial Period.

TRANSLATION: During the first year, the artist shall record a series of songs that total approximately 40 to 50 minutes in playing time. The company may ask the artist to record more songs during the first year, provided that the total running time of these songs is no more than another album's worth.

REALITY: If the label doesn't like the songs, they can insist the artist record more. In fact, even if they *do* like them, they can ask for more songs, provided that the total playing time of the album of songs doesn't exceed the normal length (40 to 50 minutes). This seems to protect the artist from giving the label more than an album's worth of material within each year, but they have ways around this as well, as you'll see shortly.

3.(b) During each Option Period, ARTIST shall jointly perform for the recording of masters the equivalent in playing time of one (1) LP. At COMPANY's election, ARTIST shall jointly perform for the recording of additional masters provided that such additional masters shall not exceed the equivalent in playing time of one (1) LP during any Option Period.

TRANSLATION: During each year in which the contract is still in force, the artist shall record songs totaling approximately 40 to 50 minutes in playing time. And again, the company may ask the artist to record more songs in that year, provided that the total running time of the new songs is about the same length (40 or 50 minutes).

REALITY: This is a repeat of 3(a), extending the same rights to the label for each "Option Period." Each year in which the record company is not happy with the work the artist submits, they have the right to ask the artist to record more and more songs until they feel they have enough "acceptable" material for a full-length album for that year. In effect, the artist must keep recording until the record company says they can stop. (Sure sounds like an employment agreement to me.)

And now for the killer clause. Pay attention:

3.(c) Provided that ARTIST shall have timely completed the recording (as hereinafter defined) of the first LP required to be recorded during the Initial Period or any Option Period in accordance with all of the material terms and conditions of this Agreement, COMPANY's election to require ARTIST to record a second LP during the Initial Pe-

TRANSLATION: Provided that the artist **quickly completes** the first album and complies with all the strings attached in this contract, the company's right to request a second album during that same year shall be made (i) within six months after the completion of the first album or (ii) three months before the end of the year, whichever comes later. But, if the artist fails

riod or any Option Period shall be made, if at all, prior to the later of (i) one hundred eighty (180) days following the completion of recording of the first LP required to be recorded during the applicable Period or (ii) ninety (90) days prior to the expiration of the applicable Period. **If ARTIST shall have failed to have timely completed** the recording of the first LP required to be recorded during the applicable Period, then COMPANY's election to require ARTIST to perform for the recording of a second LP during such Period may be made, if at all, at any time prior to the date the applicable Period would otherwise expire. **Notwithstanding the foregoing,** if ARTIST shall have **failed to timely complete** the recording of any such first LP for reasons solely caused by COMPANY or solely within COMPANY's control, then COMPANY's election to require ARTIST to perform for the recording of a second LP during the applicable Period shall be made, if at all, not later than ninety (90) days prior to the expiration of the applicable Period.

to deliver the album **in an amount of time that the company thinks is reasonable,** then the company's demand for a second album could be made at **any time before the end of that year.** If, however, the artist is unable to complete the first album during the year because of something the company did (or failed to do), then the time limit for the company's request for the second album must be made at least three months before the end of the year.

REALITY: Although written in a very contorted way, this basically means that the label can ask for two records within one contract year. This is the case even if the artist was not able to complete the first record due to a screw-up on the part of the label. The label also has up to six months after receiving the finished recordings to ask for this second record. This effectively extends the time of the contract, since the six-month deadline could fall after the end of the contract year. As a weird form of concession, the label agrees that if the album can't be completed because they, the label, screwed up somehow (like not giving the artist recording money or not approving of the producer and the studio, as you'll see in a minute), then they only have three months before the end of the year to request a second album. Well, that's a relief.

3.(d) ARTIST shall record masters for COMPANY hereunder in a recording studio selected or approved by COMPANY at such times and with such individual producer as COMPANY may designate or approve. COMPANY shall advise ARTIST of the financial terms of any agreement with any producer and ARTIST shall have the right to approve such financial terms, **which approval ARTIST shall not unreasonably withhold.** Moses Avalon shall be the producer of the first LP required to be recorded during the Initial Period of the Term of this Agreement.

TRANSLATION: The artist shall record the album when the company says, where the company says, and with a producer that the company will choose for the artist. The company is required to tell the artist how much they are paying the producer (and tagging onto the SSC) and how many points from their end of the deal they are giving to the producer. The artist shall have the right to object if they think it's too much, **but not too strongly or they will be in breach of this agreement.** Moses Avalon will produce the first album of the first year.

REALITY: The artist is *working* for the label, period. The label says how much it will cost (i.e., how much the artist will owe them) and who will be in charge. The artist can object, but they'd better not get pushy about it.

3.(d) (cont'd) ARTIST acknowledges that COMPANY has advised ARTIST of the financial terms of COMPANY's agreement with Moses Avalon and that ARTIST approves of same. The masters recorded by ARTIST hereunder shall consist of ARTIST's newly recorded joint studio performances of material selected or approved by COMPANY and not previously recorded by ARTIST. Each such master shall be subject to COMPANY's approval as commercially satisfactory for the manufacture and sale of records. Upon the request of COMPANY, ARTIST shall re-record any selection until a **commercially satisfactory master** shall have been obtained.

TRANSLATION: Even though in the last paragraph the artist agreed to be reasonable about objecting to how much the company would pay the producer, here the artist acknowledges in advance that the financial terms of the company's agreement with Moses Avalon are A-okay. The songs recorded by the artist for this record shall consist of new material, approved by the company and not previously recorded by the artist. Each song shall be subject to **the company's standards of quality.** If the company requests it (and they will), the artist has to re-record any song until an album of songs has been completed that **the company thinks it can easily sell.**

REALITY: The label has complete control of every element of the artist's recordings.[5]

But even though the label has complete control of the recording from jump street, they still insist on a massive *six-month* grace period after the delivery of the record before rejecting it and requesting a second record. Mind you, if they exercise this right, it could now be a year and a half after the artist has signed and quit their day job before they have to start recording this second new album. What does the label offer as a means for the artist to earn a living in the meantime? Not much.

[5] Which by definition makes the contract an employment agreement in most states in the United States.

3.(e) ARTIST shall complete the recording of the first LP required to be recorded during the Initial Period or any Option Period within six (6) months following the commencement of the applicable Period. ARTIST shall complete the recording of any additional masters required to be recorded during the Initial Period or any Option Period within sixty (60) days following COMPANY's request therefor, unless COMPANY shall otherwise advise ARTIST. **Notwithstanding anything to the contrary contained** in this Agreement, COMPANY shall have no less than one hundred and fifty (150) days following the date of ARTIST's completion of recording and COMPANY's acceptance in accordance with all of the terms and conditions of this Agreement of all the masters required to be recorded by ARTIST during any contract Period within which to exercise its immediately succeeding option to extend the Term.

TRANSLATION: The artist has to complete the first album of each year within the first six months. The artist has to complete the recording of any additional songs that the company insists they record within 60 days following company's request, unless the company specifically says they don't have to. **If anything else in the contract contradicts the next half of this sentence, then what follows is the prevailing rule:** The company has *at least* five months after the completion of each album, and their acceptance of all the additional songs and recordings that they requested, in which to decide whether or not to renew the contract for the next year and thus to extend the term.

REALITY: The artist has to complete an album within the first six months of the beginning of each contract year. The label has five months to reject it, and then the artist has 60 days to remake it (good luck). After this, the label gets another six months to exercise their option to reject the new record and dump the artist. How is this possible if the label has exercised their option from paragraph 3(c) to wait six months and then ask for the second record from the first contract year? If this happens, the artist will now be in year two of the agreement and have to record the second album for year two while re-recording the first album from year one *at the same time!* The way this is phrased, the label can keep the artist engaged in recording for several years before releasing anything to the public. And they can do this every year for a minimum of five years.

Timetable

Artist signs with label	Jan. 1, 2005
Artist completes first album	June 1, 2005
Label rejects first album and requests more recordings. Artist begins re-recording first album and starts recording second album	Jan. 1, 2006
Artist completes re-record of first album	April 1, 2006
Artist completes second album	June 1, 2006
Label releases first album while requesting a re-record of second album, while artist begins recording third album	Jan. 1, 2007
Artist finishes re-recording second album	April 1, 2007
Artist finishes third album	June 1, 2007
. . . and so on and so on	till 2012

❷ Conclusion

We can now have a bit more compassion for artists who seem to have "sold out" after their first record. They have the years before they are signed to prepare for the first record, but only one year to prepare their second record, and six months to prepare their third. The absurd time constraints make it nearly impossible for the artist to achieve this production schedule at all, let alone with any degree of quality. Don't forget, a working artist or band is touring for six months out of the year, so they're doomed to be in breach of this agreement. If they don't comply with the above schedule, then they don't get their royalty increases and stay at the old rate. Thus the fraud.

Since any record label is usually required to release only *one album per year*, the label gets to keep the second recordings and can release them whenever they want to—even after the artist has flown to another label. Hence things like "previously unreleased masters" hit the market long after an artist has retired or the band has broken up.

If all this isn't bad enough, all the fancy legalese turns a five-year/five-album contract into a 7½-year/14-album contract (since the extension of the term and the "acceptance" of albums are related). Every time the label asks for a new record, they automatically extend the option period by six months (6 months x 5 albums = 2.5 years additional term time).

And this is only the first three paragraphs of a 25-paragraph agreement. Today most similar clauses are not that severe—largely due to progressive and more insistent lawyering, not record companies becoming more benign. Watch out for new and improved incarnations of the above as new areas of law like "digital transferring/transmission" and "electronic rights" start to creep into recording agreements.

But remember, many lawyers let their clients sign this exact agreement (or some version thereof) for years. Now go back, reread "Lawyers," page 6, and make sure you have a good one.

>Miscellaneous Myths and Untruths

Nothing so needs reforming as other people's habits.

—Mark Twain

CHAPTER NINETEEN

⊖A & R Dogma

I f you haven't thrown down this book in disgust, then you are ready for this next chapter. In the next pages we'll dissect some of the conventional wisdom that gets passed around on how to make it in this game. As we'll discover, much of what musicians receive in the way of well-meaning advice is irrelevant or just plain wrong.

⊖ A Good Promotional Kit Is the Key

Totally false. I have heard many stories to the contrary from friends who work in A&R departments. They rip open the package, listen to the tape, and then, if they like the music, look at the materials. If they don't like the first song on the demo, they toss the entire package without ever looking at it. If the picture doesn't match the type of music, they toss it as well.

One friend said to me, "A good early warning sign of a clunker tape: If the package looks too well put together, neat and pristine, it probably sucks. Bands who put together elaborate promo kits are trying to compensate for something."

Conversely, it's often the tape with an illegible, torn label with no information that seems to have a more compelling allure to it—provided the music is good, of course. (There are exceptions, so don't go getting extreme with this philosophy.)

Work on the music. That's what will grab the A&R person's attention. It's like the old cliché about dating (one that I hope the female readers will find cute rather than sexist): It's been said that a woman decides in the first five minutes after meeting a date whether or not she's interested. The rest of the evening, or subsequent dates, are merely for confirming her decision.

My experience has taught me that A&R people are similar. Their first impressions are the strongest. They decide in the first viewing, dare I say in the first 60 seconds of the first two songs, whether or not they are going to sign an act. The rest of the meetings, showcases, and conversations are just part of the courting game, helping the A&R person feel secure in their decision.

Take it with a grain of salt if you wish, but experience has shown me that despite all the business factors that play a role in what bands to sign, A&R people usually go with their gut.

❷ Gigging a Lot Is Good Exposure to the Industry

Many new bands think that if they get gigs in the best clubs in town, they're assured of eventually being exposed to the right people. They're right, but is this a good thing? In planning the strategy of an act, it's a good idea not to make them too visible too soon. This destroys the allure that is necessary for A&R interest. Yes, A&R wants to sign a working act, but not one that has been working too long.

The rationale is that if they have been out there for a couple of years and no one has signed them, there must be a reason. You should by now understand the insecure position of the average A&R person. This issue of a band being "too visible" and "too accessible" is all they need to tip the delicate scales of rejection. A band that seems too eager can destroy the thrill of the chase that A&R people enjoy. Remember, they want to discover something new and exciting—that's what gets them fame and bonuses. Signing an act that has been knocking around for a deal for a couple of years is about as exciting as going home with the drunk person that has been hitting on you all night at a bar.

This is especially true in the major cities, where about half of the signing for major labels is done. The lines below, by two distinct but equally quoted prophets, illustrate the logic one should apply to attracting A&R.

The prophet is without honor in his own land.
                                          — Jesus

*I'd never belong to a club that would have
me for a member.*   — Groucho Marx

Solution: Many savvy managers try to book their up-and-coming acts in the suburban areas outside the major music cities such as New York and L.A. Not only do the venues tend to pay more, but the audiences are far more appreciative of a big-city act coming out to them than the city folk are about hearing "just another local band from the sticks." In this way the act can build up a better following. When the time comes to showcase for the record companies in the city, an artist's manager will canvass the suburban areas where the artist is popular. The hope is that their crowd will drive in to see them. This pads the audience for the A&R people and gives them a better impression of how hard the band has been working at aggregating *real* fans. That's what they want to see, not a club filled with relatives and significant others.

❷ Second Sendings

A second sending is when a band has been rejected and then follows up with a second CD several months later. Despite the party line—that A&R people are always open to hearing your latest—the truth is that they rarely change their minds.

At this point the band is better off changing their name than sending a new tape, basically for the same reason described above—they're not fresh anymore. So make sure that your first foot forward is your best. If they don't say yes within a few months, you're better off moving on to another A&R person or label. But saying yes is an elusive thing, as you'll see in the next paragraph. However, there are almost as many exceptions to this rule as there are examples of it.

❷ "We Love It, But . . ."

Show business in general and the music business in particular is an arena where yes usually means maybe and maybe usually means no. For this rule, I promise you, there are few exceptions. It is very frustrating for me to listen to artists tell me that the label they solicited loves the tape but they have "filled the roster for that month," or they think it needs a remix and then they'll reconsider it, or "the vocals aren't strong enough but the music is great," or the classic "Can we hear more material?" All of these mean they didn't like it.

I know this is hard for many artists to hear, and it isn't easy to say, but it's true. The fact of the matter is that if the A&R department really thought you were great they would offer to sign you—period, no matter what the circumstances. The only exception to this could be that they are considering another act with a similar sound. In this case, their request for more material could be legitimate.

In my experience, when a person in the music business is excited about what they hear, they tend to ask important buying questions, like what does the artist look like, how did they record this tape, and are they playing out right now? When they think it's not for them, they say, "We love it, but . . ."

The real reason for this waffling doesn't cast entertainment professionals in a very good light: it's simply done out of fear. People don't tell you what they honestly feel because they never know who might be where in a year or two. The manager to whom an A&R person says "I hate it" this year might be the director of his label next year. There is also the possibility that the "passed over" artist gets signed and does well on another label. A&R people can't afford to be wrong. Their entire perceived value is based on their ears.

In all fairness, there are many A&R people who rise above these shortcomings, but these are things that artists and producers should be aware of. Odds dictate that if an A&R man says "no" (however he phrases it), he has a 95% chance of being right even if he thinks the tape is good. Ninety-five percent of all artists fail for one reason or another. So why take a risk unless it looks and sounds really good?

Yes means maybe. Maybe means no.
No means call back.

⊘ Labels Sign Bad Acts for Tax Write-Offs

Nonsense. This myth is probably perpetuated by sour-grapes bands who hate to see their friends get signed and not them. A&R signs bad acts often enough to make a person wonder what their agenda is, but the idea that a record company, which generally operates on a small profit margin anyway, would sign an act and spend half a million dollars just to avoid paying taxes is absurd. Anyone who tells you this has no understanding of how corporate taxes work and has even less idea how the politics of labels work. If a major label wanted a tax write-off, there are much deeper wells they can go to than signing a bad act. They could just press about 500,000 CDs of one of the loser acts they already have (every label has at least one). The records would ship back from the stores, and not only would they get a tax deduction, but they would also be able to charge more return fees to that artist's recoupment account. (See "The Major Label Deal from the Artist's Point of View," page 63, for what a recoupment account is.)

I think this concept started because in the '80s there was a lot of funny accounting going on in the record industry (and there still is). A&R people would ask for kickbacks from the producers in exchange for large advances. If this was the A&R person's agenda, then it didn't matter if the band was good or not. To cover up this type of fraud, the labels themselves may have started the rumor that they signed a bad act for tax purposes. Maybe it helped them save face with their parent holding companies, whose primary concern is where all the money is going.[1]

[1] See "The Big Picture," page 293.

The other possibility is that the tax write-off signing is being confused with a very real phenomenon—the mercy signing.

The Mercy Signing

A&R people build up relationships with various producers and managers over time. Let's say that during the course of one deal the A&R person asks the producer to step away from the act. The producer may agree to do this if the label signs another of his other acts with no questions asked. If the relationship is strong, the A&R person will do it.

Another type of mercy signing is when a relationship between the A&R person

---

SHOOTING BLANKS

To give you an idea of the extent of A&R paranoia, I'm reminded of an experiment done by a trade magazine several years back. They sent a false promo kit around to several labels with a *blank demo tape* inside. Out of the 15 submissions to major labels, only one called them on it. The rest sent back a form rejection letter that basically read, "We think this shows potential but we are currently not signing any new acts this year."

and the manager is a very long one and over the years the manager has given that A&R person first look at all of his choice acts. If the signings have been profitable for the A&R person, then the manager would not hesitate to ask that the label sign a clunker and then drop them later so that the manager can get a commission and pay some bills.

Also, most managers' contracts have a clause that states that if the manager is not successful in getting the artist signed within a period of time (usually not more than two years), then the artist is free to go. It is not unknown for the manager to persuade an A&R friend to sign the act at the very end of the contract to a "development deal," thus extending the manager's hold on the artist. The deal will usually take several months to negotiate. In that time the manager will continue to collect money off the artist for their personal appearances, royalties, or any other income.

Make sure the person representing you has your best interests at heart.

A twist on this scenario is when an A&R person is being pressured to sign someone because the manager has told him that if he doesn't, then that manager or producer will never bring him anything in the future. If the A&R person values the relationship, he could be pressured into signing the act where before he was ambivalent about it.

Unless the label is truly convinced that the act is good, any pressure used in manipulating them to sign an act will usually mean that the artist will not receive the label's full attention and dedication. This is not always the case, and there are numerous examples where the sleeper act on a label's roster turned out to be a winner, but in general the mercy signings tend to get dropped shortly after the record comes out.

By the way, indie labels don't have the money for this sort of bullshit. They tend to sign only what they believe in, so an artist on an indie can expect a higher level of commitment.

❯ SoundScan Tells All

SoundScan is a service owned by Nielsen, the company that computes TV ratings. SoundScan uses the barcodes on CDs to register sales at record stores. The correlated data contributes to the *Billboard* chart listings, as well as to much of the market research that record companies use to determine which artists are worth keeping under contract.

Many times you hear that when so-and-so has a hit, they quote the sales numbers from SoundScan. Indies and emerging artists think that if they can get lots of people to buy their records, then they will track well on SoundScan and be discovered by a major.

If only it were true.

The number of stores that report to SoundScan makes up less than half of the record-buying outlets in the country. Generally, only the big chains and several well-placed mom-and-pop stores participate in their tracking system. To compensate for this, SoundScan assigns "multiple numbers" to some of the most remote stores that report to them. This means that if you buy one record at a store with a X3 multiplier, that purchase will count as three purchases. On the other hand, if a record is bought at a large chain in the city, it might count only as one or even half a sale.

Learning which stores have high multipliers is part of gaming the SoundScan system. So it does not follow suit that the SoundScan charts are either an accurate reflection of real sales or that each store is participating in the system on a level playing field.

What SoundScan doesn't put in their advertising is that they would probably ignore a surge in sales from an underdog (or unlikely) indie band, until the indie label (or act) could prove that the sales were legitimate.[2]

This, of course, would take several days or weeks to tabulate; and SoundScan revising a chart once it's published is about as rare as politicians admitting a mistake.

However, this does not mean that SoundScan is useless. SoundScan is like what someone once said about democracy: It's the worst system in the world except for all the others. But there are plenty of other charts besides SoundScan's that cost far less and make good stuff to stick in a press kit. (See "Other Types of Charts," page 118.)

[2] This was confessed to me by a SoundScan representative.

❷ Illegal File-Sharing Is Killing the Music Business

On the surface this point seems rather obvious to the labels: record sales are way down and peer-to-peer file-sharing is the new variable. Therefore it must be the cause. Poor choices in A&R, bad marketing, or new attractions (like computer games) for the youth market's disposable income would never enter into the minds of major-label top brass. These days they seem far more interested in large public stock offerings as a way of making money than they are in the art of music itself.

Naturally, the real answer is a bit more complex.

First, people who say "the music industry is dying" are not taking into consideration the $2 billion in new revenue created by ringtones and the fact that revenue from master licensing in film and TV is reaching all-time highs. Songs that used to be licensed for motion pictures at $20,000 a pop are now commanding fees of $150,000, some over $1,000,000. TV advertising negotiations often begin at $500,000 for use of a hit single and climb up from there. This is where the record companies make their highest margin of revenue, not off of CD sales. Since the early '80s, CDs, tapes, and singles have been little more than a device to recoup the R&D costs for creating tomorrow's catalog. So if I'm right (and I am), what's with the big lies about file-sharing killing the business?

Are Sales Really Down?

It depends on when you start your clock.

If you only examine 2002–2005, yes. During that time there was a total 12% drop in unit sales. (Although there's more to this as well, as you'll see in a minute.) However, if you look at the period of 1997–2002 you see an increase of about 9%. And if you go back five years before that, 1991–1996, you see a drop again. It seems that the industry works in cycles (like most other industries): seven-year cycles that catch their breath every three to four years or so. This is nothing to worry about.

The truth is that sales of physical recordings are going through some awkward transitions and may possibly become obsolete. But, if you want to understand whether file-sharing is having a real financial impact on this *one* element of the music business (ignoring everything else like: publishing, concerts, licensing, merchandising, sponsorships, etc.), you have to learn two new words. "Sales" is the first one of them. I know you thought that you knew the meaning of this word, but as you'll see, the RIAA says you don't.

If you carefully read the RIAA website during 2003–2004 you would have noticed that every time the RIAA complained of large drops in "unit sales" it includes international sales, not strictly domestic sales. But every time it spoke of domestic "losses" it was speaking ONLY of "units *shipped* in the U.S." to record stores. But, at the exact same time that this **statement** was being proliferated, SoundScan was reporting an increase in U.S. sales from the years 2003–2004.

- For the first quarter of 2003 SoundScan registered 147,000,000 records sold.
- For the first quarter of 2004 SoundScan will report 160,000,000 records sold.

That's 13,000,000 more units, almost a 10% increase in U.S. sales since the previous year. What gives? Can both SoundScan and the RIAA be right? As it turns out—yes!

The secret: The RIAA reports "a sale" as a unit *shipped* to record stores, not necessarily one that is actually sold to a customer, whereas SoundScan reports units sold to the consumer *at the point of purchase*. So, we're talking about apples and oranges, or to be more accurate, sales and "sales." In simple numbers it works like this: If last year Johnny shipped 1,000 units but sold only 700, and this year Johnny shipped 900 units but still sold 750, Johnny is experiencing a 10% drop in "sales." This is what the RIAA wants the public to accept as "a loss."

I never got an MBA, but, by my math, shouldn't a lower shipment-to-sales ratio mean fewer returns, and shouldn't that also mean an *increase* in record company profits and artist royalties, not a decrease? Isn't tighter inventory management a good thing?

Here's where we have to learn our other new word, "profits." RIAA's press releases sometimes interchange the word "profits" with "sales," in hopes that you don't really know the difference. Most people don't. "Sales" is the amount of units you distribute, for which you got paid and which didn't get returned. "Profit" is the difference between the cost of producing/marketing something and what you sold it for. "Sales" refer to a number of units, whereas "profit" is a vig between costs and purchase price.

There is no way for the public to investigate the claim of "lower profits," since record companies do not publish their profit/loss statements in a public forum. In fact, they don't even report their costs to the RIAA in any official way. So, in real terms, profit could "go down" if they decided to spend more on advertising, for example, or to increase the salaries of their executives,[3] or lower the price of the CD to retailers. However, the Egghead Box on pages 106-107 shows that some costs in manufacturing have gone up and that record companies *did* see a probable profit loss since 2001 in this area, but it has nothing to do with file-sharing. It's due to the rising costs of mechanical rates and artists negotiating better royalty rates.

So Are There Real Losses?

Maybe, but the public will never be able to figure them out due to this confusion, deliberate or not. And if there are losses of CD sales, it's impossible to determine if *illegal* file-sharing plays a significant role in the decline because there are so many other factors that play roles in the changing ways people buy and listen to music, like *legal* digital distribution.

Regardless, "lost sales/profits/revenues" has certainly been a great excuse for majors to clean house of overpaid executives and rally the government to make rulings in their favor. Let's not be too harsh on them for being this manipulative—the jobs they are trying to save are not just theirs. They're yours too. (See "Record Industry Slumps Are the Direct Result of Poor A&R Decision-Making," page 278, for more on this.)

[3] While some major labels like Warner Brothers and BMG fired about a third of their staff due to "revenue losses" in 2003-2004 they also paid out record-high bonuses to their top brass.

●ASCAP vs. BMI: PRO Pontification

(If you're not familiar with what a PRO is, see page 37 before reading onward.)

● Preface

Let me start off by making one thing perfectly clear: Even though this entire chapter is about scrutinizing the pitches from the two main U.S. Performing Rights Organizations ("PROs")—ASCAP and BMI—without them it would be a bleak world for writers of popular music and the music business would lose much of its ability to be economically viable. Investors use projected money paid from PROs as a significant incentive for taking risks on new talent. If ASCAP and BMI were not in position, emerging artists would face even bigger hurdles when it comes to developing their careers, and pop music as a commercial artform would suffer.

Aside from collecting the money due writers and publishers, PROs also give grants to charities, help writers get loans and health benefits, give career advice, and showcase new talent. They will also make sure that writers get paid their share of royalties even if a writer is unrecouped with his publisher.[1] I think that's a biggie considering how slanted the industry generally is against the little guy. So, do not confuse the cheeky attitude I'm taking here—in order to make a point about honesty and choice—with one of an extremist who

[1] ASCAP started this policy and BMI followed shortly after. If you are unfamiliar with the concept of "recoupment," see Publishing Deals, page 81.

thinks these companies should be dismantled or indicted. These are far and away worthwhile entities. But you can read all about this good stuff on their websites. Here's what you will not read.

Quick disclaimer: All percentages and references are from 2003–2004 research. Things change annually.

➤ Overview of the Battlefield: The Players and Their Game

If you own a bar or radio station and want to play *only* your music that you wrote (or no music at all), then you don't need to bother dealing with a PRO. But if you want to play popular songs and they happen to be written by BMI, ASCAP, or SESAC members (which most all popular songs are), then you need a license from at least one and possibly all of them.

PROs grow powerful by enforcing a section of the Copyright Act that requires commercial establishments (clubs, radio stations, TV networks, sports arenas, etc.) to pay a fee in order to have popular music performed in their venue.[2] The strength a PRO has to enforce this part of this law depends almost exclusively on getting writers and publishers of the most popular music to join their organization, thus granting the PRO the right to collect these lucrative performance fees.

You can only join one, so say them all, and so the rivalry is fierce. Each spends millions a year to gain the trust of writers with claims that they are the best at collecting and distributing these fees. To help create a benevolent atmosphere they like to call themselves "societies," as in "Performing Rights Societies." It sounds far friendlier than "organizations" or "corporations," but, in reality, they are not organic communities like MySpace or Friendster, and when it comes to collecting their money they are no friendlier than unions.

In regard to membership, ASCAP and BMI are not very selective, either. If they could find some way to sign only successful writers, they probably would. But it's hard to know who will be the next big hit-maker, and since signing a new writer costs nothing more than photocopying a one-page contract, they take the only other logical marketing approach—they try to enroll *every writer*, often at conferences and often right on the spot. Thus the process of assigning some of your most valuable rights is made as painless as filling out a simple form.

To make this route even more natural and seamless, many industry veterans will casually tell you that choosing between ASCAP and BMI is like choosing between Coke and Pepsi—a consoling, oversupplied analogy that, taken to heart, can cost

[2] Section 114, a good read if you're having trouble sleeping. The law only applies to music that is protected by copyright, not public domain music like classical pieces.

a writer a great deal of money. It's a safe bet that many of the people who say this have never taken the time to do an analysis of their differences. But in fairness to the guilty, both ASCAP and BMI do little to discourage the Coke/Pepsi analogy. It keeps the public focused on a two-party choice and distracts us from looking too closely at the differences between them and between their mutual competitor, SESAC, the other PRO (the RC Cola, I guess). It's also possible that until the comparative work done for this chapter of *Confessions of a Record Producer*, there never had been a critical analysis in a mainstream publication to suggest otherwise.[3]

In regards to SESAC, for many years their membership grew by invitation only, and most of their members were soundtrack and classical composers. SESAC's market was so niche that neither ASCAP nor BMI considered them a real threat. But SESAC of late has entered the game. They are pursuing applications from established songwriters and giving substantial advances for a commitment. Bob Dylan's announcement that he was leaving ASCAP and going to SESAC fired a significant warning shot across the bow of the two-party landscape.[4] They currently claim about 5% of the market. However, I'm assuming that many of you reading this are probably not on the SESAC invitation list *yet*, so SESAC is not, with occasional exception, included in this comparison between your only practical choices, ASCAP or BMI.

❷ Should You Bother to Join Either of Them?

ASCAP and BMI will both tell you it is irrational *not* to join one of their organizations. They collect the bulk of all the performance royalties in the U.S., and you cannot get your share unless you are a member. In their pitch they will make it sound as if your music is already out there earning money and the PRO is just holding it for you, like a bank, waiting for your application. But the truth is that unless you wrote a popular song or composed a soundtrack for a TV show like *The Simpsons* you are unlikely to see any significant royalties, even if you are a member.

Regardless, I'd have to say that, under the right circumstances, joining a PRO is wiser than not. Sure, you could stay independent and make your own PRO—"Joe's Performing Rights Organization" or something cute like that—and try to collect money only on Joe's songs from the many places that pay PROs. It's exhausting; you'd have to prove that every establishment you approach for money was definitely playing Joe's music, and then, in all probability, unless you are a superstar songwriter, you will not fare any better than if you join ASCAP or BMI.[5]

For practicality, the real question is not *should* you join, but *when* and *which*

[3] **Kudos to Backbeat.**

[4] **The amount of the advance was never publicly disclosed, but rumor suggests it was in the area of $1,000,000. Some have told me $9,000,000. Either one is a lot for a PRO to give on spec.**

[5] **In the future, Internet-based systems might allow a venue to license directly from a writer with ease. When that happens PROs will have to rethink their position in the music community. But that day is not around the corner just yet. Perhaps by the next edition of *Confessions*.**

one. Many people new to the industry think they should sign up as soon as they can. The lavish events that both ASCAP and BMI host make one think that joining means there is an *immediate* chance to collect money. I'm not so sure this is true. Even if you are a member you only get paid if:

(1) There is money to collect for *your* musical works and, more important...

(2) If you meet their requirements to receive money *after* you join.

This means it's entirely possible that after you commit to one, your song(s) could be earning money for your PRO but the PRO is paying you *nothing in return.* So, unless one offers you a financial incentive, I don't see this choice as a real dilemma until and unless you have written music that fits one of the criteria below:

- Recorded by a significant artist and the album is about to be released.
- Placed in a movie soundtrack that is about to be broadcast on a major TV network.
- Used as a theme for a series that is about to be broadcast on a significant TV network.
- Currently getting *a lot* of play on *commercial* radio or podcasts or has been tracked by a reliable service as being downloaded (legally) thousands of times.[6]

Notice that all four items above are happening *now* or about to happen in the *near* future. Not things that have happened in the past or will happen in a year or two. Both PROs have pay-out systems that tend to respect events that are *around the corner* (more on this later). If you had a hit five years ago and are first thinking about joining now or you've just been signed to a major label but you haven't even recorded your first album yet,[7] don't expect to have any real negotiating leverage. Also notice what's <u>NOT</u> on my list above, writing the music for:

- A TV commercial.[8]
- A soundtrack for a movie that has only seen a theatrical or direct-to-video distribution in the U.S.[9]
- Independent films that show at festivals *only.*
- A hot regional artist's indie release.

[6] Podcasts? Iffy. I'm being progressive by adding this to my list. ASCAP has a podcast license, but, even with it, as of this writing there is no easy way to properly license a piece of music for a podcast, and PROs do not seem to be making an aggressive play to collect on this medium. Yet.

[7] On major deals the time spread between signing and first release can easily be a year or two. See the subchapter "Speed Trends" in the chapter "The Independent Record Deal from the Point of View of the Artist."

[8] Most commercials are composed as "work-for-hire buy-outs," making the producer or advertising agency the author, or at best, if the writer has leverage, the co-author. Thus, with exceptions that are rarer and rarer these days, "jingle" writers don't get much by way of PRO royalties. But don't worry; they are usually well compensated with other fees.

[9] No PRO in the U.S. collects from movie theaters. In Europe and other parts of the world they do.

For reasons you're about to learn, these circumstances tend to not track on either ASCAP's or BMI's systems. However, any of the bottom four could someday metamorphose into the top four. If so, which you join could make a radical difference in your income. Since joining is really the only bargaining chip you have, I say wait a bit, see which way the wind blows for your career, and carefully consider all the points below.

❯ Who Pays More

When it comes to *advances*, BMI has been known, on rare occasions, to offer non-recoupable ones (called "guaranties") to superstars, whereas ASCAP's internal policy is emphatically that they will not.[10] So, on the front end BMI is definitely more generous. On the royalty end, however, its gets very amusing: each claims to pay *more* than the other.

Unfortunately, there are myriad stories about songwriting teams where one writer was ASCAP and the other one BMI, and their royalties for a particular song were very different. In the past the PRO with the lower payment would make up the difference.[11] But the fact that it happens at all begs this question: How can any discrepancies occur if they are like Coke and Pepsi? Clearly learning which PRO pays higher royalties under what circumstances is significant. Two factors weigh in here.

(1) How much your PRO spends to collect your money (covered in the next section below about "nonprofits").

(2) The method the PRO uses to calculate what they owe you.

Let's look at number two first.

What's That Floating in the Pool?

You'd think, in this high-tech world where NASA could track the exact location of a space capsule the size of a closet on the lunar surface *in 1968*, that tracking exactly how many times your song plays on local radio and TV *today* would not be so difficult. But apparently it is.[12] Neither ASCAP nor BMI can say with exactitude how many times or places a piece of music is performed. Instead, TV and radio stations are asked to keep "logs"[13] of what music they broadcast and how long each performance runs. PROs then combine these logs with "surveys'" done by people who are paid to monitor the airwaves. They listen for what composition is played when and where.

Each PRO has its own monitoring group with its own methodology for cre-

[10] However, ASCAP paid Alicia Keys a $1,000,000 *re-coupable* advance to join. It took her less than three years to repay them. Good call ASCAP.

[11] Unfortunately this does not always happen, and according to my sources, it's happening less and less. Why? One reason is that some writing teams deliberately join opposite PROs to game the system.

[12] Irony alert: To pull off this miracle, NASA used computers with less processing power and memory than an iPod.

[13] Also called "cue sheets."

ating "surveys." Although both claim that their tracking methods are 95% accurate, experience suggests that survey systems are far from comprehensive. They often miss performances in less-than-traditional as well as non-commercial venues. So if you're expecting a check because your song played 10 times on a college radio station, don't hold your breath. Even if it was 100 times, you'll likely get $0. Same goes for Public Radio and local cable stations: Forget it. And that's just the beginning of the bad news.

After PROs collect all the money that the surveys/logs and an independent audit confirm they are owed, it's combined into "pools" and each applies its own dice-'n'-slice formula for paying members. In this "pooling system" a general rule of thumb is, the more plays of your music that show up in surveys/logs/cue sheets, the more "credits" you earn. Credits = $$$.[14]

But, although ASCAP and BMI have very different methods of how they translate credits into dollars,[15] the one thing their systems have in common is that each is "weighted" towards groups who generate the most revenue. So, to turn the pooling system into a "canteen" analogy, since a canteen holds a finite amount of water, some people are going to get credits for a few sips more at the expense of people who are going to get a few sips less. And instead of one credit for one sip, it works out like this: The more sips from the canteen you take, the more credits you earn to take a *big gulp*. And in fact this is what generally happens with PRO money. The rich get richer faster.

Several arguments on the Internet about this issue claim the difference for songwriters versus instrumental composers on ASCAP can be quite alarming: as much as 3:1, meaning that for every dollar that a traditional pop song makes, an instrumental composition, performed in exactly the same way, makes about 33 cents.[16] ASCAP does not deny this. They stand by their system and argue that this is a sort of financial democracy; some types of music are simply worth more financially than others, therefore earning more credits in larger, more lucrative pools. It makes sense. A pop song, for example, will likely be used in radio and show, in TV promos, and a film soundtrack or two. This is clearly worth more than a film score that will not ever be played on pop radio (unless it's *Star Wars*) and will show up only in places where the film it was composed for is broadcast. Regardless, if you're the person on the shallow end of this small pool, it wreaks of elitism. (See Who Controls ASCAP, page 266.)[17]

BMI implies that in their calculations the discrepancies between radio play of a pop song and an instrumental piece are not drastic. But this implication, designed to make them seem more fair than ASCAP, actually has the opposite effect if you consider who owns BMI: the same people who are supposed to

[14] ASCAP has of late begun to incorporate electronic data gathering systems (Media-Guide) to help improve the accuracy of their surveys.

[15] ASCAP's method segregates the money into individual pools for each source and then applies their credit system. BMI mixes all the money together first and then applies their credit system to the entire pool.

[16] For more, do an Internet search on "ASCAP controversy."

[17] A side point worth noting is that with PROs in Europe and other parts of the world, a pop song and an instrumental piece are treated the *same way*.

pay them—*broadcasters*. (See Who Controls BMI, page 265.) It begs the question: Does BMI go easy when it comes to distributing royalties for their biggest revenue source—pop songs—thus weighing the pool a bit more towards the group that earns the least—composers?[18] Absurd, says BMI. But, if you're a BMI writer and your first hit lasted only a week or two on Top 40 radio, don't start shopping for a Ferrari. You're likely looking at a check in the low triple digits, if anything.[19]

So, who pays more to whom? For now, here are some simplified, general answers:

- If you plan to be earning money from pop songs on the radio you may prefer ASCAP.
- If you plan to be earning money from copyrights that are instrumental soundtracks in films and TV, or in Broadway musicals, you may prefer BMI or SESAC.[20]
- The above is the opposite of what many people will tell you. (Especially BMI.)

Also worth considering is the unique philosophy that influenced each PRO when constructing their pooling formulas. For example, as of last year, ASCAP's calculations don't factor in your history with them. They don't care how long you've been an ASCAP member—ten years or ten days. Their system is purely based on number of credits earned in *that exact pay-period*. Their applied philosophy:

If you got a hit you get a split.

In contrast, BMI's math tends to favor their successful writers who are *time-honored* over those who are new to their system. The longer your music is earning money for BMI the more credits you earn. So on BMI:

If you're new to the game, your check might be lame but… if you once had a hit you can still get a split.[21]

How might ASCAP and BMI's different philosophies affect your consideration? A few thoughts:

- If you think that people who were lucky enough to get big hits in the past don't need bonuses that earn them extra cash *today* at the expense of sophomore writers who just got their first big break, you

18 To learn more about how the PROs add up and pay out money the best book is *Money, Music and Success*. It's lengthy, but if you can wade through it, there is more information in that book regarding the PROs than in any other book on the biz. But consider the source: one of its authors is an attorney who also is an ASCAP executive.

19 Examinations of BMI royalty statements were the references for this conclusion.

20 From BMI's 2005 press release: "BMI composers accounted for 75% of the music on all network prime-time shows and composed the music to the majority of the Top 10-grossing films of the past year."

21 References: interviews and the book Music, Money and Success.

may prefer ASCAP's system. But…

- If you think that a songwriter with a history of hits and who has been loyal to his PRO doesn't deserve to get tossed aside simply because a one-hit wonder got lucky one year, you may prefer BMI's system. Also…
- To help compensate for injustices in their system, ASCAP gives away about $2 million each year in awards to members who have "distinguished" themselves but who didn't show up in that year's surveys. BMI has a similar policy although it's not spoken about. If you think that PRO money should only go towards those who statistically "earned" it and not to those who are good at brown-nosing upper management, you may prefer SESAC.
- Regardless, they cannot and should not be analogized to Coke vs. Pepsi.

Bottom line: as a result of "weighed pooling systems" used by ASCAP and BMI, some writers float on a raft with mai-tai in hand, while others tread water with a lead weight tied to their ankles.

We're a Nonprofit, So You Can Trust Us

Since both ASCAP and BMI pay their overhead *first,* before they apply their individual pooling and credit formulas to distribute your royalties, the other important factor in how much you, as a member, will get paid is how much each organization spends to collect your money.

On music industry panels, reps from both ASCAP and BMI will say things like "We're a nonprofit organization." Sometimes I have even heard reps from either say, "We're a better choice than SESAC because SESAC is a *for-profit* company and we're a *not-for-profit.*"[22] This is designed to make you think that they spend the *bare minimum* on collecting your money and pass 100% of the balance on to their members. As an added value, when people think of nonprofits the word "charity" is usually not far behind. So this claim also creates the subconscious impression that people at ASCAP and BMI are somehow in this business for purely altruistic reasons. In truth, ASCAP and BMI are among the richest entities in the music business.

The creativity of this nonprofit claim is revealed by looking at the actual legal definition of "nonprofit." To be a nonprofit you only have to ask the IRS for "nonprofit status" and meet their minimal qualifications; the main one is that after you pay all your expenses, any remaining money must be paid out to your members or your cause, thus leaving no "profit" left to distribute to you or your stockholders and no profit to pay taxes on. This is true even if you have 99 cents worth of expenses on every dollar you make and give only a penny to your cause. The caveat

[22] By the way, I've heard SoundExchange make this same nonprofit claim against their competitor Royalty Logic.

being that it must be 99 cents' worth of "legitimate and necessary expenses."

Compliantly, ASCAP and BMI both claim that after their necessary expenses they pay out *all remaining money* to their members, leaving no "profit" to distribute to stockholders at the end of each year. So, what do the PROs consider "necessary" to spend your money on? A few facts:

- The CEOs of both ASCAP and BMI make salaries well into the mid-level six figures (maybe seven figures with bonuses).
- Both have offices in prime real estate in Manhattan and Los Angeles whose rent approaches the millions per month. Executives are paid quite well too.
- Both throw expensive parties designed to rally new members and give away huge cash awards.
- Everything above costs each PRO about $100,000,000 *a year* in "expenses."

Big parties? Huge salaries? Fancy offices? A hundred million bucks a year in overhead? Does this sound like a charity or like a nonprofit? Are any of these expenses truly "necessary" to collect performance fees that are due them *by law*?

Now, the IRS has an entire department set up to expose fake nonprofits that overspend and underreport. If they catch one, the company could lose its nonprofit status and be subjected to hefty fines and penalties. Yet, would you believe that neither ASCAP nor BMI has ever been stripped of their nonprofit status or paid any fines related to fraud of this nature? How do they get away with it?

I'll explain.

BMI reps may tell you over drinks that they are a "nonprofit organization," but their website and press releases say something a bit different. They state that they are a "non-profit-*making*" corporation that operates on a "nonprofit *basis*." (Emphasis mine.) It almost sounds identical, especially if you've been partying a bit. But this is the same kind of semantic distinction the law requires food companies to make on their packaging, with phrases like "cheese-*food*" and "orange juice-*drink*," when most of its ingredients are artificial.[23]

Truth: The BMI you join as a writer/publisher is a standard, typical, run-of-the-mill, garden-variety "domestic business corporation." A senior vice president inside the company confided in me that it is *not* a 501c3 (the IRS code for a tax-exempt nonprofit).

In regard to ASCAP, here's where it gets somewhat forensic. There is more than one entity incorporated in New York State with the name "ASCAP" and 1 Lincoln Plaza as their address. These entities appear, from the state's database, to be *for-*

23 One I'm sure readers of this book are familiar with is the use of the words "digital quality" to help bolster the credibility of a piece of audio gear. Another example is words like "organic," often used to market food. The "California Organic Standard" requires food to be prepared under certain guidelines. But many companies simply use the word "organic" hoping that the consumer will not know the difference. In reality, "organic" simply means "made from carbon," which all human food is.

24 I tried to explore it in my research. The best answer I could get from ASCAP reps was, "It's for the protection of our members."

25 Although both BMI and ASCAP maintain modest nonprofit "foundations," which give away a few million a year, these small divisions have nothing whatsoever to do with the collection of over $1.3 billion a year in performance fees and the distribution thereof to its members. They are completely separate from the main branch that has writers and publishers as members.

profit. What these different entities do, why they were formed, and who's involved have not been publicly explored.[24]

So the answer to the question of how do ASCAP and BMI avoid jeopardizing their nonprofit status is quite simple: *neither of them was officially a nonprofit corporation to begin with.* (The ASCAP you join isn't even incorporated, it's a "membership organization.")

Therefore they are not misrepresenting anything to the IRS. Only to you.[25]

Bottom line: In reality ASCAP and BMI are not charities and don't really emulate the lifestyle of them, either. PROs who tell you they are "nonprofit-making" are playing a word game and taking advantage of your ignorance on this confusing subject.

Okay, So We're Not Really a "Nonprofit." Big Whoop. We Still Act Like One, Right?

Maybe. In a real tax-exempt nonprofit there are regulations about how much the company can filter for expenses. But in a nonprofit-*like* scenario, only your conscience is your guide. Because they are not real nonprofits, what they claim as an "expense" is not subject to government oversight, and we can never know for sure if, when each spends $100,000,000 a year, it's truly necessary.

However, the fact that each pays themselves and their vendors *first, before they pay you* is one element of being nonprofit-like that they readily embrace. To massage this fact and to help create the charitable atmosphere, both PROs are very philanthropic; they give a great deal of money to the music community in the form of donations, showcases, and grants. But, keep in mind the structure of a nonprofit—expenses first. And some of these "give-back" items are calculated as "expenses." Considering the weighted pooling systems discussed in the previous section, I would hope that long before they start giving away your money to the needy, they take care of their own struggling writers first; y'know, make sure that everyone who trusted them, everyone whom the pooling system may have overlooked, each gets at least a small slice before the PRO splurges on showcases or so the kids in Compton get a new piano. Do they? Unfortunately for their members, no.

Now, I'm all for charity. I give money myself to several, but it's *my choice* and it comes out of money I can afford to donate, *after* I pay for my family's needs. The PROs, however, act as if they know how your "family" feels and that you'll certainly want to help new artists and the needy, instead of widening the pool so you can make a few bucks. I mean, isn't that how you feel? Oh, wait... they never asked you how you feel, or gave you a choice to opt out, in case your priority is to first help *your* family? Well, then, let's look at how much of your money, in the name of PR, they are being generous with.

ASCAP claims to have the highest cost/payout ratio (called a "cost/benefit ratio") of any PRO in the world—13.5%, meaning that 86.5 cents of every dollar they take in goes to their members. BMI claims on their website their overhead is only 15%, meaning that 85% goes towards their members.[26] These are acceptable percentages that one might expect from any legitimate *tax-exempt* nonprofit, like *Save the Children,* that pipelines donations to underdeveloped nations, so it's no surprise that the PROs would emulate such a percentage. But is it true? What if they are exaggerating by only a small half-point or so? Just to be contrary, let's explore a hypothesis:

By looking at the difference between the collection rate that one PRO used to charge radio stations—about an average of 6 cents a spin—and what they used to pay the writers who earned enough credits in that pool to see some of this money—about an average of 5 cents a spin—their cost/benefit ratio was somewhat lower—around 83/17 in the member's favor (at least for radio plays): a three-point difference.

Now, it's entirely possible that this particular area was disproportionate to other areas where their cost/benefit ratio might have been 90/10 in the member's favor, thus eventually averaging out to what they claim: about 85/15. However, radio royalties make up a substantial portion of a PRO's business. If their real cost/benefit ratio is about 83/17, then BMI was slipping an extra $1.5 million in their pocket to be used for "expenses." (That pays for a few extra showcases.) If it was *not* true, then BMI has some explaining to do: Why was the ratio on their largest revenue source, radio, disproportionate to their overall stated cost/benefit ratio?[27] Both PROs claim this type of thinking is paranoid. Do you think it is?

The Department of Justice and Federal Trade Commission don't. Both agencies have had periodic investigations into PROs. Hearings have yielded new regulations. To keep things kosher both PROs now use high-profile accounting firms to audit their annual financial statements.[28] They will both announce this proudly because the general perception is that a Certified Public Accounting firm would never stick its neck out and look the other way if their clients were skimming.

But the reality is that CPAs are not "investigators." They don't work for the government, nor are they really a public trust. They merely take the information given to them by their clients and prepare an opinion about how truthful it is, similar to what H&R Block does with a personal tax return.[29] Simply put, if you lie to your CPA it's not really his job to dig very deeply to try and catch you. Only to question you if there is an obvious discrepancy in what you provide to them.[30]

26 The 2005 press release states they lowered it to 14.2%.

27 ASCAP does not charge by the spin; they take the buffet approach and use a fixed price per year for all-you-can-play (called a "Blanket License"). But since both PROs are required by law to be comparable, it's reasonable to assume that this analysis could apply to ASCAP as well.

28 However, tax returns are not audited.

29 Well, this is a very simplified answer. Audits are far more comprehensive than preparing a tax return, but the point still stands.

Bottom line: Operating on a "nonprofit basis" is no guarantee that a member will receive more money than with a "for profit" company. In fact it could easily mean the opposite. (See the chart on page 39 for a crude example of this concept.) Since how much they spend bears a direct relationship to how much is left for you, here are a few fiscal policies to consider. And remember when reading them that when they brag about how much they "give back" they are hoping you forget that it's *your* money they are giving back with.

- BMI has more recruiting offices than ASCAP and therefore more salaries. ASCAP has fewer national offices and far fewer employees. If you like a lean, fiscally unadventurous administration you may prefer ASCAP.
- BMI gives advances and has relationships with banks to get their members loans against *possible* future earnings. If you think that giving speculative money to emerging talent is too big a risk to take with your royalties, you may prefer ASCAP's purist *if you got a hit you get a split* philosophy.
- BMI has tie-in marketing campaigns with industry trades and equipment makers to give their members "free" subscriptions and "discounts." As you know, there is no free lunch. BMI sponsors these and justifies it as an expense. If you think this is a waste of your money, you may prefer ASCAP.
- BMI throws (on average) more lavish showcases than ASCAP. They also sponsor songwriting workshops, grants, and scholarships galore for emerging writers. If you think exposing the industry to new talent (other than ones you're connected to) is not something you wish to involuntarily subsidize, you may prefer ASCAP.
- ASCAP sponsored a "matching donations" campaign for victims of Katrina, 9/11, and others. It also spends millions each year in "outreach programs" to bring music to poor school districts. If you feel giving your money to disaster charities is a decision that you would like to save for yourself and not subsidize involuntarily, you may prefer BMI. However...
- BMI's nonprofit sister company (the "BMI Foundation") gives away millions each year to other nonprofit organizations for music programs in underdeveloped areas. If you think that teaching a kid in Mozambique how to play the marimba is not what a PRO should be doing with your money, you may prefer ASCAP.

Final score: Unlike other comparisons in this chapter, here there is a clear distinction. ASCAP's expenses are annually about $11,000,000 *lower* than BMI's.[31] They spend far less on overhead and frills and are not as quick to play Robin Hood with your royalties. Whether or not this is a good thing ultimately depends on your politics and how you personally define a PRO's responsibilities to the music business community over their members.

❯ So, Who Owns These Guys?

I don't know about you, but I think it takes real chutzpah to blur the boundaries between "nonprofit" and "nonprofit-making" when vying for your money and to spend so lavishly while some members get little to nothing. More than anything it makes me very curious to know who exactly controls these entities.

Who Controls BMI

The legal name is Broadcast Music, Inc. It is a New York "domestic business corporation" originally filed in 1939. This corporation has established itself in other states such as California and Florida. Because it is a closely held, private corporation (few shareholders and no public stock), there is little documentary evidence of who controls it.

On the BMI website's FAQ there are only scant clues as to the existence of a board, and no clue as to shareholder identity. Most of what is ascertainable is from court papers of lawsuits filed against the corporation. Here's what they reveal:

When BMI was originally incorporated in New York the stockholders were the TV networks CBS and NBC and a couple of other smaller entities. CBS sold their interest in BMI years ago, and other stock has changed hands over the years. The records of these transactions are not publicly available. However, in a brief filed with the Supreme Court involving the now famous Napster case, we know that Meredith Corporation, Clear Channel, and Gannett Co., Inc. (through a wholly owned subsidiary) own as much as 10% each of BMI stock. Meredith Corporation is one of the nation's leading media and marketing companies, with businesses centering on publishing, television broadcasting, and interactive marketing. Gannett Co., Inc., is one of the largest diversified news and information companies in the world, with 102 daily newspapers and 21 television stations covering 17.9 percent of the nation. With over 1,200 terrestrial radio stations Clear Channel is the largest conglomerate of radio and live venues in the continental U.S.

This is only what we can definitively prove. Who knows where the BMI octopus's tentacles reach under the covers?

Is there anything wrong with a PRO being owned by several major media conglomerates? Many think so. Many believe that this is like the fox guarding the hen house since these are the very same companies that BMI is supposed to extract almost *three-quarters of a billion dollars a year* away from and into the pockets of their writers and publishers. A rather obvious conflict of interest.[32] As a safeguard, from time to time government agencies look in on BMI's practices. They have appointed a Federal Magistrate who tries to see that BMI is sticking to the guidelines in their bylaws (ASCAP has one of these too, also the result of government oversight committees)—one lone judge who we have to hope is not the type to get starstruck, bored, or easily "incentivized" to overlook things.

It's possible that in the future, this conflict may force some of these media giants to sell their interests in BMI. Then we'll get to see how BMI's collective bargaining really works when they have to negotiate with an *actual* adversary.

Who Controls ASCAP

ASCAP is another animal entirely. While BMI is owned by the very entities they seek to extract money from (broadcasters) and their members have *no* say in how this money is split up, ASCAP likes to tell people that they are a true "democracy," owned by the members of its society—the writers and publishers. It has an elected board of directors and a voting membership. If you want a voice in how your PRO works, you have no choice but ASCAP, *in theory.*

In reality, the process to get on the ASCAP board is, to use a polite word, *moderated.* The articles of ASCAP require signatures from "five-eighths of one percent of the total writer or publisher members of the society" to qualify for the ballot. Since ASCAP has about 220,000 members, that would mean that over 1,000 signatures are necessary—far more than the 25 signatures that were required only a few years ago. By way of a comparison, you or I or anyone can run for President of the United States, but in reality, you need many signatures, and that just gets you on the ballot. Getting elected is another campaign entirely.

ASCAP management is also less than helpful when it comes to assisting you in getting the signatures you need. They don't publish a list of members who have voting status. Yes, that's right—not all members get to vote. So, if you're saying to yourself, "I know at least 1,000 people in ASCAP; I'll just ask all of them to sign my petition," surprise, surprise—there's a good chance that many of them probably are not eligible to participate in the "democratic" process. Why? Because ASCAP's voting privilege is only available to those who earn "credits." You must have songs that have shown up in their surveys before you get a vote.

And to make matters worse, ASCAP's system is not a true democracy in that you

32 However, it's worth noting that conflicts like this are everywhere in the music business: Big Four distributors who own publishing companies, production companies who own management companies, and law firms who represent parties on both sides of a negotiation.

do not get one person, one vote. It's one vote *times your earnings*. Someone with a lot of credits gets a stronger vote than someone with only a few. So, Billy Joel might get exponentially more voting power with *his one* vote than Joe Blow gets with his one vote. This would be equivalent to a system where if the average American makes $100,000 a year and you make over $1,000,000 a year, your one vote for President of the United States counts ten times more.

So, in truth, saying that ASCAP is owned by its members is about as accurate as saying the U.S. Government is "of the people and [controlled] by the people." It's certainly controlled by some of "the people." But which ones?

ASCAP's board has 24 seats. To be fair and balanced, they have divided them equally between publishers and songwriters. But because of ASCAP's "democratic process," the board has remained in the majority control of a small group of songwriters who possess massive voting credits over the other board members, who are publishers. They and they alone can change the credit/pooling system that currently shows greater favor to pop songwriters than musical composers. If you're a songwriter you want this, regardless of how fair it is. If you're a publisher you may have serious issues.

Bottom line: Both PROs have made it either impossible or virtually impossible for the power structure to be usurped. They are each owned by entities or groups who make decisions based on the personal agenda of their boards. So, how does all this affect which you should join?

- ASCAP's claim that they are a democracy "owned by their members" is, in practice, a non-issue unless you are a superstar. Their system is a bureaucracy that will be about as frustrating to deal with as the DMV. But you can appeal within their system, if you have the patience. If you want a PRO with less red tape and where policy can be changed quickly if you know the right people, you may prefer BMI. But …

- BMI's "government" is a closed door. You have no voice. As a result, BMI has much more latitude in how they spend your money. If you like the way they spend it, great. But if you don't and you don't play golf with a board member, you have only your beer to cry in. (See previous section on how the PROs spend your money.) If you want a PRO that has to answer to some legislative oversight and where you have a chance, however slim, to make changes in policy, then you may prefer ASCAP.

- ASCAP's weighted pooling system can be changed only by board approval—a long, involved process—and before any change is implemented they are required to inform all members. So, the system does not change very often or in any significantly radical way, but when it does you will always know it. And since their contracts are only a year long, if you're unhappy you can easily switch to BMI.

- BMI's Star Chamber management makes it easier to issue advances and compensate for "discrepancies" in the case of writing teams where the same song has earned different payments from ASCAP and BMI, and their weighted pooling system can be changed at any time with relative ease and can respond to ebbs and flows of the changing market. But, unlike ASCAP, BMI is *not* required to inform the members of any shifts prior to their implementation. So if changes happen, by the time you find out they will already have affected you. BMI's contract is a three-year commitment, during which time changes can and *often do* happen. If you like a stable system that despite its flaws is predictable, you may prefer ASCAP.

❯ The Bully Factor

Finally, there is this to consider. I call it the *bully factor*. This means, how aggressive do these companies behave when collecting money? ASCAP's website calls itself "the world's leading performing rights organization" even though it's not justified either in money or membership. BMI's pushes the "nonprofit" bullshit a lot harder than ASCAP and likes to rub ASCAP's irrelevant, elitist history in your face as a selling point.[33] Both can be very hostile about their viewpoints when competing with each other, but how about when dealing with your clients and your audience—the venues and the people who attend them to enjoy your music?

Now, keep in mind, the Internet didn't make music thieves of normal people. History reveals that people will steal music if they think they can get away with it or if they are just too unsophisticated to see that music protected by copyright is private property. It's a PRO's job to hunt down and get money from all the horrible people out there who try to sneak by and play music in public without paying their share. (Like the Girl Scouts of America; see below.) And, in fairness to the PROs, it isn't a job for a nice, understanding group. Radio stations aside (because they have always paid), venues once stole music:

- by hiring pianists to play songs and not pay the writers a cut
- by having unregistered ("hot") jukeboxes that were not affiliated with an accounting agency
- by stealing sheet music and by flat-out refusing to pay the PROs and taking them to court

33 Prior to the 1960s ASCAP's system favored pop music and discriminated against R&B artists. (Black artists, in other words.) This has not been the case for 50 years now, and the board members who presided at that time are long gone. BMI likes to remind the public of the fact that they never discriminated. This argument would be like the Ford Motor Company reminding car buyers that America never had death camps in World War II, like the Germans and the Japanese.

The formation of collective PROs brought strength in numbers. In the 1950s–1980s they began to use their legal muscle to force establishments to pay annual license fees for use of their entire catalog. Soon every bar, radio station, club, luncheonette, and even hot dog vendor if he had an AM radio on at his stand, was on the PRO radar.

When a new bar or club decides to "perform" music, a PRO agent, say one from BMI, will either show up in person or write a letter demanding money for a license. If a venue refuses, then the PRO will threaten to sue. The venue eventually caves in, often after spending thousands in legal fees, and agrees to an annual license. (Anywhere from $200 to $5,000, depending on its size and other factors.) They think their troubles are over. The following week they will get a visit from the other big PRO, ASCAP, and the process begins again. When ASCAP is finished, it's SESAC's turn. (Can you imagine the chaos if every songwriter and publisher seceded from the three PROs in favor of their own "independent" one?)[34]

But in the mid-1990s restaurants fought back and won a substantial legal victory over the PROs by arguing that the music they play is "fair use,"[35] and should not have to be licensed. Even though the new ruling only applies to smaller eateries, this defeat still cost PROs and their writers about $200,000,000 a year, they claim. To make up the loss, PROs began to get tough with others who use their writers' songs, often without regard for the public relations consequences.[36]

- In the fall of 1996 ASCAP shook down the Girl Scouts of America for a license to sing "campfire songs." This resulted in the GSA deleting "Puff the Magic Dragon" and other favorites from their songbook.
- NASA was contacted for a license by copyright holders of "Mustang Sally" (registered with BMI) after astronaut Sally Ride sang "ride, Sally, ride" during a press conference—while orbiting the Earth. They claimed their territory is "the known universe."
- ASCAP has been known to threaten legal action for the singing of "Happy Birthday to You"[37] at ice cream parlors and children's birthday venues.
- In 2002 BMI sued a bar for having karaoke night without a license. One of the "infringing" songs named in the complaint was "God Bless America." (Ironically an ASCAP song.)
- In 2004 BMI supported one of its publishers when they sued a website (JibJab.com) for using a political satire song, "This Land Is Your Land," as the basis for a new political satire.

And finally and most audaciously…

34 Actually, more than one economist has argued that if even ten people tried it the entire system would collapse and very few would get any money.

35 "Fair use": a provision in the Copyright Act that allows a person to use work protected by copyright without payment to the author or permission.

36 These items have been in the press, but the details have not been investigated.

37 In case you didn't know, "Happy Birthday to You," by sisters Mildred and Patty Hill, is still protected by copyright and will be until about 2050. It's registered with ASCAP.

- In 1999 BMI requested that *record stores* pay for a license for playing CDs while customers shop and having in-store performances of pop artists to promote new releases. The stores flat-out refused, daring them to sue. BMI opted not to.

At one time in the 1930s, many states, including Nebraska and Wyoming, passed laws prohibiting the collection of music licensing fees. About 30 other states also followed suit.[38] Why didn't you already know any of this? Because while the media loves to lambaste the RIAA for suing file-sharers, the PROs seem to attract only a tenth of the bad press for their sometimes extreme interpretation of copyright law.

Meanwhile, both ASCAP and BMI in 2005 Capitol Hill testimony claimed that life was "unfair" to these billion-dollar agencies because the government "forced" them to issue a license to anyone who wants one, no matter how tasteless the use, while allowing SESAC the privilege of being able to pick and choose who gets to publicly perform their catalog.[39] This is basically like saying, "We (ASCAP and BMI) service 95% of the market because the government forces us."

SESAC scoffs at this and claims that being able to refuse a license is small advantage considering that both ASCAP and BMI have used "unfair" and brutally "anticompetitive tactics" to try and drive them out of business. They have claimed publicly:

- That both ASCAP and BMI have a secret policy wherein if a writer leaves either of them to go to SESAC, the PRO they left will withhold money.
- ASCAP and BMI use predatory pricing by giving away free licenses for digital broadcasts, something that SESAC claims they cannot afford to do.
- That ASCAP and BMI allow incorrect information to be maintained in databases, thus impeding the accurate distribution of license fees.
- That ASCAP and BMI have deliberately excluded them from participating in the planning stages of a "master PRO" that would govern the Internet and digital performances, cutting down the expenses that are duplicated by having multiple PROs.

The SESAC complaint list goes on and on.

38 Federal courts have ruled that even if a State law prohibits a PRO from trying to collect, they can still do so under Federal law. (Nebraska vs. Remick Music, 1946 and Ocasek vs. Hegglund, 1987)

39 Look up "Consent Decree" for more on this.

⊘ Conclusion: So Which PRO Is Right for You?

It's hard to say whether your choice of PRO will be the most important decision that you make in your music career, but it is up there with what I call the "big three decisions":

- What label you sign with (if any)
- What publisher you sign with (if any) and
- What musical direction you decide to take (if any)

So it's worth more than a casual coin flip or basing it on which rep got to you first with a drink ticket or an invitation to play at a showcase.

The right choice for you may ultimately boil down to a few considerations, but the main one is probably whose philosophy you relate to more. To compare the world of U.S. PROs to our two-party political system, I would say that ASCAP is the more "conservative" PRO in that they have leaner expenses and a more fiscally cautious approach to spending their members' money. BMI is more of the liberal "rock 'n' roll" PRO with a *we got it, so we're spreadin' it around* philosophy.[40] I don't think in this regard one is better than the other, just different.

Ironically, the very people who are more attracted to BMI's philosophy—pop writers whose careers can be a feast-or-famine roller-coaster ride—are better served by ASCAP's pooling system. And classical composers—who are quite probably more conservative and have longer, more stable careers—are better served by BMI's calculations.

On a broader scale, some tech gurus are saying that both mega PROs will soon be a thing of the past once Internet-based technology makes it possible for venues to do "direct licensing" from writers.[41] The technocrats never seem to want to give us a timeline for this prediction, however.[42] It may happen someday, but don't hold your breath or plan on this as an excuse to avoid making a decision about joining one of the current PROs. My philosophy for predicting the future has always been:

Technology may advance at the speed of light, but it's filtered through the speed of bureaucracy.

---

40 Although more competition may force them to tighten their belts. In December of 2005 they announced that they had cut back their expenses.

41 Some believe that a standard "compulsory license" for performances will be the answer to all the complex new forms of media who need to license music. This would diminish the PRO's bargaining power substantially. See the "Publishing" chapter, page 81 for more on what a "compulsory license" is.

42 I tried to in my new book, Million Dollar Mistakes. See the last chapter, called, "The Future of Music and Its Enemies."

Though the technology exists for the large conglomerates to cut out a middle-man, that doesn't mean that they will want to. If you build it, they don't always come, and if they do come, it's generally very slowly and over time. Large corporations like dancing with other large corporations. They feel safe in knowing that things are handled, in their view, "professionally."

Now, a personal comment: I have tried not to seem like I'm favoring either ASCAP or BMI in this chapter. But I would like the reader to note that in verifying my facts for what you have just read, representatives of ASCAP, knowing that I was going to write something sobering, were forthcoming and cooperative. I wish I could have said the same for BMI. All they would give me was a press release. That might be worth something to some of you.

Only time will tell if ASCAP and BMI will grow more powerful or outgrow their usefulness. Much of this will depend on whether or not its members, as well as the Department of Justice and the Federal Trade Commission, agree with the PRO agenda and the methods they use. But you can see how creative their pitches can get when the booty is worth only $1.3 billion a year. As digital broadcasting evolves, the stakes will grow into the tens of billions a year. I can't wait to then see how competitive things get for the "societies." I for one I plan to keep a front-row seat, with popcorn and drink in hand.

Coke, anyone?

CHAPTER TWENTY-ONE

⊚Production Boners

Next, let's take a look at some of the myths that can trip you up in the recording studio.

⊙ You Need a "Master Quality" Demo to Get a Deal

"Master quality" is perhaps the most misused bit of jargon that circulates within the industry, next to "digital." The term master quality and whether or not an artist gets signed are unrelated. I know of many artists who were signed on the basis of 4-track demos made in their living rooms.

In a recording contract, the term master quality will be used to describe the level of quality that the label will accept for commercial distribution of the final recording. This clause is in there to prevent the producer or artist from taking a hundred-thousand-dollar advance and delivering a 4-track Porta-studio final mix.

In these contracts the term "master" means the final version from which all other copies will be made. It does not necessarily mean 24- or 48-track digital recordings, although those are the norm. On the contrary, record companies have been known to release the original 8-track *analog* home recordings if the sound is good enough. So the de facto definition of master quality can only mean a recording that the label deems acceptable for commercial distribution.

Since labels have, at one time or another, deemed all formats of recording acceptable, there can be no specific definition of master quality that relates to the number of tracks that are used or whether the recording is analog or digital. So if the label can't define what format a master recording should be recorded in, how can they only accept master quality for submissions? You see the paradox?

⊜ You Must Record on a Digital Medium with at Least 100 Tracks

While we're on this subject, I want to dispel another myth concerning master quality. A federal judge once said, in his decision concerning a pornography case, that he couldn't define pornography, but he knew it when he saw it. It's the same with "master recordings." Since so many records have been done on so many different formats over the years, no one can really use a particular format to define master quality. The only thing you can do is use your ears. If it sounds like a record, it is a record—period.

Far more important than the number of tracks that are available is the quality of each track and the quality of the equipment used to deliver the audio signal. I'd rather have eight quality analog tracks to produce with than 100 poor ones, digital or not.

To prove my point, here are a few examples of hit records that were not recorded on large formats:

Dark Side of the Moon—Pink Floyd 8-track
Abbey Road—The Beatles 8-track
Sgt. Pepper's Lonely Hearts Club Band—The Beatles 4-track
"Brown Sugar"—The Rolling Stones 4-track
"Sweet Dreams Are Made of This"—Eurythmics 8-track
"Stairway to Heaven"—Led Zeppelin 8-track

"Respect"—Aretha Franklin 4-track

Look Sharp!—Joe Jackson 8-track

ABC—The Jackson 5 .... 4-track

Most pre-1975 Motown records.. 3-track

❯ Why the Cassettes Sound Muddy

Well, aside from the fact that CDs sound cleaner than tapes in general, there is a more tragic reason why commercially produced analog audiocassettes tend to sound awful.

CDs are digitally transferred to each copy. Since it's a pure digital transfer, that means that there is no generation loss from copy to copy. It also means that each machine will receive the information exactly the same way as the previous machine.

With tapes, however, the duplication process is quite different. The music is transferred to a large tape loop. This loop is put in a bin that winds the tape over the playback head very fast. As it spins, the music is transferred to many cassettes simultaneously at high speed. The faster the dubbing speed, the lower the fidelity. This should be familiar to anyone who's made double-speed cassette-to-cassette copies on their home stereo. You will notice a loss of fidelity and additional hiss at only two times the normal speed. Usually, full-length records are transferred at 32 times the normal "reel" speed.

The other drawback is that the record heads of the cassette machines that are recording the music often fall out of alignment. The duplication house is supposed to align them daily, but there are usually hundreds of them, and whoever is in charge tends to slack off. This leads to poor cassette reproduction, which, unfortunately, represents a little over a third of the artist's sales. (According to the RIAA, in 2001 U.S. artists sold roughly twice as many CDs as cassettes.)

There is little anyone can do about this, because record companies won't pay for slower "real-time transfers" of the album due to the added cost. This is why your homemade "bootlegged" tapes of CDs often sound better than the official commercial ones.

CHAPTER TWENTY-TWO

⊕Marketing Mishigas

After the record is completed, the marketing department gets their crack at figuring out how to best represent the artist to the public. Most of the time it's of benefit to the artist. But sometimes . . .

This section looks at the strengths and weaknesses of the marketing process.

⊜ Lots of Airplay Assures Big Record Sales

Hopefully. While there is a direct correlation between radio play and sales, it would not be uncommon for a song to become a "radio hit." The term has an obvious meaning. It's when a song gets put on many playlists—either because the label has promoted it to many stations or because the station manager likes and believes in it—but the record stores can't seem to sell the record. This happens a lot with sophomores (an artist who has a great first record but a less than successful second record). The radio will play it to death, but the airplay won't translate into record sales.[1]

Then there are the classics like "Wild Thing," which is still played over and over on the radio but sells barely any records. Or, more commonly, dance records,

[1] Unless it's part of a compilation album.

which do well in the clubs and on the air but don't translate into big sales at the stores as one would think.

The reverse can be true. Just because the radio doesn't play a record doesn't mean that it isn't selling. *Enigma* got very little radio play comparatively but sold over a million copies.

➤ "We Get to Say What Our Album Cover Will Look Like"

Are you sure? Read your contract carefully. If it says, "The artist will be consulted for final approval," that means all the label has to do is ask you what you think; it doesn't mean that they have to take your advice. If it says, "The artist will contribute to the cover art design," that means that you can submit something, but again they don't have to use it.[2] Whatever way you think you can get control of this, there is usually a loophole that will let the label get around it. Labels rarely, if ever, give up the right to decide how to package a new artist. Deal with it, and try to rationalize that they want you to sell the most records that you possibly can, so they're on your side even if it seems they're not.

[2] See "Legal-ease?," page 227.

➤ Record Industry Slumps Are the Direct Result of Poor A&R Decision-Making

Every time the record industry has a bad year, the rhetoric is the same. "It's because the labels have lost touch with their market. They don't know good music when they hear it." I disagree.

In most cases these stories are generated by music journalists who have an ax to grind with major labels. Often the records that they give poor reviews to sell the most. Conversely, the records they give the best reviews to often go nowhere. Who can say why?[3]

In the years that record sales have been universally deflated there is usually an outside force that interfered. In 1996 every major paper ran a story stating that were it not for Alanis Morissette and Hootie and the Blowfish, the industry would have sold almost no records. Journalists seem to overlook the coincidence that 1996 was also the big boom year for home computers and the public's fascination with the

[3] For some odd reason, good reviews in the mainstream papers and magazines seem to be the kiss of death for an album. Underground reviews apparently carry more weight. This is probably because most young record buyers don't trust mainstream media's taste in "good music."

RIPPIN', BURNIN', DOIN' TIME

You're not going to believe this one. The Recording Industry Association of Amerika (RIAA), asserting their position that all "file sharers" should get nothing less than capital punishment, tipped off a district attorney about a 19-year-old student who was "sharing" Pink Floyd's *Dark Side of the Moon* (a record just about everyone owns anyway) with about 3,000 other fellow students. The goat was a graphics-design freshman at Oklahoma University. The DA seized his computer and placed him under arrest. The student pleaded no contest to a misdemeanor charge of "unlawful advertisement or offer to distribute sound recordings" and was fined $5,000. He also had to forfeit his computer, monitor, and hard drives so they could be destroyed.

The irony is that while another college student was heralded on the cover of *Time* magazine for creating Napster, the ultimate file-sharing system with millions of users, this art student—with only a campus-full of exposure—will now have a criminal record. Can somebody explain this to me so that it makes sense?

Internet. Also, for the first time in recent years, television hit with shows that grabbed a young audience (*Friends* and *The X-Files,* to name two).

The record industry functions on surplus income. That's why it markets itself mostly to the under-20 crowd; they have no mortgages or child support payments and plenty of cash for fun stuff. The last great upset in record sales came in the early '80s. Critics once again claimed that it was because record companies were putting out junk. This was also the same time that Baby Boomers (who fueled record sales throughout the '60s and '70s) were now buying homes and having babies of their own. Coincidence?

The good news is that pendulums swing, trends come around, and for every bad year there usually follows a year of "great growth." The executive turntable rotates and the new generals take the credit for what is, by and large, the natural ebb and flow of commerce. There's no business like show business.

CHAPTER TWENTY-THREE

⊙Getting Credit Where Credit Is Due

On major-label albums credit is more coveted than people realize. A&R people typically want executive producer credit. Engineers and writers typically want coproducer credit. Key musicians hired for overdub sessions have often argued that their contributions to the material constitute a coproduction or cowriter credit. DJs, who are part of rap groups, have hired lawyers claiming that the turntable they "play" is a musical instrument and therefore they should be paid a union wage for session work and credited for it. Singers whose vocals have been sampled and used for other records have sued if they didn't get credit on the sampled record. Studios have bargained with producers to include them as the studio of record on an album just so they can tell their clients that "this hit was recorded here."

It can get brutal. Here are a few guidelines to credit—how to get it and when to watch your back.

⊙ Look for the Union Label

My first paying job in the music industry was as a sideman playing on the soundtrack of a motion picture. I was only 17, and as you can imagine I was quite excited; it was my first recording session, and it was at Sigma Sound, where Billy Joel and Aerosmith were recording their albums at the same time. I was put in a glass booth and did my thing. It was cool.

When the session was over, I was asked to sign a piece of paper that required me to join Local 802 of the AFM (see page 42). The dues would have cost me everything that I earned for doing the session. But aside from that, I didn't want to join a union that I knew would do nothing to get me work. I declined to join, as did many other first-timers on the session.

ROCK AND TUNA TEKI ROLL

In the mid-'80s I was working for a Japanese production company owned by one of the major distributors. We manufactured karaoke music.

They had set up shop in a midtown studio in Manhattan and were hiring union musicians left and right for sessions, but were paying them only $20 per hour. (And believe me, they worked them.) Twenty dollars an hour doesn't even come close to the union minimum scale of about $300 for a three-hour session. But the company didn't care. This was their deal, and they weren't putting a gun to anyone's head to take their money.

I can recall many top musicians coming through those doors for work every day—musicians who play in TV bands and on commercials for thousands of dollars were showing up at this company to pick up an extra couple of hundred off the books for pocket cash.

The AFM eventually found out and paid the studio a visit to speak to the Japanese project director. The conversation was very short. The director screamed to the union representative in Japanese and broken English that he didn't care about their "fucking union," and to "get the fuck out" or he would have him "arrested for trespassing."

The union threatened to pull the cards of anyone who worked for this company again. So from then on, the musicians used fake names on their invoices. Since they weren't getting credit on a karaoke record, they didn't care.

The law of supply and demand will always prevail over organized policies.

When the record came out, I ran to the record store and bought the album. I couldn't wait to see my name on a record, especially such a popular one. But when I ripped open the cellophane and looked at the liner notes, I saw that my name wasn't mentioned. In fact, the credit for the work that I had done had been given to someone else.

Imagine my disappointment and anger.

I called the production company and spoke to a woman that I had become friendly with. She did some inquiring and told me that since the recording sessions were union sessions, only union people were allowed to get credit. The person listed where my name should have been was a union session player who never even set foot in the studio with us.

In retrospect, I should have joined the union, because the credit was more important than the money, and the union does guarantee certain rights. This was not explained to me at the time, however. But the idea of only giving credit to union players is not uncommon. In fact, most major labels insist that their recording artists join the union. And, by agreement with the union, any player who doesn't join will not receive credit on the record, even if they're part of the established band.[1] Sometimes the joining dues are paid for out of the artist's advance, sometimes not, but for this reason alone the union gets members. No one wants to pass up a major label credit for a few hundred bucks.

[1] The established band is really the band as a corporate entity, see page 224.

This insistence that starving musicians spend hundreds of dollars to join an organization that offers little by way of health benefits and does not guarantee work is one of the last old-economy rituals to fade away and also shows the callousness that big business takes toward labor. At the same time, record companies offer even less by way of pension plans, or any form of assistance in helping the artists they exploit. So unfortunately, even though the union may not be the musician's best friend, it's the musician's only friend.

Incidentally, indie labels don't usually engage in this kind of policy, and it's my guess that majors will stop soon. The connections between unionized labor and corporate management are thinning day by day in this country. As the connection thins, so does the union's power. One particularly colorful example of the thinning process is illustrated in the "Rock and Tuna Teki Roll" sidebar.

In the area of Latin music this matter of credit has become a major cancer. Most albums that are recorded on major labels' Latin imprints are not done under a union contract. So a musician getting proper credit as well as proper pay is an uphill battle.

❯ Major Label Philosophy on Giving Credit to Sidemen and Engineers

Musicians are protected to some degree by the fact that they have a union. Unfortunately, they're the only group in the music industry that has this privilege. Engineers, producers, recording studios, programmers (sometimes classified as keyboard players), DJs (who claim the turntable as a musical instrument), and writers are not unionized and have no voice to assert their right to be credited for work; they are at the mercy of the record labels.[2] Unfortunately, unless the producer submits the credits, the label often doesn't make any effort to discover who actually worked on the record.

[2] Writers receive protection from credit fraud because miscrediting the writer of a song can have serious consequences. (See "The Myth of Copyright Protection," page 179.)

"WE'LL FIX YOUR CREDIT ON THE NEXT PRINTING"

On one record that I engineered early in my career, the producer forgot to include my engineering credits on two songs. Since both songs charted, I was anxious to get my name where it belonged. I called the label, but they wanted proof that I had worked on the record. My next step was to call the producer. He swore that he submitted my name; the label said otherwise. The producer wrote a letter to the label asking that my credit be added in the next printing. I also had the recording studio where we cut the record fax the session reports to the label. I had to sign those reports—*indisputable proof that I did the work.* The assistant to the A&R director finally said that they would change the liner notes in the next printing. They never did. Even if the assistant was being sincere about changing the notes in the second printing, turnover in the record biz is so high that in all likelihood he probably quit or was fired shortly afterward. The new person would not have been left a memo to deal with such an insignificant problem, so it would get shoved under the rug forever.

The record to date has sold several million copies.

As you might guess, producers don't consider policing their underlings' credit a high priority. Producers generally like to take credit for as much as they can. There are exceptions, and it is important to quickly ascertain what type of producer you are working for and deal with your credit from there.[3] I have been shafted so many times on this issue that the exact spelling and description of my credit is outlined in my contracts.

[3] See "Control Freaks," page 30.

Labels complain that record buyers don't read credits and that they take up too much space, costing the artist money for the additional panel of the packaging jacket. Labels will use this as leverage to get the artist on their side of the argument, but it's total bullshit. It doesn't even cost a penny to put an extra panel on a CD. The unspeakable fact is that labels and producers just aren't that enthusiastic in general about giving credit. Believe it or not, giving credit means exposing themselves to liability.

How, you ask? It's simple but sad. When a record is a hit, everybody who was even in the neighborhood when it was made comes out of the woodwork to say that they had something to do with it. People will even try to claim that they cowrote the song. Obviously, if they have a credit on the record, the label can't say they never heard

SONGWRITERS' CREDIT

Writers are, under most circumstances, protected under the law against fraudulent credit being assigned to their song. However, there are cases where songs are done as work-for-hire and the employer puts their byline on the song and doesn't include the original writer's credit. I believe that there's something evil about this, but apparently it's legal.

In fact, one very large entertainment company has been known to ask the writer of a song to sign over the complete copyright and byline even if the writer does not work for the company and the song pre-existed the film project it's being bought for. The legality of claiming that a pre-existing song could be work-for-hire is, at the moment, questionable and will remain so until someone takes this company to court. This is not likely to happen for two reasons: (1) the company is extremely powerful, and (2) a copyright infringement case would be held in federal court—lots of time and money and no punitive damages even if the songwriter prevails.

of them, so they are forced to deal and settle with the individual. This doesn't happen a lot, but it happens often enough to make labels wary about giving credit indiscriminately. As a result, proper credit for the talent on great records is not given or, worse yet, is stolen. It's not uncommon for credit to be given as a favor in exchange for a favor that is owed.

❯ How to Get Even

Legally, there is little anyone can do to get record companies to print complete or even accurate credits in the liner notes of records. When my credit was omitted from that multiplatinum record I mentioned in the sidebar, I went to an attorney to discuss my options. According to him I could have sued the record company for "publishing false information." This would have to be done as what's called a class action suit. This means I would be filing suit in the name of every person who bought a record and was potentially misled by the information the label falsely printed.

As you can imagine, this would be hard to prove, and wouldn't do much for my reputation either. Plus, a victory wouldn't necessarily amount to much money for me.

A personal civil suit, my other option, would have required me to prove that the omitting of my credit cost me money personally. Even though it might seem obvious to most that not having a major label credit could cost an up-and-coming professional money, proving it in a court of law is another matter. So I let it go.

But, I discovered through the process that there is one way around the system, but you have to be ballsy and sneaky. However, I have been advised that I must tell you **NOT TO DO THIS. THIS IS WRONG. IT IS BAD. DON'T DO IT. I AM NOT RECOMMENDING THAT YOU DO THIS. THE PUBLISHERS DO NOT RECOMMEND THAT YOU DO THIS. THE BOOKSTORE WHERE YOU BOUGHT THIS BOOK DOES NOT RECOMMEND THAT YOU DO THIS.**

But in case you're still interested, here's how it goes . . .

Record companies hate to redo the printing plate of the liner notes (known as the mechanical) once it has been approved. The liner notes are all drawn by the art department, which is part of the production department at the label.(Note: "Production department," when used to describe a part of a record company, has nothing to do with the production of the recording. It's just the department responsible for the final assemblage of the CD and its packaging.)

If you have friends who work in the company that is putting out the record that you want credit on, have them find out who is the artist drafting the mechanical. It may be more than one person, but it doesn't matter—the more there are, the better it is for you. Just find one of them. These people are usually paid very little, and they are easily bribed with concert tickets or free goods. However, no amount of money will bribe them unless there is a way for them to cover their ass in case of discovery.

This can be handled simply by faxing a memo with the letterhead of a management agency directly to the art department. The memo should be marked with an important person's signature forged on it and should state the credit that must be added. Example:

> To: **Lori Rubinstein (low-paid employee/conspirator**
> **in the art or production department)**
> From: **Gleason Management Inc./Jason Gleason**
> **(important name that everyone will recognize)**
> Re: **Addition to liner notes for Johnny Rock Star album**
> ***Give Me a Break***
>
> Please be advised that the name Moses Avalon should be added to the
> engineering credits.
> **—Jason Gleason/Management for Johnny Rock Star**

Your conspirator will add the credit and then give the entire mechanical to the head of the production department, as usual, for their approval. The head of production in a major label will, in all likelihood, not even question the addition, because such last-minute changes are done frequently and he or she will have five projects going at a time, all with deadlines. If they do question it, Lori, the fictional conspirator, will show them the memo.

The VP of marketing is next in the approval process. They will have even less of an idea if it's right. If they do question it and call the management company, they will find out that it's a fraud. This could be a problem, but all that will happen is that they will delete the credit and you will be no worse off than you were before. Your friend will be covered, because a lowly mechanical artist would have no way of knowing if the memo was or wasn't real. With no one to blame, all departments will chalk it up to another prankster trying to get one over on a record label. But knowing human nature, and our natural tendency to do as little as possible to make waves, they will probably approve the final draft without even questioning the change. By the time anyone realizes that the credit is unauthorized, the CD will be on the shelves in the record store. If you've read my discussion of the way the distribution chain works, you should be able to guess why the record company will never recall the records for a liner note error. If you're laughing at this little plot, laugh at this: I am personally aware of over 20 situations that were resolved in exactly the manner I've just described.[4]

The lesson to be learned:

Low-paid employees make excellent spies.

[4] The publisher has requested that I put a disclaimer here stating that presentation of this incident is not an endorsement of it. In other words, don't try this. You could be arrested.

❯ The "Coproduction" Credit

As bands gain more clout, they will want to produce their own recordings. It's not uncommon that the band and engineer end up doing most of the producer's work anyway. The riff goes something like this: The producer says to the engineer or artist, "I have to do some things. I'll be back in a couple of hours. Record the vocals, okay?" Of course, they will oblige. But what does "record the vocals" mean? If the engineer or artist must decide which takes to keep and which to do over, doesn't that mean they're doing the producer's job? The answer is yes, definitely.

It happens that way because snagging a major credited producer if you're not a top act is not all it's cracked up to be. Here's why:

If the producer they have seduced with a lot of money also has other acts that he or she is producing, the artist may find that the one really in charge of making the record is not the producer but the producer's assistant.

Big producers prioritize their jobs. They will give most of their attention to one big project but let their engineer or a protégé attend to the lesser ones. Only if the lesser act is lucky will the producer even take the time to personally okay the tracks before they go to the label for final approval.

But if the engineer or artist voices a dissenting opinion that they deserve recognition as a producer, they can generally be pacified with a coproducer credit.

Here's the catch-Coproducers are not listed on the *Billboard* charts as one of the producers of the song. (Nor do they get any points.) In essence, the credit serves only as a résumé builder (much like the vice presidency of the United States). What they should be asking for is a line that reads, "Produced by Joe Producer and Johnny Rock Star" (or "and Eddie Engineer").

CHAPTER TWENTY-FOUR

⊘Industry Census

The ridiculous myth that everyone seems to accept at face value is that the record industry is a small place and everyone knows everyone. This is completely unfounded. The people who still say things like this are the ones that have been in the business for years or even a couple of decades. They deal with the same people constantly and think that it's a small community. Indeed, when they were starting out in the industry, it was much smaller. In the '60s there were only about 20 or so legitimate labels and about a hundred independents. There were maybe 30 A&R people worth talking to.

Nowadays there are about 1,000 labels in this country alone. About two or three new ones spring up every month, as a couple of others fade away. While it's true that the distribution pyramid is getting more bottom-heavy and the people at the top are therefore more elite, the structure of the industry has changed and made these people less significant than they might want to admit. Currently there are about 35 labels that could be called "majors," which would include several one-deeps that have made outstanding names for themselves, like Jive and Verve. Combined, these 35 companies create seats for approximately 1,287 executives.[1] Yes, we've grown quite a bit since the '60s. But leaving these 1,287 folks aside, you no longer need a major label to break an

[1] Up from 1,260 since the 2001 edition of *Confessions.*

act, as we saw in "The Vanity Label," page 151. The indie distribution channels are getting more effective by the day, and things like iTunes and Yahoo make it possible for artists to market themselves with a bit of ingenuity and a fraction of the budget that was once needed. Online e-tailers like Amazon also make it possible for anyone to distribute themselves. With these new entities, the network of nepotism has also expanded greatly, giving powerful jobs to a massive new base of people. The local college radio DJ now plays a more-than-insignificant role in breaking a record in a region, as do bloggers that cover local music scenes. This means that when you size up the populace of the industry you have to include these people as well.

There is no way one can say this is a small industry when you include all of the people who contribute to the success of a record. If you include the indie promoters, the indie publicity people that the artist hires, the local and regional DJs and their program directors, the engineers and mastering house, e-tailers, digital distributors, and the secretaries and office support people who work for these entities, you can figure on well over 1,000 people who help contribute to the success of a record and an industry whose population is in the neighborhood of about 500,000 nationwide.

So while we're discussing the makeup of the industry I thought I'd give a few special interest groups something to chew on.

➲ Are All the Powerful People in the Business Jews?

I have been witness to many a conversation with Jewish folk bemoaning the fact that they wish there were some truth to the stereotype: that there is a powerful network of Jews who hire each other and meet secretly to direct the major trends in the record business. But this is not true, and anyone who still believes it is the case hasn't done their homework. If one were to take the time to do any research, they would see that Jews are a minority in this and every other business, as they are a minority in the world (about .03% worldwide). It does, however, seem that there are an awful lot of Jews in the entertainment industry. Without going into a history of minority life in America, I offer this simplified explanation.

Most of the music industry revolves around New York and L.A. These two cities have the largest population of Jews in the world—even more than Israel. New York has about two and a half million Jews out of its eight million people. This means that the odds are about one in four that any person you meet, regardless of their profession, will be a Jew. But I can assure you that in places like Nashville (the other U.S. music industry capital), London, Munich, Chicago, Minneapolis, Seattle, Austin, Latin America, and Canada, the situation is quite different.

Also, one has to remember that the Jewish community in this country rose largely out of poverty, like most immigrant communities, and found it hard to get decent paying work. Because of discrimination, many Jews who made it out of the ghettos of New York (where over 90% of all Jewish immigrants entered this country in the late 1800s and early 1900s) started working in new industries where the status quo had not yet been established—like the entertainment industry. Over the years, as the community grew, so did its power base. Of the 35 major labels, and their 1,287 executive positions, about 20% are occupied by those of the Jewish persuasion. Most of them occupy positions in A&R and finance. On the surface this might seem like there are Jews everywhere. But one must also consider two other important factors. First, in the indie record world the ratio of Jews in the driver's seat is considerably smaller—less than 5% in the CEO positions. Also Latin divisions of the majors are almost completely Jew-free.

The other important thing to note is that most major record companies are owned by larger multinational holding companies. These companies do not directly decide which bands to sign, but they do determine if the president of the label will have his or her job next month. The boards of directors of these companies are the real power in the music industry. With the exception of Gerald Levin at Time-Warner, no chairman of the board or chief executive officer position in these companies is held by a Jew. And out of the 62-odd members of the combined board of directors of the companies that own the Big Four, only 11 have names that even sound Jewish. (See "The Big Picture," page 293.)

❯ Are Women Discriminated Against in the Music Business?

It would be easy to jump on the activist bandwagon and talk about the discrimination that women face in business. But this is a book about naked truth, not political correctness, so I won't insult your intelligence by candy-coating this important issue.

The long hours required to excel in this industry make it hard for anyone who's planning a family to succeed, regardless of their sex. By way of a stereotype, since women tend to have a stronger instinct toward family, they are naturally going to be affected more by this than men.

While I'm sure that the lion's share of discrimination stories do have truth to them, I tend not to see big business discriminating against women specifically as much as I see it keeping down all contenders in general. I view it as more of a class struggle than a race or sex struggle. The fact of the matter is that record companies are so greedy for good product that if someone put a hit on their desk, they wouldn't care if it was produced by a woman, a man, or a chimpanzee.

When assessing the degree of effectiveness or presence that women have in the industry, it has to be remembered that women in the workforce in general are quite new. It is only since the 1960s that women as a class have expressed an organized interest in forgoing the conventional roles of wife and mother and opting for the high-pressure, corrupt, power-hoarding careers that men have long enjoyed. Dismantling any power structure, especially the male-dominated workforce that has had over 10,000 years to evolve to its current standard, is a long process; in 1990 there were fewer than five women in CEO, COO, or CFO positions at the 35 major labels. But by 1997 that number climbed to 16[2] and has remained stable since then. Today almost 31% of the major labels have women in VP/national director positions, and more than a third of them have women as VPs of A&R. Of the 1,287 executive titles offered by the Big Four, 400 of them were held by women in 2004.[3] That's approximately one in three executive positions held by the fairer sex. And if you look at two-deep labels, the percentage of women in the driver's seat increases. Compared to other industries, like finance, medicine, and law, the music industry—with its 31% ratio—is highly progressive.

As producers, women's struggle is harder. Even female A&R representatives tend to prefer a man in the producer's chair. I'm sure this will change as more women make the bid to be producers and it becomes less unusual to hire women for this position, but this will not be a battle that is easily won. Most artists are men (rather testosterone-driven ones at that) and will probably have trouble accepting a woman as having control over their record. No amount of social reconditioning is likely to change this attitude anytime soon. If I may wax psychological for a moment, in my experience many women artists—for whatever reason—also seem to prefer men as the father figure in the studio.[4]

As managers, however, women seem to fare much better. According to *The Music Business Registry*,[5] out of the 4,387 people listed who call themselves managers, 1,785 are women, almost one-third. And this percentage is climbing yearly.

[2] That's 16 out of the (approximately) 35 major labels, or roughly half the ndustry.

[3] Down from 410 since the 2001 edition of *Confessions*.

[4] If you think I'm full of it, look at the production credits on the jacket of any powerful female recording artist's CD. You'll be hard-pressed to find a woman's name credited as the producer, unless it's the artist naming herself as a producer.

[5] *The Music Business Registry*, published twice a year, lists the names and contact information for producer's, managers, and A&R persons. http://www.musicregistry.com

CHAPTER TWENTY-FIVE

❯The Big Picture,
or the Record Industry from the Point of View of the Rest of the World

Newspapers love to print huge numbers describing the record industry's annual worth. Four billion a year, $8 billion a year, $12 billion a year. I've seen it go as high as $40 billion. But what real meaning do these numbers have? Unless you know the cost-to-profit ratio, they have zero meaning. A company can earn $1 billion in one year, but if it cost $999,999,999 to run the company, then they made only a dollar. Think this is a far-fetched example? It's not. In 2001 Sony Music took in almost $5 billion in sales. But after expenses, they were left with only $400 million—about 8 cents on the dollar.

So what does this have to do with getting a record deal? Nothing. This chapter has nothing to do with record deals. It's a bird's-eye view of the industry and will probably not have much to do with your day-to-day operations in music. So why is it in this book?

Obviously I think there is value in understanding the big picture of business and how our financially small but emotionally powerful industry fits into the global puzzle, so this chapter is more theory than anything else.

Santayana said, "To predict the future you must look at the past." I have my own interpretation of that: The key to making money is understanding trends. The key to predicting trends is understanding how big players interpret their past mistakes.

❯ Do Record Companies Really Make Any Money?

The answer is not as obvious as you might think. If you look at entertainment shows, you'd expect that the music business is alive and healthy, with everyone making zillions of dollars. Careers are built and huge salaries paid to executives, artists, and other pros. But does it make money for the one entity footing the bill—the parent record label? This is a difficult question to answer, since we don't know exactly how much money they make after they pay out all those huge advances and salaries. But we can use some information that is public to build a gauge. For example, when MCA was sold to the Seagram beverage company for approximately $10 billion— a shockingly high price to those in the know—it sent ripples throughout the industry and gave other multinationals the expectation that they could sell their record divisions for high prices. EMI and WEA both restructured, trimming the fat to make them lean and attractive to hungry purchasers.

When the smoke cleared, there were none. EMI was considered substantially more successful than MCA, yet even at an asking price of only $9 billion ($1 billion lower than MCA's closing price) it could get no takers. For a company that's supposed to earn $7 billion a year, this is fairly pathetic.[1]

What's the Story?

The answer lies in how these companies fit into the portfolios of their parent companies and how they fare over the long haul. Observe:

MCA has been sold four times within 15 years for a cumulative price of over $18 billion. Yet it hasn't earned anywhere near that in the same time period.[2] If Seagram had an agenda other than profit for owning MCA, they may have not cared whether the company actually makes money by selling records. As history reveals, the position of MCA/Universal in Seagram's portfolio made them an attractive buy for media giant the Vivendi Corporation in 2001. They sold to Vivendi for a substantial bonus to the company's key players, even though Universal had not increased profits since they were originally bought by Seagram. In the Warner deal of 2005, even though the company failed to sell enough stock to pay off its debt, the engineers of the deal managed to pocket millions in broker fees.

Whatever the financial details, the fact remains that record companies are not necessarily bought because their record sales are profitable, as illustrated below.

[1] A general rule of thumb in finance is that if the earnings of a company over a five-year period can surpass its sale price, it's a good buy. Thus, EMI would have earned $35 billion over five years, making the $9 billion asking price very attractive.

[2] This example is somewhat exaggerated to make a point. In truth, profits were earned upon each individual sale of the company. However, in the 1980s the value of many companies was based on estimates of their future earnings potential rather than their present actual earnings. Ofttimes estimates were a bit optimistic.

Loss Leader

"Loss leader" is an old retail expression. Its roots come from the ploy of having a giveaway item that draws one into a retail store, after which the patron would be sold other things. A crude but simple example might be the "free" prize one finds in the bottom of breakfast cereal for children. (All right, I admit it, I still buy them, too.)

Several of the multinationals that used to hold major label record companies found that there was a synergy between record sales and other products they manufactured. For example, Sony and PolyGram (which was owned by Philips until 1999) co-own the patent on the compact disc. Every time a CD is manufactured they each enjoy a small royalty. It doesn't matter if the records sell in a store or online—they get the fee at the manufacturing end. By this gauge it could be argued that the artist and the musical content on the CD is a loss leader[3] (sometimes called, in the corporate world, a "support function") for generating activity in the CD-manufacturing business, thus earning money for the company's patent division. It is not surprising, then, that in 1999 Philips sold PolyGram. One probable reason is that the patent on the CD is soon to become public domain. Without patent royalties, Philips probably doesn't see the sense in keeping the company in its family.

Another example is RCA, whose record division in the 1950s lost money consistently and was kept running solely because RCA also manufactured record players.[4] Radio airplay stimulated sales of record players. This may seem far-fetched, but believe me, it isn't. Big business looks at the big picture. For example: A major book retailer claimed in a 1995 statement that book sales were hedging back and that the mainstay of their profit came from the sale of coffee to people browsing while in the bookstore. As a result, this particular chain of bookstores has become little more than a library that serves cappuccino.

Another wild example of a loss leader comes from the movie industry. Theaters claim that they make little or no money on ticket sales, and that the $100 million blockbuster is just a loss leader, or support function, to bring in the crowds so they can sell popcorn and soda.

In the retail world of record sales, Virgin MegaStores provide an indication that CDs alone cannot justify the cost of building a large outlet. They feel they have to offer the buying public a "shopping experience" to get them in the mood. Tower Records, HMV, and Specs have all experienced financial hardship in recent years. A partial solution has been to start carrying merchandise other than music: T-shirts, posters, CD-ROMs, even Calvin Klein cologne.

[3] There is an odd similarity between the expression "loss leader" and the expression "lost leader." The latter is an audio term. It comes from the protective length of paper or plastic film at the beginning and the end of reel-to-reel recording tape. The film is called "leader" because it leads the way for the rest of the tape through the transport mechanism. The actual leader tape is considered worthless. Bad recordings are still cynically called lost leaders even though in digital technology there is no actual tape.

[4] Originally called Victrolas; way back then, the Radio Corporation of America merged with the Victor record company to form RCA Victor.

Does all this mean that movies are just two-hour commercials for selling junk food? That books are bait for selling coffee? Or that great recording artists are just an excuse to sell T-shirts and collect patent royalties? On a personal level I would like to think not, but the naked truth is, it depends on how your bread is buttered.[5]

In the 1998 first edition of *Confessions* I made this prediction in this very spot: "As far as music retail goes, in the future you will probably see multi-media stores replace old-style record stores. You will have a sort of supermarket of entertainment." I thought I was talking about ten to fifteen years down the line. How wrong I was. It happened in about half that time. Entertainment companies are merging into fewer but larger incarnations of themselves. In the final analysis the entertainment supermarket will probably emerge for no other reason than it will make financial sense to do it.

Here's a more recent and relevant example: According to the annual report of Internet giant AOL/Time Warner, in the fiscal year 2000 their record division earned about $4 billion. But after expenses WEA, the distribution company owned by AOL/Time Warner, was left with only a measly $500 million. And from that they had to pay taxes. That sucks—especially when compared to the Internet portion of AOL/Time Warner, which earned $7.7 billion and managed to keep about a third of it. AOL's interest in buying Time Warner was for their music catalog and cable TV distribution. Perhaps they planned to offer subscribers free downloads from the entire roster of WEA artists as an incentive to join America Online. If so and the record division lost money, they wouldn't really care that much. It was about subscribers. But this plan fell apart. When AOL stock plummeted in 2001–2003, they initiated a sell-off of Warner Music and eventually let it go for below book value. Many artists were dropped in the downsizing.[6]

Does this story affect how you go about shopping for a label? You betcha. An artist on a label that's going through massive consolidation and changeover is always in danger of being cut from the roster.

Looking at the business this way allows you to rephrase the question that leads off this section. The question shouldn't be, "Do record companies really make any money?" but rather, "How does owning a record company help make money for its owner?"

5 Wouldn't it be really wacky if it turned out that breakfast cereal was the loss leader/support function and that the manufacturer's real intention was to sell the little cheap toy inside? Keep a sharp eye out for the realities of this joke in the next few years.

6 Warner Music was let go from its parent company AOL/Time in 2005. Although a private investor group raised $750 million so that they would not have to be tied to another multinational conglomerate, they failed to come close to raising the total "assessed" value of $2.3 billion. People in the know just didn't think it was worth the price tag.

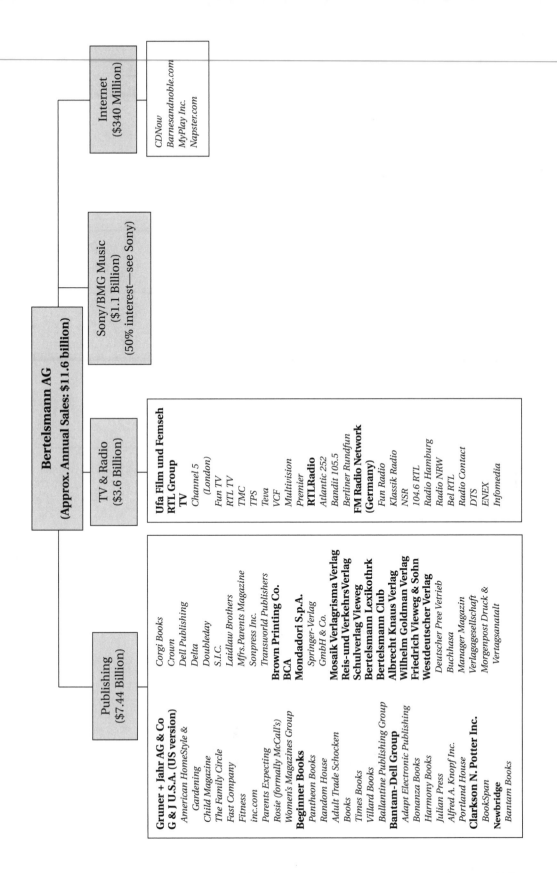

Bertelsmann AG (Approx. Annual Sales: $11.6 billion)

Publishing ($7.44 Billion)

Gruner + Jahr AG & Co
G & J U.S.A. (US version)
American HomeStyle &
  Gardening
Child Magazine
The Family Circle
Fast Company
Fitness
inc.com
Parents Expecting
Rosie (formally McCall's)
Women's Magazines Group
Beginner Books
Pantheon Books
Random House
Adult Trade Schocken
  Books
Times Books
Villard Books
Ballantine Publishing Group
Bantam-Dell Group
Adapt Electronic Publishing
Bonanza Books
Harmony Books
Julian Press
Alfred A. Knopf Inc.
Portland House
Clarkson N. Potter Inc.
BookSpan
Newbridge
Bantam Books

Corgi Books
Crown
Dell Publishing
Delta
Doubleday
S.I.C.
Laidlaw Brothers
Mfrs.Parents Magazine
Sonpress Inc.
Transworld Publishers
Brown Printing Co.
BCA
Mondadori S.p.A.
Springer-Verlag
  GmbH & Co.
Mosaik Verlagrisma Verlag
Reis-und VerkehrsVerlag
Schulverlag Vieweg
Bertelsmann Lexikothrk
Bertelsmann Club
Albrecht Knaus Verlag
Wilhelm Goldman Verlag
Friedrich Vieweg & Sohn
Westdeutscher Verlag
Deutscher Pree Vetrieb
Buchhasa
Manager Magazin
Verlagagesellschaft
Morgenpost Druck &
  Vertagsanatalt

TV & Radio ($3.6 Billion)

Ufa Film und Femseh
RTL Group
TV
Channel 5
  (London)
Fun TV
RTL TV
TMC
TPS
Teva
VCF
Multivision
Premier
RTL Radio
Atlantic 252
Bandit 105.5
Berliner Rundfun
**FM Radio Network
(Germany)**
Fun Radio
Klassik Radio
NSR
104.6 RTL
Radio Hamburg
Radio NRW
Bel RTL
Radio Contact
DTS
ENEX
Infomedia

Sony/BMG Music ($1.1 Billion) (50% interest—see Sony)

Internet ($340 Million)

CDNow
Barnesandnoble.com
MyPlay Inc.
Napster.com

Warner Music Group & WEA
Purchased for $2.4 Billion in 2005

Warner Strategic Marketing

ATCO
Avenue
Bad Boy
Cadence Christian
Casey Kassem Presents
Chicago Kid
Curb
Asylum
Delicious Vintage Vinyl
Earthbeat
Erato
Finlandia
Garden City
HBO/WEA
Hightone
Hillsboro Jazz
Jade
Kid Rhino
Legion
Lightyear Entertainment
Major League Baseball
Maranatha

MCA
Milan
Musiteca
Nonesuch
Rap-A-Lot
Rhino
Music For Little People
EarthBeat
RuffNation
Spring Hill Music Group
Sybersound
Select-O-Hits
Niche
Teldec
Time/Life
Top Sail
Vector
VP

Warner Group

Warner Bros.
Festival Mushroom
Sixshooter
Sonic
Giant
London-Sire
Maverick
Q Records
Quest
Reprise
Warner Bros. Nashville
Warner Music Latina
Warner Publications
Word Entertainment
Word
Word Gospel
Myrrh
Squint
Everland
Unison
DaySpring
Canaan

Atlantic Group

Atlantic
La Salle
Vice
VP
East/West
Elektra Asylum
Elektra Entertainment
Esperanza
Lava
Modern

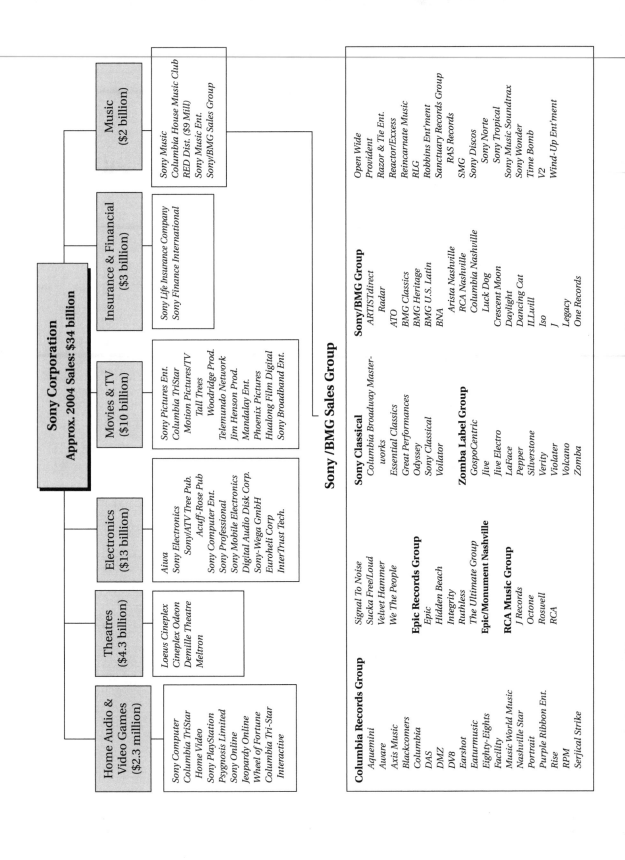

Sony Corporation
Approx. 2004 Sales: $34 billion

Home Audio & Video Games ($2.3 million)	Theatres ($4.3 billion)	Electronics ($13 billion)	Movies & TV ($10 billion)	Insurance & Financial ($3 billion)	Music ($2 billion)

Home Audio & Video Games ($2.3 million)

Sony Computer
Columbia TriStar
Home Video
Sony PlayStation
Psygnosis Limited
Sony Online
Jeopardy Online
Wheel of Fortune
Columbia Tri-Star
Interactive

Theatres ($4.3 billion)

Loews Cineplex
Cineplex Odeon
Demille Theatre
Meltron

Electronics ($13 billion)

Aiwa
Sony Electronics
Sony/ATV Tree Pub.
Acuff-Rose Pub
Sony Computer Ent.
Sony Professional
Sony Mobile Electronics
Digital Audio Disk Corp.
Sony-Wega GmbH
Euroheli Corp
InterTrust Tech.

Movies & TV ($10 billion)

Sony Pictures Ent.
Columbia TriStar
Motion Pictures/TV
Tall Trees
Woodridge Prod.
Telemundo Network
Jim Henson Prod.
Mandalay Ent.
Phoenix Pictures
Hualong Film Digital
Sony Broadband Ent.

Insurance & Financial ($3 billion)

Sony Life Insurance Company
Sony Finance International

Music ($2 billion)

Sony Music
Columbia House Music Club
RED Dist. ($9 Mill)
Sony Music Ent.
Sony/BMG Sales Group

Sony /BMG Sales Group

Columbia Records Group

Aquemini
Aware
Axis Music
Blackcomers
Columbia
DAS
DMZ
DV8
Earshot
Eaturmusic
Eighty-Eights
Facility
Music World Music
Nashville Star
Portrait
Purple Ribbon Ent.
Rise
RPM
Serjical Strike
Signal To Noise
Sucka Free/Loud
Velvet Hammer
We The People

Epic Records Group

Epic
Hidden Beach
Integrity
Ruthless
The Ultimate Group
Epic/Monument Nashville

RCA Music Group

J Records
Octone
Roswell
RCA

Sony Classical

Columbia Broadway Master-
works
Essential Classics
Great Performances
Odyssey
Sony Classical
Voilator

Zomba Label Group

GospoCentric
Jive
Jive Electro
LaFace
Pepper
Silverstone
Verity
Violater
Volcano
Zomba

Sony/BMG Group

ARTISTdirect
Radar
ATO
BMG Classics
BMG Heritage
BMG U.S. Latin
BNA
Arista Nashville
RCA Nashville
Columbia Nashville
Luck Dog
Crescent Moon
Daylight
Dancing Cat
ILLwill
Iso
J
Legacy
One Records
Open Wide
Provident
Razor & Tie Ent.
Reactor/Exxess
Reincarnate Music
RLG
Robbins Ent'ment
Sanctuary Records Group
RAS Records
SMG
Sony Discos
Sony Norte
Sony Tropical
Sony Music Soundtrax
Sony Wonder
Time Bomb
V2
Wind-Up Ent'ment

Vivendi Universal
Approximate 2004 Sales: $7.5 Billion

Bottled Water

Vivendi North America
Co. Sierra Spring Water
Co. Culligan Int.
Co. EverpureUS
Filter ArrowheaDavco
Div. Davis Pordcuts
Mcallen
Pip & SupplyAqua
AllianceMetcalf & Eddie
Seagrams Beverage co.

Telecommunications/Media/Games
($2 billion)

Canal
Canal Satellite
VUP Investima
Aprovia
Edition Nathan
Edition Bordas
Usine Nouvelle
L'Acution Mtunicpale
Librairia Larousse

Multithematiques
Palanete Cable
SECA
TV SportMonte Carlo
TMC
Tele+

Cegetel SA

NBC/Uni (joint)
Universal Studios
Radar Pictures
Universal Amphitheatre
Universal Pictures
Focus Features
History Channel
Sci-Fi Channel
Wet n' Wild
USA Networks
A&E Networks
Biography Magazine
Womps Bar & Grill
Vivendi Universal Games
Blizzard
Knowledge Adventure
Sierra Ent.
Dynamix Inc.
Papyrus Racing

Construction
(1.4 billion)

Compagnie
Generale Des
Eaux
Campenon
Bermard
Sade

Music
($3.6 billion)
(90% ownership)

UMVG Distribution

Concord Records
Concord Records
Concord Picante
Peak Records
Playboy Jazz
Stretch Records
Concord Jazz
Fantasy
Contemporary
Good Time Jazz
Kicking Mule
Milestone
OBC
OJC
Pablo
Prestige
Riverside
Specialty
Stax
Takoma

Geffen Records
413
Chess
Drive Thru
Fiddler
Flawless
Flicker
I Am

Geffen
DGC
Experience Hendrix
Radioactive
Raukus
Never So Deep

Interscope/A&M
A&M
Interscope
Almo
Aftermath
Amaru

Beat Club
Cherry Tree
Flip
G-Unit
Kickball
Nothing
Ruff Ryders Ent.
Shady
Vagrant
Weapons of Mass Ent.

Universal Music Latino
CJ Latin
Flow Music
Fonosound
Gold Star
Guitian
Infinity
Karen
Latin World
Mas Flow
Music Haus
Musimex
New Records
Perfect Image
P1

Island/Def Jam Music Group
American Recordings
Def Jam
Def Jam South
Def Soul
The Inc.
Roc-A-Fella
Island
Kemado
Mercury
MonarC
Murder Inc.
Roadrunner

Universal Motown Group
Bad Boy
Blackground
Brushfire
Casablanca
Cash Money
Cherry
D Block
Enjoy
Fo' Reel
Moonshine Conspiracy
Platano
Big World
Music Up
Protel
Revolú
RMM
Universal Music Latino
Vale Music
Vivamusic
Motown
Next Plateau
Polydor
Republic
Rocket
Street
Strummer
SRC
Strummer Recordings
The Ultimate Group
Universal

19 Records
ABKCO Records
ARK 21
Mondo Melodia
Bungalo
Disa
Procan
DreamWorks Nashville
DreamWorks Records

Fonovisa
DMY
Garmex
Oro Musical
Platino
Hollywood Records
Lyric Street
Mammoth
Skaggs Family
Ceili Music
Lideres Records
Ole Music
Machete Music
Los Cangri, Inc.
VI Music
Palm Pictures
Pyramid
Sybersound

Thump Records
B-Dub
Discos Fama
Thump Street
UMG Nashville
DreamWorks Nashville
Lost Highway
Mercury Nashville
MCA Nashville
Rounder
Bullseye
Heartbeat
Marsalis Music
Philo / Zoe

Universal Classics & Jazz
Classics
Decca
Decca U.S.
Decca Broadway
Deutsche Grammophon
Archiv
ECM
Philips
Mercury Living Presence

Universal Music Enterprises
Chronicles
Hip-O Records
New Door Records
Universal Special Products
UTV

Universal South
Univision Music Group
Univision Records
Fonovisa Records
Ramex
Varese Sarabande Records
Fuel 2000
Sunswept Music
Water Music
Verve Music Group
Blue Thumb
GRP
Impulse
Verve
Verve Forecast
E2 Music
Empire
Walt Disney Records
Buena Vista
Walt Disney Records
Disney Sound

Fontana Distribution

301

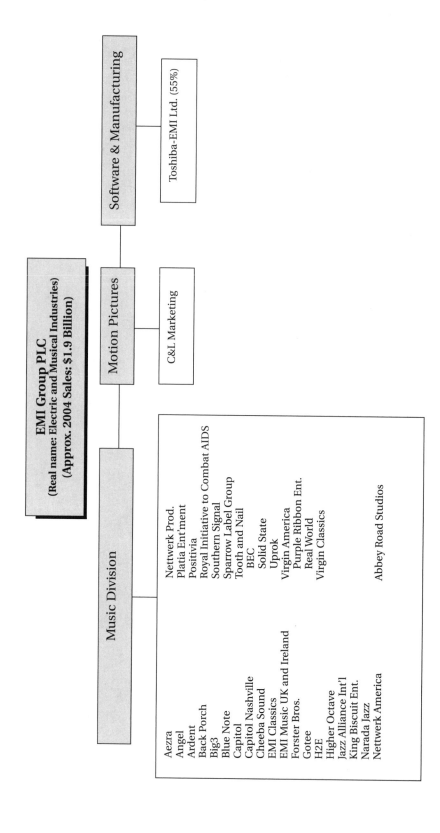

EMI Group PLC
(Real name: Electric and Musical Industries)
(Approx. 2004 Sales: $1.9 Billion)

Music Division

Aezra
Angel
Ardent
Back Porch
Big3
Blue Note
Capitol
Capitol Nashville
Cheeba Sound
EMI Classics
EMI Music UK and Ireland
Forster Bros.
Gotee
H2E
Higher Octave
Jazz Alliance Int'l
King Biscuit Ent.
Narada Jazz
Nettwerk America

Nettwerk Prod.
Platia Ent'ment
Positivia
Royal Initiative to Combat AIDS
Southern Signal
Sparrow Label Group
Tooth and Nail
BEC
Solid State
Uprok
Virgin America
Purple Ribbon Ent.
Real World
Virgin Classics

Abbey Road Studios

Motion Pictures

C&L Marketing

Software & Manufacturing

Toshiba-EMI Ltd. (55%)

⊜ A Map of the Financial Universe

How does the record industry look from the point of view of the parent holding companies? Look at the family trees on the previous pages and you'll get an idea of the big picture. Notice that the record division in most cases brings in the lowest, or close to the lowest, amount of revenue and profit compared to other holdings.

If the trees above are a bit confusing, check it out in a more fluid form. Below is a breakdown of the parent company portfolios that hold the major record distributors as they were up till 2004. This oversimplified chart shows how the money trickles down. All of the figures, taken from publicly available data, are for 2001 and some from 2004. In the Appendix there are the same family trees as they appeared in 1998 and 2001. Look how the industry has changed and who owns what today as opposed to just a few years ago.

None of the companies breaks out record sales alone, excluding other items like music publishing. Even so, the figures should give you a picture of what's going on. The set of numbers represent the total amount of money earned by the division and the amount left over after that division paid its operating expenses (excluding taxes, etc.)

AOL/Time Warner Inc. 2001 ($37.3 billion)

	Total earned	After expenses	Cents on the dollar
America Online	$7.7 billion	$2.3 billion	30 cents
Cable	$6 billion	$2.8 billion	47 cents
Movies	$8.1 billion	$800 million	10 cents
Networks	$6.8 billion	$1.5 billion	22 cents
Publishing	$4.6 billion	$700 million	15 cents
Music	$4.1 billion	$500 million	12 cents

Vivendi Universal 2001 ($44.3 billion)

	Total earned	After expenses	Cents on the dollar
Telecommunications	$4.6 billion	$1.1 billion	24 cents
Internet	$42 million	<$162 million>	–3.8 cents
TV & movies	$7.8 billion	$682 million	11 cents
Environmental services	$23 billion	$3 billion	14 cents
Publishing	$3.1 billion	$434 million	14 cents
Music	$5.8 billion	$1 billion	17 cents

Sony Corporation 2001 ($58.5 billion)

	Total earned	After expenses	Cents on the dollar
Electronics	$44 billion	$2.0 billion	4.5 cents
Games	$5.3 billion	−$400 million	−7 cents
Movies & theaters	$4.4 billion	$30 million	.67 cents
Insurance	$4.3 billion	$100 million	2 cents
Other small stuff	$3.2 billion	$100 million	3 cents
Music distribution	$4.9 billion	$20 million	<.5 cent

Since Bertelsmann AG and EMI Group are not public companies, only total earnings numbers are available.

[7] This number is from the annual reports of these companies. It may or may not match the calculations to the right.

Bertelsmann AG ($21 billion[7])

BMG Entertainment (film, TV)	$10.5 billion
Music distribution	$4.0 billion
Publishing (magazines, newspapers, books)	$7.7 billion
Dot-coms	$0.34 billion

EMI Group PLC (formerly Thorn EMI PLC) 2001 ($3.7 billion)

(Electric and Musical Industries)

EMI Music	$3.7 billion

The Walt Disney Company ($27.4 billion[6])

Walt Disney is not a major label; it is listed here purely out of respect for the 300-pound indie giant.

Theme parks and resorts	$6.8 billion
Broadcasting	$9.1 billion

"Creative content" (including films, records, and consumer products) $9 billion (33%)

(Note: Estimated annual sales for Walt Disney Records were $50 million.)

What Does the Above Teach Us?

It costs a typical major label about $8.50 in overhead to make a single dollar. Because the record industry is probably really worth about $10 billion a year in before-expense sales, that may sound like an idle complaint—but consider the alternatives: paper, oil, gas, military contracting, and other commodities. These industries are worth $15 to $50 billion a year after expenses, and they don't have anywhere near the same overhead that the music industry does. What all this means is that at the end of the day it costs more to make less in the record game.

This is nothing new; the profits in music have always been questionable. But in the past there was always a secondary business to offset the losses. Things are different now, because most large companies have sold off the unprofitable parts of their empires in the mergers and acquisitions of the 1980s. Those who bought the record divisions rationalized that they could make these enterprises work if they could just keep their overhead down—something they have been unable to do. When the reality of this settles in, the corporations will look to sell.

What keeps the record game going is the allure. Crown jewels like U2, Bob Dylan, the Rolling Stones, Madonna, Eminem, and other cash cows attract large multinationals to gobble up what they think are money-making ventures; the sale is made, and lots of new money flows. Then, after several years, the attractiveness of owning a glamorous liability wears off. During this phase a new mentality emerges: "Sign hits or get the ax." Naturally one can't sign hits every day, so the policy mutates into one of damage control—giving away as little as possible to each signed act. This also means paying off as few people as possible and cutting out the middlemen, like producers and managers, whenever possible.

In time, the budgets shrink, favors are hard to come by, and eventually the record company is sold off, starting the process all over again. In the interim more artists, producers, executives, and lawyers make their mark while Papa Bear Holding Company figures out how to get out of the mess it bought into.

But can this kind of game continue? Eventually, won't everyone know that big profits in the world of major labels is somewhat of a fallacy? The answer is yes, they already do. But major labels are presently trying to redefine their roles in the brave new digital future and are experiencing the most far-reaching transformations that they have ever known in their 50-year history. When the restructuring is over, there will likely be fewer jobs in middle management (like A&R, artist relations, and promotions) at big record labels and more splinter record labels (which many call indies and I refer to as one-deep and two-deep labels) with ties to Big Four distribution.

⊘ Major Label Family Trees ("The Big Four") as of 2005

```
Quick Key:
BIG FOUR DISTRIBUTOR
Parent label (major)
      One-deep label (imprint)
            Two-deep label
                  Three-deep label
```

UNIVERSAL MUSIC & VIDEO DISTRIBUTION (UMDV)

19 Records
ABKCO Records
ARK 21
    Mondo Melodia
Bungalo
Concord Records
    Concord Records
        Concord Picante
        Peak Records
        Playboy Jazz
        Stretch Records
    Concord Jazz
    Fantasy
        Contemporary
        Good Time Jazz
        Kicking Mule
        Milestone
        OBC
        OJC
        Pablo
        Prestige
        Riverside
        Specialty
        Stax

        Takoma
        Volt
Disa
    Procan
DreamWorks Nashville
DreamWorks Records
Fonovisa
    DMY
    Garmex
    Oro Musical
    Platino
Geffen Records
    413
    Chess
    Drive Thru
    Fiddler
    Flawless
    Flicker
    I Am
    Geffen
        DGC
        Experience Hendrix
        Radioactive
        Rawkus
    Never So Deep
Hollywood Records
    Lyric Street
    Mammoth
    Skaggs Family
    Ceili Music
Interscope/A&M
    A&M
    Interscope
        Almo

Aftermath
    Amaru
    Beat Club
    Cherry Tree
    Flip
    G-Unit
    Kickball
    Nothing
    Ruff Ryders Ent.
    Shady
    Vagrant
    Weapons of Mass Ent.

Island/Def Jam Music Group
  American Recordings
  Def Jam
    Def Jam South
    Def Soul
    The Inc.
    Roc-A-Fella
  Island
  Kemado
  Mercury
  MonarC
  Murder Inc.
  Roadrunner

Lideres Records
  Ole Music

Machete Music
  Los Cangri, Inc.
  VI Music

Palm Pictures

Pyramid

Sybersound

Thump Records
  B-Dub
  Discos Fama
  Thump Street

UMG Nashville
  DreamWorks Nashville
  Lost Highway
  Mercury Nashville
  MCA Nashville
  Rounder
    Bullseye
    Heartbeat
    Marsalis Music
    Philo / Zoe

Universal Classics & Jazz
  Classics
  Decca
  Decca U.S.
    Decca Broadway
  Deutsche Grammophon
    Archiv
  ECM
  Philips
    Mercury Living Presence

Universal Motown Group
  Blackground
  Brushfire
  Casablanca
  Cash Money
  Cherry
  D Block
  Enjoy
  Fo' Reel
  Moonshine Conspiracy
  Motown
  Next Plateau
  Polydor
  Republic
  Rocket
  Street
  Strummer

SRC

Strummer Recordings

The Ultimate Group

Universal

Universal Music Enterprises

Chronicles

Hip-O Records

New Door Records

Universal Special Products

UTV

Universal Music Latino

CJ Latin

Flow Music

Fonosound

Gold Star

Guitian

Infinity

Karen

Latin World

Mas Flow

Music Haus

Musimex

New Records

Perfect Image

Pi

Pina

Pimient

Pina Records

Planet Rhythm

Platano

Big World

Music Up

Protel

Revolú

RMM

Universal Music Latino

Vale Music

Vivamusic

Universal South

Univision Music Group

Univision Records

Fonovisa Records

Ramex

Varese Sarabande Records

Fuel 2000

Sunswept Music

Water Music

Verve Music Group

Blue Thumb

GRP

Impulse

Verve

Verve Forecast

E2 Music

Empire

Walt Disney Records

Buena Vista

Walt Disney Records

Disney Sound

EMI MUSIC MARKETING (EMD or EMI)

Aezra

Angel

Ardent

Back Porch

Big3

Blue Note

Capitol

Capitol Nashville

Cheeba Sound

EMI Classics

EMI Music UK and Ireland

Forster Bros.

Gotee

H2E

Higher Octave

Jazz Alliance Int'l

King Biscuit Ent.

Narada Jazz

Nettwerk America

Nettwerk Prod.

Platia Ent'ment

Positivia

Royal Initiative to Combat AIDS

Southern Signal

Sparrow Label Group

Tooth and Nail

    BEC

    Solid State

    Uprok

Virgin America

    Purple Ribbon Ent.

    Real World

Virgin Classics

WEA CORP. DISTRIBUTION (WEA)

ATCO

Atlantic

    La Salle

    Vice

    VP

    East/West

    Elektra Asylum

    Elektra Entertainment

    Esperanza

    Lava

    Modern

Avenue

Cadence Christian

Casey Kasem Presents

Chicago Kid

Curb Group

Asylum

Delicious Vintage Vinyl

Earthbeat

Erato

Finlandia

Garden City

HBO/WEA

Hightone

Hillsboro Jazz

Jade

Kid Rhino

Legion

Lightyear Entertainment

Major League Baseball

Maranatha

MCA

Milan

Music for Little People

    EarthBeat

Musiteca

Nonesuch

Rap-A-Lot

Rhino

    Music For Little People

RuffNation

Spring Hill Music Group

Sybersound

Select-O-Hits

    Niche

Teldec

Time/Life

Top Sail

Vector

VP

Warner Bros.

    Festival Mushroom

    Sixshooter

    Sonic

Bad Boy

Giant

London-Sire

Maverick

Q Records

Qwest

Reprise

Warner Bros. Nashville

Warner Music Latina

Warner Publications

Word Entertainment

Canaan

DaySpring

Everland

Fervent

Myrrh

Squint

Unison

Word

Word Gospel

SONY/BMG SALES COMPANY (Sony/BMG)

ARTISTdirect

Radar

ATO

BMG Classics

BMG Heritage

BMG U.S. Latin

BNA

Arista Nashville

RCA Nashville

Columbia Nashville

Lucky Dog

Columbia Records Group

Aquemini

Aware

Axis Music

Blackcomers

Columbia

DAS

DMZ

DV8

Earshot

Eaturmusic

Eighty-Eights

Facility

Music World Music

Nashville Star

Portrait

Purple Ribbon Ent.

Rise

RPM

Serjical Strike

Signal To Noise

Sucka Free/Loud

Velvet Hammer

We The People

Crescent Moon

Daylight

Dancing Cat

Epic Records Group

Epic

Hidden Beach

Integrity

Ruthless

The Ultimate Group

Epic/Monument Nashville

ILLwill

Iso

J

Legacy

One Records

Open Wide

Provident

Razor & Tie Ent'ment

RCA Music Group

    J Records

    Octone

    Roswell

        RCA

Reactor/Exxess

Reincarnate Music

RLG

Robbins Ent'ment

Sanctuary Records Group

    RAS Records

SMG

Sony Classical

    Columbia Broadway Master-
      works

    Essential Classics

    Great Performances

    Odyssey

    Sony Classical

    Vivarte

Sony Discos

    Sony Norte

    Sony Tropical

Sony Music Soundtrax

Sony Wonder

Time Bomb

V2

Wind-Up Ent'ment

Zomba Label Group

    GospoCentric

    Jive

    Jive Electro

    LaFace

    Pepper

    Silverstone

    Verity

    Violator

    Volcano

    Zomba

⊜Record/Pause

As a closing summary I've composed a checklist of many common pitfalls that a recording artist, producer, or small label owner could encounter. It's the Murphy's Law of the recording industry, if you will, and it's compiled from listening to 20 years of fuck-ups and fish stories. Remember, the wise man learns from other people's mistakes. If you can make it through this list, you're assured to make mountains of money and have lots of great sex.

⊛ Checklist for Disaster

(Note: Each of these things is guaranteed to have actually happened more than once.)

√ **Band members can't get along.**

√ **No consistent direction in the band's music/no good material.**

√ **The manager/producer working with you dies and ties up your contract in probate court.**

√ **The lawyer handling the negotiating of your record deal gets fired or moves, leaving your contract in limbo.**

√ **The advance from the label doesn't cover the cost of making the record.**

√ The studio you're recording in has a flood and it destroys your masters. Oh, yeah, and they recently canceled their liability insurance.

√ The label's distributor moves warehouses and loses your stock of CDs.

√ The A&R person who signed you is fired or dies and the new person filling their shoes is less than interested in you.

√ After two years of recording your masterpiece album, it is finally released and it sounds two years old.

√ The radio station that your label had a great relationship with changes its format.

√ Long hair is back and you just got a buzz cut to be hip.

√ The record is doing well, but the lead singer wants to do a solo project next.

√ While on tour the entire group is arrested by a local sheriff for DWI and knocking up his underage daughter.

√ The producer won't deliver the master to the record company until he gets more money.

√ The artist won't show up for a session or photo shoot until they get more money.

√ One or both of the above delay the record's release and the marketing window closes.

√ The single that the record company picks is the most atypical song on the record. It's a hit and the band's credibility is destroyed.

√ The label goes into Chapter 11, tying up your royalties and contract in bankruptcy hearings.

√ The artist, after one record, decides that they can produce the next record themselves. Oh yeah, and they don't need a manager telling them what to do, either.

√ You sold over 20,000 CDs through your local record store, but they have no receipts and it didn't show up on SoundScan.

√ Some Internet cyber-dweeb puts your single on an online bulletin board and everyone's downloading it, royalty-free.

√ You've sold a million records, but the label's cost for promotion was so high that you still owe another half a million dollars before you get royalties.

√ Your label merges with its parent distributor and trims the fat off their roster—you're on the cutting room floor.

√ Your indie label can't pay you because their distributor won't pay them, or went out of business.

√ You get a letter from the lawyer of some drunk you hung out with one night, and he's decided he helped you cowrite that new hit song of yours.

√ Some other band with the same name decides to sue you for trademark infringement.

❯ Final Word

In closing this book I would like to leave you with a somewhat philosophical thought: We are perched at a new age of our industry. Technology has lifted the veil of secrecy from record sales and has made it possible for anyone with a phone line to reach thousands with their message. New laws will alter the way artists will be paid, and electronic media may permanently change the way we buy and listen to our favorite songs.

There is something odd about change. We talk passionately about wanting it until it starts to become a reality. Then a deep-rooted fear of the unknown sets in as our status quo dissolves. We hope it's for the better.

Regardless of corporate influence, pop music responds to the values and needs of each new generation. If we look at modern music in this way, we must conclude that it is not just a "business." It is a key barometer of how our culture evolves. If we agree with that statement, then those who commit to music as a career accept an important contract with their fellow human beings—the power to influence.

If you've read this book carefully, you have more information and tips than most people when they started out in this business. Use your new knowledge wisely. Make a difference. The movers and shakers who have had ongoing hits in this industry are constantly evolving and keeping on top of what's fresh. This is important. Do not lose touch with the market. Whether you're a producer, manager, lawyer, A&R person, label owner, session player, sideperson, engineer, or writer, remember:

Half of being smart is knowing what
you're dumb at.

While you grow older, your client,
the record buyer, is forever young.

Peace.

> Appendix A: Family Trees of Big Six Distributors as of January 1998

Compare these charts showing what the industry looked like a few short years ago to the current status as shown starting on page 297. See how the industry has changed and who owns what now versus then.

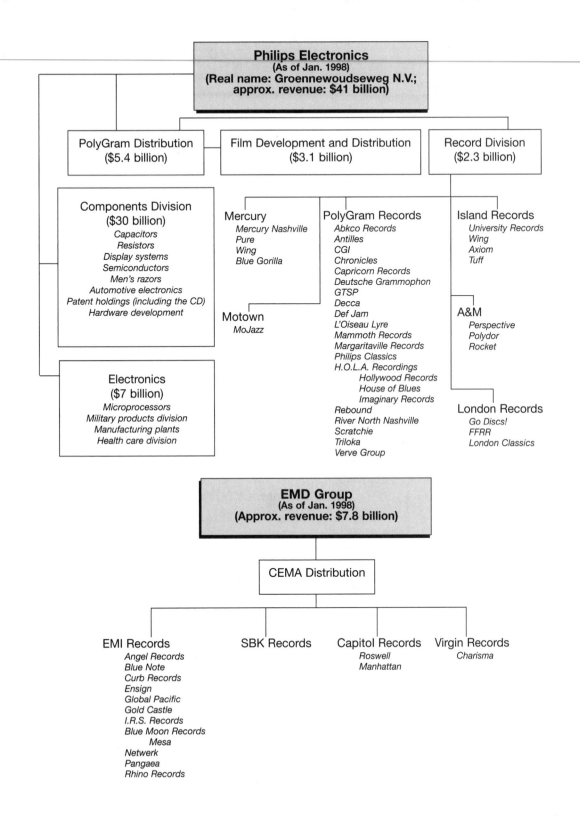

Philips Electronics
(As of Jan. 1998)
(Real name: Groennewoudseweg N.V.;
approx. revenue: $41 billion)

PolyGram Distribution
($5.4 billion)

Film Development and Distribution
($3.1 billion)

Record Division
($2.3 billion)

Components Division
($30 billion)
Capacitors
Resistors
Display systems
Semiconductors
Men's razors
Automotive electronics
Patent holdings (including the CD)
Hardware development

Mercury
Mercury Nashville
Pure
Wing
Blue Gorilla

Motown
MoJazz

PolyGram Records
Abkco Records
Antilles
CGI
Chronicles
Capricorn Records
Deutsche Grammophon
GTSP
Decca
Def Jam
L'Oiseau Lyre
Mammoth Records
Margaritaville Records
Philips Classics
H.O.L.A. Recordings
   Hollywood Records
   House of Blues
   Imaginary Records
Rebound
River North Nashville
Scratchie
Triloka
Verve Group

Island Records
University Records
Wing
Axiom
Tuff

A&M
Perspective
Polydor
Rocket

London Records
Go Discs!
FFRR
London Classics

Electronics
($7 billion)
Microprocessors
Military products division
Manufacturing plants
Health care division

EMD Group
(As of Jan. 1998)
(Approx. revenue: $7.8 billion)

CEMA Distribution

EMI Records
Angel Records
Blue Note
Curb Records
Ensign
Global Pacific
Gold Castle
I.R.S. Records
Blue Moon Records
   Mesa
Netwerk
Pangaea
Rhino Records

SBK Records

Capitol Records
Roswell
Manhattan

Virgin Records
Charisma

Bertelsmann AG
(As of Jan. 1998)
(Approx. revenue: $14 billion)

BMG Music
$5 billion

BMG

Reunion
Time Bomb
Bad Boy
Career Records
Private Music
RLC
The Children's Group
CMC International
Critique
Logic
Miramar
Musicmakers
Restless Records
Robbins Ent.
Wind-Up Ent.
V2
　　　Gee Street
Volcano Recordings

RCA Records

Beggars Banquet
Big Time
Bluebird
Dedicated
Grunt
LMR
Milan
Nashville
Novus

Windham Hill

Windham Hill Jazz
Dancing Cat
High Street
Hip Pocket
Open Air
Rabbit Ears

Arista Records

LaFace
Bad Boy
Career
Dedicated
Rowdy
Time Bomb

Imago Entertainment Group

Gruner+Jahr Publishing
($7.3 billion)

Baby Care
Home Video
Family Circle
McCalls
Doubleday
Dell Publishing
Transworld
5% of America Online

Sony Corporation
(As of Jan. 1998)
(Approx. revenue: $43.3 billion)

Research
($2 billion)
Thinfilm coating
Etching systems
High purity metals
& materials

Sony Electronics
($10 billion)
Aiwa

Telecommunications
($3.5 billion)
Semiconductors
Logistics services

Sony Entertainment
($4.6 billion)
Columbia Pictures
Tri-Star Pictures
The Peter Guber Co.
Barris Productions

Ceramics
($6.2 billion)
High-tech very
pure ceramic eas-
ings for electronics

Sony Music
($2.9 billion)

Sony Records

Chaos	*Hall of Fame*	**Columbia**
Soundtrax	*Heartcry*	*Def Jam*
Sony 550	*Higher Ground*	*Relativity*
Crescent Moon	*Hoppoh*	*So So Def*
OKeh	*Hudlin Brothers*	*Sony Discos*
Tri-Star Music	*Immortal*	*Sony Tropical*
Sony Classical	*Independent*	*Stonecreek*
Soho Square	*Lucky Dog*	*Word Gospel*
Sony Wonder	*Myrra*	*Word Nashville*
Chrysalis	*New Deal*	*Yab Yum*
Big Cat	*Q Division*	**Epic**
Crave	*Ruffhouse*	*Lifestyle*
Creation	*Slam Jamz*	
Flavor Unite		

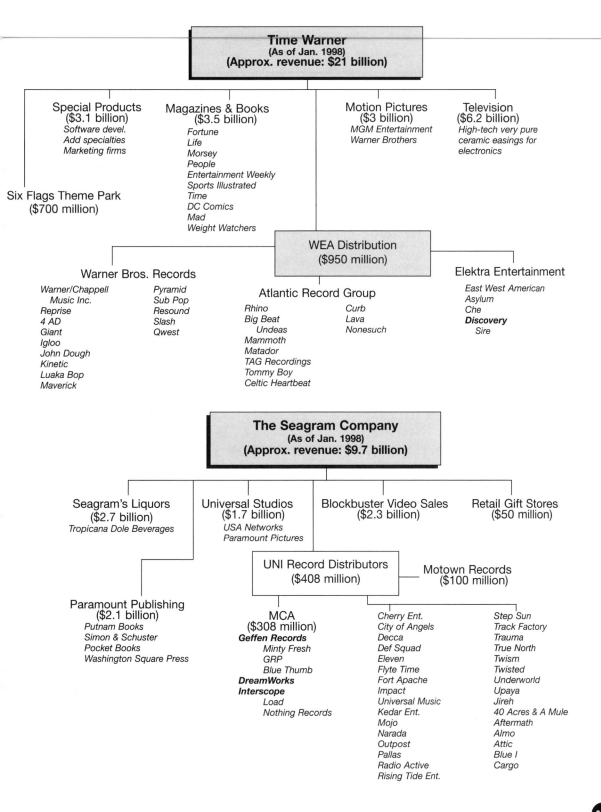

Time Warner
(As of Jan. 1998)
(Approx. revenue: $21 billion)

Special Products
($3.1 billion)
Software devel.
Add specialties
Marketing firms

Six Flags Theme Park
($700 million)

Magazines & Books
($3.5 billion)
Fortune
Life
Morsey
People
Entertainment Weekly
Sports Illustrated
Time
DC Comics
Mad
Weight Watchers

Motion Pictures
($3 billion)
MGM Entertainment
Warner Brothers

Television
($6.2 billion)
High-tech very pure
ceramic easings for
electronics

WEA Distribution
($950 million)

Warner Bros. Records

Warner/Chappell
  Music Inc.
Reprise
4 AD
Giant
Igloo
John Dough
Kinetic
Luaka Bop
Maverick

Pyramid
Sub Pop
Resound
Slash
Qwest

Atlantic Record Group

Rhino
Big Beat
  Undeas
Mammoth
Matador
TAG Recordings
Tommy Boy
Celtic Heartbeat

Curb
Lava
Nonesuch

Elektra Entertainment

East West American
Asylum
Che
Discovery
Sire

The Seagram Company
(As of Jan. 1998)
(Approx. revenue: $9.7 billion)

Seagram's Liquors
($2.7 billion)
Tropicana Dole Beverages

Universal Studios
($1.7 billion)
USA Networks
Paramount Pictures

Blockbuster Video Sales
($2.3 billion)

Retail Gift Stores
($50 million)

UNI Record Distributors
($408 million)

Motown Records
($100 million)

Paramount Publishing
($2.1 billion)
Putnam Books
Simon & Schuster
Pocket Books
Washington Square Press

MCA
($308 million)
Geffen Records
  Minty Fresh
  GRP
  Blue Thumb
DreamWorks
Interscope
  Load
  Nothing Records

Cherry Ent.
City of Angels
Decca
Def Squad
Eleven
Flyte Time
Fort Apache
Impact
Universal Music
Kedar Ent.
Mojo
Narada
Outpost
Pallas
Radio Active
Rising Tide Ent.

Step Sun
Track Factory
Trauma
True North
Twism
Twisted
Underworld
Upaya
Jireh
40 Acres & A Mule
Aftermath
Almo
Attic
Blue I
Cargo

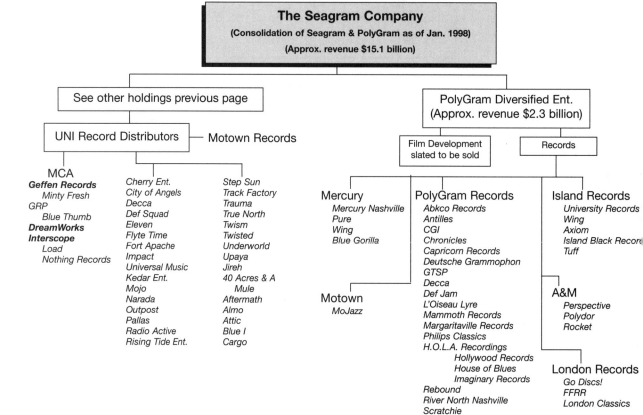

The Seagram Company
(Consolidation of Seagram & PolyGram as of Jan. 1998)
(Approx. revenue $15.1 billion)

See other holdings previous page

PolyGram Diversified Ent.
(Approx. revenue $2.3 billion)

UNI Record Distributors — Motown Records

Film Development
slated to be sold

Records

MCA
Geffen Records
Minty Fresh
GRP
Blue Thumb
DreamWorks
Interscope
Load
Nothing Records

Cherry Ent.
City of Angels
Decca
Def Squad
Eleven
Flyte Time
Fort Apache
Impact
Universal Music
Kedar Ent.
Mojo
Narada
Outpost
Pallas
Radio Active
Rising Tide Ent.

Step Sun
Track Factory
Trauma
True North
Twism
Twisted
Underworld
Upaya
Jireh
40 Acres & A
    Mule
Aftermath
Almo
Attic
Blue I
Cargo

Mercury
Mercury Nashville
Pure
Wing
Blue Gorilla

Motown
MoJazz

PolyGram Records
Abkco Records
Antilles
CGI
Chronicles
Capricorn Records
Deutsche Grammophon
GTSP
Decca
Def Jam
L'Oiseau Lyre
Mammoth Records
Margaritaville Records
Philips Classics
H.O.L.A. Recordings
    Hollywood Records
    House of Blues
    Imaginary Records
Rebound
River North Nashville
Scratchie
Triloka
Verve Group

Island Records
University Records
Wing
Axiom
Island Black Records
Tuff

A&M
Perspective
Polydor
Rocket

London Records
Go Discs!
FFRR
London Classics

ACKNOWLEDGMENTS

The music industry is a place that attracts many who claim to be of high moral character. I have been fortunate to know some of the few who really live up to that claim. The making of a book like this does not come without great personal sacrifice. I would first like to thank all of those who, despite potential derision, supported and applauded this effort. They deserve my eternal thanks and the appreciation of all who enter the business of music.

First and foremost a good friend, Pat Cameron, who, along with Matt Kelsey at Backbeat, had the vision and bravado to give this project a chance. Jim Aikin, my first editor, for his talent in turning a phrase and whose irritating demand that I back up every fact in this book will probably keep me out of court. Richard Johnston, the editor on this edition, because anyone who puts up with my crap deserves recognition. Renee, my research assistant, who spent tireless hours in the public library looking up names, dates, and obscure elements of copyright law. Some important lawyers: Richard Wolf, a barrister of undying righteousness who found time for me. Matt from Greenberg Traurig and Rick at Warner Bros., the two most honest lawyers in the business, who helped keep me honest when entropy proposed otherwise. Michael Ostroff at Universal, who was more honest than I expected, and Neville Johnson, who just gets me, God help him. My first agent, Donald. Dick Gabriel, and his desire to make a difference. R.B., a royal pain in the butt who gave a smart-ass engineer a shot and taught me that Allah loves all. My engineering mentor, John H., who showed me how to set up a mike, and that new does not necessarily mean improved. Doug, who looked at my early scribbling and thought I had something worth pursuing. Shasti, my spiritual sister, whose illustrations do not appear in this book. Brian, my oldest friend, who indulges me in the sport of arguing (I have that $20 I owe you). Additional thanks go out to the following for their uncompensated contributions to keeping this book accurate: John Luongo for his keen eye and math skills; JM at Middle Ear; Lauren, my buddy on the inside; Jennelynd, wherever you are—you started all this; Josh at Intouch; Dean—please resurface; the two dudes at SpinArt; Mike Baker; Stan Soocher; JJ French; Steve Addabbo; Bruce the gnome; all the affiliates of www.MosesAvalon.com; the educators at music schools everywhere who do not get enough credit; and anybody whose name I've forgotten. Thanks to all.

Finally, my mother, who raised me right, teaching me to tell the truth, the whole truth, and nothing but the truth. And my wife and best friend, whose support and inspiration make every day worth living.

You are all a credit to the human race.

WHO IS MOSES AVALON AND WHAT IS THE MOSES AVALON COMPANY?

Mr. Avalon began his career as a New York record producer and recording engineer. His combined work of producing and engineering with Grammy® award-winning recording artists has earned him several RIAA Gold & Platinum record awards. His soundtrack compositions have been used in films that went on to win outstanding achievement awards at Cannes, The New York Expo, and WorldFest. Today he is an artist's rights activist, author, educator, and consultant. Mr. Avalon has also acted in an advisory capacity to the **Senate Judiciary Committee in Sacramento**, the **Department of Justice**, and two **State Attorney General's** offices, in their campaign to help legitimize areas of the music business. His syndicated newsletter, *Moses Supposes*, which features satirical editorials on the inner workings of the music business, reaches thousands of subscribers each month. He is an active lecturer around the world and CEO of **The Moses Avalon Company**, a music business consulting firm and artist's rights advocacy organization. Through the Company Mr. Avalon and a team of advisors help and educate emerging artists about progressing their career and safeguarding their rights. The Moses Avalon Company also handles established artists for such things as expert witness testimony, contract analysis, and dispute resolution. His advocacy efforts can be reviewed at www.MosesAvalon.com.

TAKE THE CONFESSIONS OF A RECORD PRODUCER WORKSHOP

Now you can learn how the record business *really* works from one of the country's leading experts at the ***Confessions of a Record Producer Workshop.*** This acclaimed two-day workshop, attended by top industry pros, reveals tricks of the trade to help songwriters and artists protect their money and their rights. Learn what the most successful artists, managers, producers, and lawyers already know:

- How to get a six-figure advance.
- Protecting songs from copyright theft.
- Using digital distribution as an alternative to a major label.
- Getting out of bad contracts.
- The latest issues regarding artists' rights, the internet, and domain names.
- Revenue streams examined up close with *real dollar values.*

Hosted live by **Moses Avalon**, author of *Million Dollar Mistakes: Steering Your Music Career Clear of Lies, Cons, Catastrophes, and Landmines.*

"I was never quite able to decode the terms and cash flow of a record deal till I did the Confessions Workshop." —Geza X, Producer, **Meredith Brooks, Dead Kennedys,** Los Angeles

"Not one single music business workshop in the last ten years comes a close second. It's worth ten times what you pay and it won't last forever." —Dave Paton, Booking Agent: **Van Halen, Tom Petty, Twisted Sister**

"The Confessions Workshop is an extremely valuable tool for the new artist who needs to be realistic about their first recording contract." —Philip K. Lyon, Attorney, Nashville, TN, whose firm represents **Kenny Rogers** and **David Allan Coe**

Don't sound like this in 10 years:

"Recording companies really, really do conspire against the artists."
—Michael Jackson

"Our record company, after selling 70 million [of our] records, still tells us we are unrecouped." **—Kevin Richardson, Backstreet Boys**

For information and calendar go to: **wwwMosesAvalon.com**